STRICTLY OLA
MY STORY

First edition

Published by SJH Publishing

298 Regents Park Road, London N3 2SZ

020 8371 4000

stjamess.org

ISBN: 978-1-906670-42-9

Cover photo: Snooty Fox Images

Cover design: bettycreative.com

Picture credit: Flynet Pictures

Printed and bound by CPI Group (UK) Ltd, Croydon, CR0 4YY

To my Mama and Tata, Janina and Dariusz.

I can never truly thank you enough for everything you have done for me, for all your love and support and for raising me in a stable household, where you taught me traditional values and to embrace whatever life throws at me. I could not have asked for better parents or role models.

Also, to James's mum and dad, Sharon and Allan – without both sets of parents, none of our success would ever have been possible.

1

'I'm going to be a dancer like that one day,' I thought, gazing open-mouthed at the beautiful women on the television screen in front of me.

I was seven years old and lying propped up on my elbows on the living-room carpet, the heels of my hands wedged under my chin as I craned my neck to watch my favourite TV show. As usual I was dressed in a well-worn grey tracksuit, my hair was tied in shoulder-length, mousy-coloured plaits and my brown eyes were on stalks as I watched the dancers glide and twirl with amazing skill around the shiny-floored ballroom.

To me, the pretty women looked like perfectly painted dolls or mannequins that had come to life. They were immaculate and captivating, and when I grew up I wanted to be one of them, more than anything else in the world. It wasn't just a pipe dream either; in my mind it was definitely going to happen, no question at all.

A presenter spoke enthusiastically in a foreign language as each new group of dancers took to the floor and, over the top of his voice, a Polish translator told me the couples would be doing some very exotic-sounding dances, like the Rumba, the Tango or the Foxtrot. The translator's detached, deadpan delivery was completely at odds with the exhilaration I felt as I gazed at our little box television, which sat on a side table in our cramped living room.

I loved every dance and found each one incredibly exciting to watch. The Samba, the Viennese Waltz, the Paso Doble, the Quickstep, the Cha Cha Cha: I was going to learn how to perform every single one of these famous Ballroom and Latin dances. Every step, every sequin, every beat of the music enchanted me. I loved the glitter balls dangling above the dance floor and the flashing, multicoloured spotlights, and I was charmed by the male dancers in their long-tailed suits, each with a shiny black number pinned to his back.

It was the women who really captured my attention, though. My eyes would be glued to them from the second the big band music started and the dancing began. The women all had deep, golden tans and the most amazing dresses, ones that I would love to wear. Their hair was slicked into elaborate jewel-covered buns or set in rhinestoned plaits and ringlets, and they all wore the most dramatic and striking make-up I had ever seen. My mum and nearly all of the other women I saw in real life wore no make-up at all, let alone ultra-sparkly eye shadow, thick smoky eyeliner, shimmering blusher and glossy red or vibrant pink lipstick. This was another world compared to the one I lived in, but it was a world within my reach, and I was going to go there.

One day, when I had just turned eight years old, I was struggling to do my homework in the kitchen while my mum peeled the potatoes next to me.

'I don't want to do this!' I said, scowling at the maths puzzles in front of me, and wishing I could watch the dancing show on television instead.

'Why not?' my big sister asked, frowning.

Monika was trying to help me with my homework, as she often did, and she couldn't understand my attitude to my school work. My sister was eight years older than me, and was 'the clever one'. At sixteen, as she was now, she already knew that she wanted to carry on with her studies, and she had her heart set on becoming a pharmacist.

'I don't see the point of maths!' I complained. 'It doesn't interest me. I hate school! I don't like any of the subjects!'

'But why do you say that, Ola?' Monika asked. 'You need to learn. You need to study. What will you do with your life?'

'I'm going to dance! That's what I'm going to do. I'm going to leave this country and I'm going to dance!'

Mum laughed gently.

'Where are you going to go, Ola?' she said, clearly not taking me seriously for one moment.

'I don't know yet, but I am going to dance and I am going to leave this country!'

Mum chuckled to herself as she carried on peeling the potatoes, and Monika gave me a sweet but slightly patronising smile and said: 'Right, Ola, but for the time being, I think you'd better concentrate on your homework…'

Our family home was an incredibly small two-bedroom apartment on the fourth floor of an eleven-storey-high block of flats in the town of Legionowo, about a forty-five minute drive from Warsaw. During World War II, our town housed a German prison camp, and, when the Warsaw uprising took place, several Polish rebels were executed in a military shelter near our local railroad line. Looking back, Legionowo seemed to have scarcely moved on from its sad and dismal past.

In all my early childhood memories nearly everything around me in the town was grey and grim-looking, and all the buildings, including my school, looked like industrial units. Our apartment block was an ugly concrete rectangle, standing in the middle of a built-up residential area that, in those days, had virtually no green space or trees around it. All the other apartment blocks in the neighbourhood looked exactly the same, having also been built in the sixties and seventies by the Communist government.

Despite this my parents absolutely loved our home and were extremely grateful to have it. They were allocated the apartment when I was born, named Aleksandra Grabowska, in September 1982. I was called Ola by everyone from birth despite being christened Aleksandra, incidentally, as it's the short name typically used by all Polish girls named Aleksandra. It was seven years before the fall of the Berlin Wall, and at the time my parents and sister were living in one room in a much older building in a town called Nasielsk, about an hour north of Legionowo.

'You brought us luck,' my mum, Janina, said to me many times when I was a little girl. 'You were our lucky charm!'

'How?'

'Because of you we were given this apartment. We would not have had it without you, and we really needed to move.'

My mum and dad and my sister Monika not only had to sleep in the same room in the old place, but they cooked and washed clothes and did everything else in the tiny living space too.

'We had to put a screen across the room to make a little bedroom space for Monika,' Mum told me when I was big enough to understand, 'and when I needed water I had to go to an outhouse and fetch it in a bucket. Then I carried it up the stairs, because we had no lift. Imagine what it was like when you came along. We had no room for a new baby!'

We moved into our new apartment when I was six months old. My very first memory is of being in a cot completely surrounded by netting; I guess I must have been about two years old. After that I have a vivid memory of smashing my head on the entrance doors to our block of flats when I was a toddler. The doors were big, framed with metal and filled with four panels of glass. I ran to push them open one day, using all my might, only to find there was no glass in the section I pushed and so I bashed my face square into the metal, at full pelt.

Mum worried about me. I was always rushing around, full of energy, and she would often say: 'I despair! Ola is capable of injuring herself in an empty room.'

As a small child I also went through a long phase of pushing other children over and taking their sandwiches off them, so even when I was three and four years old Mum had to strap me in the buggy whenever she took me out. I'd always want to get out and I'd have hysterics, straining against the straps and pushing and kicking until I'd be hanging by the reins over the side of the buggy.

'What can I do?' Mum said to Dad. 'She has so much energy! She is so stubborn!'

Dad was the parent who generally dished out the discipline when it was needed, and he occasionally took out a belt and hit the furniture with it if I was very naughty. Dust would fly out of the sofa and I'd get the message: Dad was angry. On occasions like that he'd call me Olka, instead of Ola. He never hit me with the belt; his intention was just to show me who was boss, to keep me in line and out of trouble. I was the baby of the family though, and I was also a daddy's girl, so I go away with most things and so the belt didn't come out very often.

'She's spirited!' Dad would say to explain away most of my wilful behaviour. 'She knows her own mind, that one!'

This was true, and when I got a bee in my bonnet about something I never gave up. For instance, I wanted a dog so I nagged my parents relentlessly for years, until they eventually agreed to get me one even though my mum hated dogs and my dad knew how impractical it was to have one in our tiny flat.

Toby was a sausage dog cross and I adored him, although I soon had a scary incident with him that shook me up quite badly. A neighbour's dog went for Toby when I was out walking him one day. I quickly pulled him behind my leg, but the other dog went for me and bit my leg, leaving me cut and bleeding. Afterwards we found out this nasty dog hadn't had its rabies injection. I had to be checked out by the doctor, I was left with a scar on my left knee and I was also wary of all dogs after that. To cap it all, it turned out my sister was allergic to fur, but despite all the problems he brought, I was still adamant that getting Toby was the best thing ever. My parents very patiently persevered and we had Toby for years; I was the little girl who had brought them good fortune, and when I look back now I can see that, right from the start, both Mum and Dad always went the extra mile for me.

I can remember feeling very loved as a child, and grateful for the life I had. My parents were kind and lovely, and I knew that other kids were not as fortunate as I was. Not all of my friends were even lucky enough to have their own bedroom like Monika and I did, and I thought we were very fortunate.

My bedroom, like Monika's, was just about big enough to fit a single bed in, and our parents slept on a sofa bed that completely filled the living room when it was pulled out each night. At a push, you could fit four people around the table in our kitchen and as for the bathroom, after going to the toilet the adults had to be careful not to knock their head on the door when they leaned forward to stand up.

The lift serving our apartment block had no door at the front and you could see each floor as you travelled up and down in the rattling metal cage. This caused lots of accidents, especially with little kids who often stuck their fingers out as they travelled past each floor. My mum and dad would warn me to keep my hands inside, but they never complained about the dangerous state of the lift. As with everything else in the building and in our apartment, it was a godsend to them, having never had such luxuries before.

'Aren't we lucky?' they would say. 'Thank goodness for Ola, our lucky charm!'

2

———

'Why do you have to travel so far away?'

Mum worked in an office in their old neighbourhood, and so she had to commute almost an hour there and back by bus and train each day.

'Because that is where my job is, Ola!'

'But why so far?'

In time I understood the State controlled accommodation back then, and if Mum and Dad hadn't taken the apartment that was offered they could have ended up at the back of the queue, stuck in their old one-room bedsit indefinitely. I never once heard my mum complain about this situation, and she's always put a brave face on when she talked about her job and her long commute.

'I am lucky to have a job,' she said. 'Not everyone is so lucky.'

My dad, Dariusz, worked as an electrician and, when I was still a young baby, he began travelling to Germany for months at a time to work on building sites, as the pay there was much better than in Poland. Apparently I'd stand in the window once I was old enough, saying 'Dadda!' and looking out for him.

'It was absolutely terrible leaving you,' he says. 'I was away for months the first time, and when I came back you didn't recognise me. Your mum was saying: 'Ola, it's Daddy!' but you just looked at me like I was a stranger who had come in off the street. It broke my heart. I sat in the living room and cried like a baby myself.'

I can picture Dad clearly when I was a child. He had a huge moustache that turned up at the ends, he was on the chunky side thanks to the stodgy diet we lived on, and he had a dodgy right leg that caused him to limp. He claimed he injured it playing football, but I think he actually twisted it on a ladder. Either way, he never had it treated and it was something he just put up with.

My mum was a very good-looking woman with blonde hair. In years to come, as she got older, she would ask my dad to dye her hair auburn for her. Like all the women I knew, having her hair coloured professionally wasn't a luxury Mum could afford. She was short in height and very curvy, and I often say that my parents were like a comedy act, because there was a lot of banter between them. They finished each other's sentences and they took the mickey out of each other very gently and naturally, all the time. It is the same to this day.

With Dad working away, Mum had to rely on Monika to help look after me. It wasn't easy for either of them. Often Mum had to queue for an hour or more at a time just to get bread and milk in our local shop. That was generally all they stocked, and when I eventually started to talk I would ask my mum if we were going to the 'bread and milk' instead of saying 'shop', as the two things were synonymous in my mind.

On one particular day, when I was just three weeks old, my grandmother heard there was meat available in a town several hours away. Whenever there was a chance of buying extra meat all the women rushed out and stood in a queue, however long it was, because you never knew where the next meat was coming from. Normally, one small box of meat would be delivered to the local shop and it would be divided up fairly between the customers, which often meant each family ended up with just a few slices of cold ham, pork or chicken.

As I was born at the end of September, it was October at this time and the weather was freezing cold. It was out of the question for my mum to take me with her on a long journey across the country, and she decided to leave me in the apartment with Monika.

'Just stay with Ola,' my mother instructed my sister when she set off early in the morning with my grandmother. 'Don't pick her up because you might drop her!'

'What if she cries?' Monika asked.

'Just give her a drink of milk, but don't touch her!'

Monika was unsure about being left in charge of a newborn baby at the age of eight but she didn't argue; there was no way my mother could pass up the chance of getting meat like this.

Typically, we ate a lot of vegetables in soups and stews, many of them home grown in my grandmother's little patch of garden, plus whatever meagre quantities of meat we could get with the tokens given out to each family by the government. These tokens came on a sheet of card that you tore off one at a time and presented to the local shopkeeper. Many shops had a special 'mother and child' queue, which was meant to move quicker than the main queue. This meant that my mum usually tried to take me shopping with her whenever she could, even though all the other mothers had the same idea and so the queue was usually not much shorter anyhow.

One day my grandad returned home dragging a whole pig into my grandmother's kitchen. It barely fitted in the room, but somehow my mum and gran managed to cut it up and cook practically every part of it. A lot of the meat was pounded thinly, covered in breadcrumbs and fried in oil to make kotlet schabowy, which is one of the most common Polish dishes, and the blood was used to make black sausages, called kaszanka. Another time my dad came home triumphant, holding a rabbit he had found running wild. He told how he killed it, and then my grandmother turned it into a rich pâté, which we all devoured.

Turning your nose up at food was unheard of, and it never occurred to me to object to any of the dishes I was presented with. I was taught to finish everything on my plate – a habit I find hard to break, even now – and if ever I struggled to do this then my dad would polish off what I left, because wasting food was absolutely unthinkable.

We always had enough to eat and I never went hungry, but the reality was you could never be sure what would be available in the 'bread and milk' the next day. This meant you learned to live in a constant state of cautious uncertainly around food, just in case supplies were cut off overnight. It meant you were trained to eat your fill at every opportunity, even if you weren't particularly hungry; that was the unwritten rule.

When I was three I started going to pre-school, which was opposite the big school my sister went to just down the road.

'Monika will get you ready and take you,' Mum said, 'as I have to go to work before school starts.'

Monika was eleven now, and used to helping look after me.

'Put your jumper on Ola,' she would say.

'No! Don't like it!'

'But Mum left it. You have to wear it!'

'No, you can't make me!'

The red polo neck was a particular bugbear of mine. Most of the clothes you could buy locally were grey or dark-coloured, and if you wanted a new tee-shirt, for instance, you had to save up some tokens and go to one particular shop where you had a choice of about three different designs which were all as dull as each other. This meant that if we ever did get colourful clothes, we were expected to really make the most of them. One of my gran's cousins lived in New York and had sent this red polo neck over as a gift, which my mum was delighted about. It was really good quality but the neck was really big and itchy and went right up to my chin, and I hated it with a passion.

'I'm not wearing that again!' I'd cry.

'Put it on, Ola,' Monika said. 'Mum left it out for you. There is nothing else to wear.'

'I hate it! I'm not wearing it!'

Somehow poor Monika persuaded me to put it on time and time again, but I never stopped protesting, no matter how many times we went through the same argument.

I was meant to have breakfast at pre-school like all the other children, but the meal was a milk soup, like a kind of porridge, which I didn't want to eat, and so I'd tell the teacher I'd already had breakfast at home. Eventually the teachers asked Monika not to feed me breakfast at home so I would be hungry when I got to school, to which she replied: 'I don't.'

'Then why is she not hungry?' the teacher asked.

All eyes turned to me, and I had no answer so I just shrugged. Looking back, I simply wasn't very interested in food and eating back then. I was a petite child and didn't need big meals, but the food was always stodgy, fried or generally quite heavy.

When I was three and a half the Chernobyl disaster happened. I was too young to understand what a catastrophic event this was, but I do remember being given a shot to drink at school each day, like all Polish children were. It was a solution of potassium iodide to protect the thyroid glands from radiation poisoning. It wasn't nice, but I did understand this was not something I could refuse.

Most days my mum would prepare a thick vegetable soup or a potato and meat stew for Monika to heat up for me after school, but if Mum came home while I was eating I'd get distracted and want to get down from the table. In the end Mum got wise to this and would hover outside the apartment until Monika gave her the nod that I'd eaten enough and it was safe for her to come in.

One of the benefits of Dad working in Germany was that he brought home huge catering-sized bags of sweets and chocolates, which he would cram into our little kitchen cupboards and would last for ages. This was the height of luxury, as there was virtually nothing sweet available to buy in our shops and if you wanted a treat or a pudding then the women would normally make something with fruit and porridge or milk and cocoa. Dad also brought cartons of fruit juice, which we couldn't get in Poland. I remember staring at the packaging because the colours were so bright and I'd never seen anything like that before. We got creams and shower gels too, and he'd bring me back pretty dolls that I loved.

'I'm not taking them outside,' I'd say when I was old enough to play out. 'The other girls will be all over them!'

Father Christmas visits Poland on Christmas Eve, and on that day you are only allowed to eat fish and you get the presents after dinner. There was no wrapping paper and the presents would just be left under a small tree, in a bag. I'd often recognise the toys I was given by my parents, because they had been Monika's before, and Mum and Dad had saved them for me, hiding them in the loft after my sister outgrew them.

When I tell James things like this he finds it quite sad, but it was just normal to me. Plenty of parents did the same thing. Survival and providing the basics like a roof over our heads and food on the table was the priority; presents, however they were come by, were a bonus.

My parents didn't ever go out to eat in restaurants and they didn't indulge in any hobbies. Socialising with friends meant occasionally having them round to the apartment to share some food together. Mum and Dad were ingrained with a 'make do and mend' mentality that meant the furniture in our apartment never changed, nothing got replaced unless it was completely worn out, and whatever could be reused and recycled was. Dental care was considered a luxury. You didn't go to the dentist for routine check-ups like children in the UK do, and I can remember that if ever I had toothache my mum would put vodka on a cotton bud and hold it on the pain, to dull it. Once she sat up all night doing that, but I still never went to the dentist.

'What mattered most was that I was loved and cared for,' I have said many times when I look back on my childhood. 'I felt safe and happy in our little apartment, and what more does a child need?'

3

'If your results aren't good you are not coming out of your room, Ola,' my dad said. 'You need to study more! You need to work harder!'

I was big enough to take myself to school now and I was late every day, even though it was just over the road. I didn't enjoy school at all and only went because I had to.

We got loads of homework and I'd be forced to spend hours in my room just to do enough to keep myself out of trouble. I disliked Polish literature the most, and had no interest in maths, science or history. The only subjects I enjoyed were art and PE. I was quite good at art and I liked PE because I was always fit and wanted to stay that way, so I could be a good dancer one day. Having started to watch the foreign dance shows I saw on TV I was forever dancing around the apartment, sometimes with Monika but mostly on my own.

'Olka! Can't you sit still?' Mum would say to me. The bigger I became the more I'd knock over her pots and ornaments, as the place was so small. 'Olka take care! And look at your slippers! They are worn out with all this dancing! Look at the holes in the toes!'

At family weddings and parties I'd get on the stage and sing and dance, and I didn't care that my singing voice was never that great. If people didn't watch me I'd stamp my foot to get attention, and if they still didn't look at the stage I'd stamp even harder until they did.

I would never have behaved that way in any other situation in my life, but I felt like a different person when I was on stage. I was naturally shy and still am today, but from an early age something happened to me when I was dancing in the spotlight. It was the same with dressing up. I absolutely loved pretty dresses, and a blue and yellow one that Dad had bought me in Germany was my all-time favourite. I'd go out and play in it and then come in and get changed two or three times, just for the fun of dressing up in something different. I felt happy in a pretty dress, like I was ready to take on the world. It was important to me to look good, and to feel good, and this was another part of being a dancer that appealed to me. If dancing was my career, I'd get to wear pretty dresses all the time, and that would be fantastic.

By this time Dad was no longer working in Germany. He had set up his own electrical business locally, with a partner, and I loved having him at home full-time. Sometimes he'd play the guitar at night, and he taught me how to play the keyboard. I loved music, and I'd dance as Dad played sometimes. This was one of the highlights of the week, because nothing else in my life really interested me.

Saturdays meant tidying my room, cleaning the apartment with my mum and going to buy whatever food we could get hold of. Sunday always meant going to church, and when I was seven I took my first Holy Communion, like all the girls in the neighbourhood. I loved wearing the pretty white dress, even though mine was short and all the other girls had longer, more extravagant dresses. I believed in God and still do, but going to church was mostly just another ritual I had to go through, just like school.

I don't remember much about the Berlin Wall coming down. At eight I was too little to take in the immediate enormity of what was happening when I saw the pictures on TV and heard my parents talking about politics. In fact, I didn't even start to understand what 'politics' were until I began to experience some of the positive effects of the demise of Communism.

'We're going on holiday,' Mum smiled.

I had never been on holiday before and I was thrilled.

'Where are we going?' I asked, wide-eyed.

'Leba, Olenka.'

Olenka was a pet name my parents used sometimes; it was endearing and cute, the opposite of Olka, which was only used when I was naughty.

'Where is Leba?' I asked, feeling happy and excited.

'On the Polish sea.'

I was brimming with excitement. We had a green Skoda that we packed with our little bags for the week and, on our four-hour journey north, Mum explained that all our meals would be included at the hotel. Dad had bought a video camera and planned to film us on the trip, and he said we would be able to have ice cream and go and paddle in the sea.

I can remember the holiday vividly. I'd never experienced anything like it. We had never even eaten in restaurants, let alone been in a hotel with all the food included.

The sea was choppy and cool but we still played in it. I remember drinking in the experience of being at the coast and feeling the sea breeze blowing though my hair. I wrote a big '90' in the sand because it was 1990, and Mum and Dad looked really happy. People in general seemed to be smiling more, and ice-creams and walks in the sea felt like treats we'd be able to have again in the future. Despite being so young I could tell something had shifted; life felt freer and easier.

Back at school I was in for the best treat ever, because I found out there were going to be Ballroom and Latin dance classes on offer, on a Saturday.

'I want to go, I want to go!' I told my mum immediately. I could think of nothing better; this was all I had dreamed about.

You had to pay for the lessons as they were not part of the normal curriculum, but I didn't think about the cost at all. Mum and Dad could see how determined I was, but even so they discussed it at length. The lessons weren't very expensive, but they weren't used to finding money for non-essentials and such a regular financial commitment was a big deal to them. Even though life was getting a bit easier, Mum and Dad were products of the past, conditioned to think carefully about every penny they spent.

Of course, they let me have the lessons, and I absolutely adored them. Saturdays became my favourite day of the week. I loved the music, I loved all the different steps I was taught and I loved the whole ceremony of dance and feeling the rhythm through my body. I imagined myself as one of the fabulous ladies I'd seen dancing in fancy ballrooms on TV. I could do it, I could learn to be as good as them. There wasn't a single dance I didn't enjoy. The Cha Cha Cha was fun, the Foxtrot was elegant to perform, the Rumba and Paso Doble were just wonderful and dramatic. I also loved the energy of the Samba and the Jive. I entered another world when I was on the dance floor. Nothing else mattered but the next step, and the one after that.

I picked up the steps easily, and the fact I'd watched hours of professional dance competitions on TV must have helped. It seemed to come naturally to me, and before long I was taking part in local competitions and loving them too.

At home I'd practise all the time. I had a pink Walkman and I listened to my sister's tapes on it as I danced around the apartment. Samantha Fox, Sabrina and Depeche Mode were my favourite artists, and I also listened to copies of dance music tapes that my teacher gave me.

'You've got to come and watch me!' I told my parents when I was due to take part in my very first competition. My mum dressed me in my best clothes, which were a red skirt, a striped tee-shirt and a green waistcoat. On the day I was dancing with one of the few boys in the class and when Mum and Dad saw me their eyes nearly popped out of their heads.

'Look,' they said, nudging each other. 'Oh my God! She is actually dancing! And she is dancing with a boy!'

I don't thing they had bargained on me having learned so much, so fast, and they were bowled over by the display we put on, even though we didn't win the competition.

'She has a real talent,' one of the teachers told Mum and Dad.

'Really?'

'Absolutely. You should think about enrolling her in a proper dance school. There's one I would recommend in Warsaw.'

Mum and Dad were proud of me and pleased I was enjoying the dancing so much, but one again they had to sit down and talk about how they were going to pay for this.

'Can we afford lessons at a proper dance school?' Mum worried.

'Not really, but we'll find the money somehow,' Dad said. 'We can't deny her this when she clearly loves it, and has a talent.'

There was also the issue of travelling to and from Warsaw, which was an hour-and-a-half round trip.

'Is this really what you want to do?' Mum asked. 'It's going to be a big commitment, for all of us.'

'This is all I want to do,' I said.

From that point on I started attending classes on a Tuesday and Thursday at the Akmana Dance school, which was housed in an old Communist building called the Palac Kultury. Dad took me there in his little car – we had a Fiat then – and my parents bought me my first pair of Supadance dance shoes, which is the brand the professionals wear. I was thrilled with them and really appreciated them. I knew shoes of any kind were expensive, because when I was younger I could remember my dad cutting the toes out of the front of a pair of slippers I owned, so I could get more wear out of them when they got too small for me.

My feet were a size two now, and still growing, but I already had bunions and sore heels all the time, from years of squeezing into shoes I'd grown out of. Nevertheless, my heart leaped every time I put my Supadance shoes on.

My parents didn't complain about money or talk about it in front of me, and one way or another they always managed to fund the lessons, fill the car with petrol and kit me out as best they could. The clothes I wore were never the best. I can remember wearing the same old leggings and tee-shirts week in week out, but I didn't care. My mind was focused on the dancing and not what I looked like or how I compared with the other dancers, the majority of whom came from much more affluent backgrounds than me.

The dance studio impressed me. I'd never been in one so big before, and it had a wooden floor and huge mirrors all around.

'Wow,' I thought every time I walked in. 'This is great. This is where I want to be!'

Each lesson was two hours long and I'd usually dance with several different boys. I wasn't concerned with who they were or what they looked like, so long as they focused on the steps and took the lessons as seriously as I did. This wasn't always the case. Several of the boys were quite flaky and sometimes wouldn't turn up on time, while others suddenly left the school with no warning.

The girls were all friendly towards me and we got on well, but I was more interested in improving my dancing skills than anything else.

'I like your bag!' I'd hear one girl say. 'Ooh, are those new leggings?' They would chat excitedly with each other about their clothes and accessories, and some of them seemed more taken by the fashions than the actual dancing itself. I didn't get involved too much, not because I couldn't afford to or didn't want to make friends, but because I was so focused on what mattered: the steps and the routines, and performing them to the best of my ability. It wasn't until I started to be entered for my first proper competitions that I realised the difference in circumstances between me and some of the other girls was actually an issue.

'I need a dress,' I told my parents excitedly when the first big competition was looming.

I was ten years old. The dance teacher had explained to me the style and type of dress I needed, and I'd seen some of the competition dresses belonging to the other girls. They were like beautiful, miniature versions of the dresses I'd seen the professional dancers wearing on television, and some of them were covered in Swarovski crystals and made of the best fabric and lace you could buy. It was a dream come true to be told I was ready to wear a proper ballroom competition dress, but once again this was a big ask of my parents.

Dad gulped and nodded. 'Leave it with me,' he said.

I knew he didn't have a lot of money to throw at a dress, but at that age I still held the innocent belief that my parents were like magicians, and could make anything happen for me.

Dad didn't let me down. He has a very artistic streak, and if he'd had different opportunities in his life I imagine he could have become an artist, a musician or even a dancer.

He was taught to sew at an early age by my grandmother, who made every stitch of clothing for all of her children. When my sister had her school prom a year or so earlier, my dad made her a fabulous dress which she looked absolutely lovely in. Now he set about making me the best dress he could for the competition.

'You will look beautiful,' he told me. 'I'll make it a special dress for you.'

Dad asked to borrow a pink and white competition dress from a girl we knew, and then he copied the pattern, bought some fabric at the market and made me the same dress in black and white. He added frills and spent days and days sewing on tiny sequins. He would pick up his needle and thread every night when he came home from working on a building site, where he'd spent the day getting his big hands dirty, fixing electric cables and wiring.

While Dad worked away on my dress, Mum would be in the kitchen making a big pan of cauliflower or potato soup for dinner. I didn't know it at the time, but every single day my parents would be stashing away whatever money they could spare to make sure they could afford to pay for my lessons and keep my dancing dream alive.

The dress was a triumph. I loved it, and even though I didn't win my first competition, I remember it with pride because I held my own. I felt fantastic, in fact, and that was all thanks to my parents' love, care and handiwork.

4

When I was still only ten years old my grandfather passed away. He was my mum's dad, and he used to do an overnight caretaker job looking after a school. After one shift he was found on the floor, having fallen and banged his head. It turned out he had a brain tumour and needed an operation to remove it. He spent three months in hospital and I went to see him all the time. He had a massive scar on his head and was paralysed down half his body, so I'd help my mum feed him soups. After three months he was allowed home, and one Wednesday after school I went to see him and lay next to him on his bed while we watched TV together. He died on the Saturday. I cried and couldn't believe he was gone.

'Can I see him?' I asked, already knowing the answer. In Poland it was and still is the tradition to lay the deceased in an open casket at home, so family and friends can pay their last respects.

'Of course Ola,' Dad said. 'It is important to say goodbye.'

Grandad was laid out in his apartment. I can still remember the sweet smell of the flowers and the candles burning in his living room. I touched Grandad's face and whispered goodbye. It was a very sad day, one I will never forget.

I had a competition coming up, just two days after Grandad died. The whole family gathered and I heard the adults and my sister all saying 'she must go! She's got to go!'

It seemed like everyone in the extended family was involved too, and despite losing Grandad so recently they were all adamant I was not to miss the competition. I didn't want to miss it, but I hadn't expected to go, in the circumstances. The dress I was wearing needed some straps sewing on, and one of my uncles said: 'Give it to me, I will stitch the straps.'

Even then my family had recognised how important my dancing was, and I felt very grateful to them. I never wanted to miss a single class or a competition ever, and even when I was sick I always turned up and gave it my best shot. In hindsight I can see that dancing had already become my life, and it was heart-warming to me that my family understood and supported me the way they did.

Mum had made my costume this time, using an old swimming costume as the base. She added a black skirt with red spots and made red straps to attach to the swimsuit. She worked really hard on it, wanting to make sure I looked as good as I possibly could, even though she was nursing Grandad every day at the time, and holding down her office job.

Before the competition Monika did my make-up and hair and, on the day, several members of the family came to support me, clapping and smiling in the audience as I danced the Cha Cha Cha.

I loved being on the floor, and I could feel myself getting a little bit better all the time. By now my dream of becoming a professional dancer when I was grown up was all I could think of, all of the time. It didn't feel like a dream any more. It had become my ambition, and it felt like a realistic goal. I was already working hard towards it. All I had to do was keep practising and keep my mind focused on the prize. I could do it; I would do it.

From this point on I did very little besides dancing and going to school. As I got older I didn't go to discos or parties, I didn't mess around with boys and I didn't get up to mischief. James finds it quite strange that I don't have loads of funny stories like he does from his childhood and teens, and he teases me that I was boring.

'I wasn't!' I protest, 'Life was just different in Poland, and it's not in the Polish blood to look for a joke in everything, or put a funny slant on things like you do.'

'That's what I said – boring!'

'No, James, it was just different.'

The English sense of humour is very different to the Polish sense of humour. Polish people don't do sarcasm or try to wind each other up in the same way Brits do, and I know now that even when James is teasing my about my childhood being 'boring' this is actually another example of the difference in our cultures and in the way we have of communicating.

You could say life was too hard and too serious for us to be joking all the time. Day-to-day living was all about survival for my parents, and for me it was about striving to carve out a career as a dancer. We were all serious about the paths we were on, because we couldn't afford to be any other way. That was the mentality my parents had, and I had inherited it. Dancing was my daily motivation, and it dominated everything in my life. I lived and breathed it and there was nothing else I wanted to do, so I had to make this work.

When I was about twelve or thirteen I started dancing with a regular partner who had also started dancing at my school in Legionowo and then transferred to Alemana Dance school in Warsaw. He lived in the same town as me and we seemed to be in the same boat, in that his parents didn't have much money either. We danced quite well together, or so I thought, but then one day he just dropped me out of the blue. I never knew why and I felt quite hurt, but I didn't let it throw me off course. I couldn't; I had to keep going.

After that I was partnered with a boy called Krzysztof Ostrowski. Krzysztof was a couple of years older than me and he was very talented and a really good dancer. I was fourteen now, and he was sixteen. I enjoyed dancing with him, everyone said we made a good team, and to tell the truth I also fancied him a bit.

From that point on I felt like my dancing had gone up a notch. I was growing up, and my confidence was growing too. My teachers were always asking me to help teach the younger children, which also gave me a boost.

'Ola, can you show this step? Ola, can you demonstrate for us?'

The steps came naturally to me and I was always happy to help.

Before long Krzysztof and I were entered for our first serious competition together – the biggest competition of my life so far.

'Dad...?' I said.

'You need a new costume?'

'Yes.'

Dad offered to make me something from scratch again, but then one of the teachers said she had a costume to sell at a cut price, so we could afford it. I loved it. The costume was made up of was a white bra with fringed trousers, and Dad made me a white skirt to match so I had a choice of two outfits. I had a short bob by then and I was really pleased with the look.

I can still remember the excitement of the day. Dad drove us to the competition venue and the adrenaline was already surging through me. It was a very long day, with about six rounds of mostly Latin dances to go through. Krzysztof and I survived each round and got to the final, which took place at about 10 p.m. at night. Mum and Dad spectated the whole competition, bringing with them a bag of ham and cheese sandwiches and gherkins to keep us going. At the end of the day we were all shattered, but euphoric.

'How do you feel?' Dad asked.

'Like I have been run over by a bus!' I replied, because that was the truth. Despite this, I approached the next competition and the next with enthusiasm, and even when I felt like I was on my last legs, I never once said I was too tired to dance.

From around that time I started going to classes every single day except Sunday, when I went to church and caught up with my studies. My school teachers were very good to me. If I'd travelled a long way to a competition they let me take the Monday off or go in late, because they understood that my dancing was more than a hobby; hopefully it was my future career.

I was now old enough to take the bus myself. One day, when I was on my way to the bus stop on my own, a man pulled over in his car and wound the window down.

'I'll give you a ride,' he said.

Something about him made me scared and I ran to the bus as fast as

I could, not looking back and holding my breath until I was safely in a seat and the bus doors had closed behind me.

My sister Monika had her first child – my niece, Dominika – when she was twenty-two and I was fourteen. Looking back, in a roundabout way, this event fuelled my dancing ambition further still. Monika was studying very hard to become a pharmacist and she had the baby before she completed her studies so it wasn't easy for her, even though my parents helped as much as they could. They saved hard and paid for a nice big wedding for her and her husband, complete with a big white dress. Sometime later my dad tried to modify Monika's wedding dress into a competition dress for me. It didn't work, unfortunately, which I was disappointed about. It wasn't that I didn't get a new dress; it seemed such a shame to have spoilt my sister's wedding dress unnecessarily, and for my dad to have put so much wasted effort into it.

I used to babysit for my sister a lot and help her out whenever I could. I remember ironing little Dominika's clothes and taking her out in the buggy. One day a lady in the park said something that made me realise she thought my niece was my baby, and I can remember feeling horrified. 'No way!' I thought. 'I don't want to struggle like my sister!'

Monika loved being a mother, despite the fact life wasn't easy for her. She was young and studying hard and of course there was limited financial support from the family, even though my parents helped as much as they possibly could.

I was dating a boy around this time, and I can remember him telling me one day: 'Ola, do you know what I want to have in my life?'

'What?' I asked, my own dreams of travelling the world, winning dancing competitions and wearing incredible costumes flashing before my eyes.

'I want to have three kids and a dog.'

I gulped and felt like I'd swallowed a stone. I quite liked this boy and we'd been dating for a little while, but this remark completely put me off him, because our ambitions were so very different and I realised that we were worlds apart in the way we saw the future. The fact I'd seen how tough it was for my sister undoubtedly added to my view. Having kids was the last thing on my mind. I wanted a career first, and not just any career. I wanted to chase my dream and live my dream, and what might happen after that was too far in the future to even contemplate.

Not long after my boyfriend made this remark about the three kids and the dog, something terrible happened. His best friend hanged himself. It was over a girl, and he did it in the basement in his family home. When I heard the news my mind raced back in time, to when I was in primary school. I had a friend who was a little boy, and I used to spend a lot of time playing with him and going round to his house. One day he didn't turn up to play with me and I didn't know why.

Mum sat me down afterwards.

'I am sorry to tell you, he has been in an accident,' she said.

'What do you mean?'

'It was on the road. He was hit by a car.'

My friend was killed, and I cried. I couldn't understand how he had been there one minute and gone the next and his death really affected me. I'd drive past his house and look at it in confusion, thinking about how I'd played for hours in there with him, and how he was now gone. It didn't seem real.

Now, with my boyfriend losing his best friend in such a terrible way, I started to think about how fragile life was. I would pass his house and feel a chill pass over me. I wanted to make the most of every minute of my life, because you never knew what was round the corner. Something bad could happen to anyone, even me, at any moment.

'Life is short,' I thought. 'You have to make the most of your life. You have to chase your happiness.'

By now Mum and Dad had got cable TV in the apartment and this meant I could watch even more dancing competitions from abroad. Allan Tornsberg and Carmen Vincelj were two of the top dancers in the world at that time, and I'd watch their every move, captivated by their skill, their fantastic costumes and their amazing stage presence.

I wanted to be Carmen, and I wanted a committed and talented partner like Allan. Many of the boys I'd danced with so far had talent and great skills, but none of them seemed to be as serious as I was about dancing. When I looked at the greats on TV I knew I needed someone who had talent as well as drive. Then one day, at a competition, I thought I spotted him.

'Who is that?' I asked another dancer.

'His name is Przemek Lowicki'.

I looked at Przemek and the way he was dancing. I could see instantly that he was a great dancer.

'I would love to dance with him,' I thought.

Whether I was good enough to partner someone like him was another matter. Przemek had better results than me from competitions so I wasn't sure he'd be interested in partnering up with me, but nevertheless I wanted to try.

'I want to ask him for a try out,' I said to my mum that day.

'Well then ask him!' she said. 'What is the worst that can happen?'

'He could say no.'

'Exactly! Just ask him.'

Nervously, I approached Przemek in training one day. His coach had already tried to put me off and had told me he was happy with his partner, but to my delight Przemek readily agreed to a try-out. My heart leaped. I knew he was really good, and I knew that dancing with him was a big step in the right direction for me. I felt a surge of optimism: we could win competitions, I was sure of it. The try-out went well. We felt right together, and very soon afterwards Przemek left his partner for me and we began to compete in small championships around Poland. I was fifteen and these contests were fairly low-key but still exciting to me, especially when we started to win and were doing very well.

In order to take part in competitions you had to earn certain 'classes', which are the equivalent of British medals. The more 'classes' we attained the more competitions we were eligible to enter. We were both keen to rise up the ranks and enter into as many big competitions as we could, because this was what we had to do if we wanted to go all the way to the top.

There was just one problem.

'How much will it cost us?' soon became the first question that crossed my mind each time we progressed to a bigger and better competition. 'How will I afford a new outfit?' I fretted.

My dancing was costing a fortune by now. The lessons alone were a major expense, and there was no way you could cut corners when it came to choosing a coach. I'd learned this the hard way over the previous few years, by witnessing first-hand how the judging system worked at competitions. Basically, the dancers who could afford to pay for the best lessons progressed faster and further, but not necessarily because they had greater skills. The fact was that the judges at competitions were frequently the same people who taught the dancers they were marking, and it was an open secret in the dance world that many judges 'favourited' the dancers who paid them handsomely for lessons.

I can remember being asked to judge in a young kids' competition in the late 1990s, and one of the officials openly directed me to favour one particular kid who was a student of his. 'No!' I said. 'I won't do it.'

I was young and naïve and couldn't believe my ears. The official looked at me in confusion, startled that I wasn't going to do what so many other judges seemed to accept as the norm. I stuck to my guns that day, but that was one small victory that was certainly not going to win the war. Unfortunately, this practice is still rife in the dance world to this day.

Przemek did not have the same money worries I did. His family was much better off than mine and could afford the best coaches and all the competition expenses. 'Come on!' he'd say enthusiastically every time the next opportunity arose. 'We have to do this competition, Ola. We have a really good chance of winning!'

'OK! I'll talk to my parents,' I said every time. In the beginning I was always optimistic that they would manage to find the money once again, as they always had done, even though I knew it wasn't easy.

Then on day, to my shock, Mum sat me down and admitted that it had become a real struggle, and she could no longer afford all the lessons and costumes I kept asking for.

'What do you mean?' I said.

I was confused and upset and was clearly too young to have fully appreciated just how difficult it was for my parents. They had backed me one hundred per cent and had done such a great job of supporting me so far that I'd come to expect them to be able to pull something out of the bag each time, no matter how hard it was.

Mum's admission took my breath away.

'I'm not saying you have to give up dancing, Ola,' she assured me. 'It's just that everything is becoming more and more expensive so we have to be realistic...'

'Realistic? How can I dance without the lessons and costumes I need?'

'We will do our best, you know we will. All I am saying is that there is a limited amount of money, and we can't promise we can afford to keep paying more and more, because, well, because we can't.'

'But you've never said this before!'

'We've never had to before. We could just about manage. We wouldn't be saying it now if we didn't have to...'

'But I need the lessons! I need to progress!'

'I know, and there is nothing we want more but what can we do Ola? We can only do our best. We'll work hard and do our very best for you, I promise, but I can't promise more than that.'

I went to my bedroom and slammed the door. My mum was embarrassed but I didn't even think about this until later because I was so wrapped up in my own worries, as teenagers are.

It was only after this that it slowly began to sink in just how tough it was for my parents to have supported me this far. My dad owned fifty per cent of the electrical company he ran with his business partner and in time I learned that Dad's partner was building his own home with the profits he made, while my parents had literally nothing left at the end of each month. Literally every Zloty Dad could afford went into my dancing. He took home the equivalent of around £100 a month in those days, and a competition dress could easily cost £100, so the sums simply didn't add up.

I should have seen it coming, but I hadn't wanted to face these facts. I'd imagined miracles would keep happening, but the reality was that I could no longer make do with a dress my dad had stitched together, or a modified swimming costume. I was rising up the ranks with Przemek and money was now a really big problem.

I didn't argue with my mum about it after my initial outburst because there was just no point. I knew my parents would give me the world if they could, but the cold reality was that their love and loyalty was not enough to sustain me, and there was next to nothing left over after paying the bills and putting food on the table.

I felt frustrated and pessimistic from this point on. Przemek and I were doing so well that we now had coaches who were willing to come over from England to give us lessons, but this became a source of anxiety and embarrassment for me. I didn't want to have to spell it out to Przemek exactly how broke we were because the last thing I wanted to do was give up, but how could we go on?

Przemek's parents had understood from the start that my parents were struggling financially, and they had very generously started to cover the cost of many of the lessons we were now having. They were happy to do this and were very kind and sensitive, but even so it was hard for my parents to be in this situation.

I couldn't see how we could go on. By now Przemek and I were both completely living and breathing dancing. We were training together every evening and all day Saturday. On a Friday night we had lessons in Olsztyn, which was a couple of hours away, with an excellent teacher who taught a lot of champions and is now a judge on Dancing with the Stars in Poland. Przemek's parents drove us there every week, and ferried us home late at night after we'd trained intensely for three or four hours.

Our teachers encouraged us to enter the Polish Youth Championships in February 1998, because they felt we stood a very good chance of doing well. Anyone can enter a competition on the open circuit, and this one typically attracted around six hundred teenage dancers. Around half the dancers would be eliminated in the first round, then half again and so on, until six couples were left to compete in the final.

I had mixed feelings about entering. I believed that Przemek and I could get through to the latter rounds because our training was going really well and we were both so dedicated. I desperately wanted to compete, but the excitement I wanted to feel was quashed when I thought about the expense. How could I do this to my parents?

The competition was being held in a big sports hall in the city of Szczecinek in the north west of Poland, several hours' drive from our home town. We would have to stay overnight, and I would need a good costume, as every girl would be in her best dress.

I fretted about the costs, and seriously considered telling Przemek it was out of the question, but then Mum took me aside.

'Ola, we know you want to do it,' she said. 'We have saved some money. We want you to take part, and we have enough to buy you a new dress.'

'A new dress?' I said, amazed and delighted.

'Yes, Ola. We will have it made to measure for you.'

Mum told me the name of the lady who was making it, and I was completely taken aback as I knew she made beautiful dresses for lots of professional dancers. For the first time in my life I was totally lost for words. I'd had a few nice dresses by now, but all of them were second hand, bought from other dancers or from the teachers and modified to fit me, which is common practice. I hugged my mum and told her how grateful I was.

'I told you we would do our best,' she smiled.

'Thank you. It means so much.'

The build-up to the competition was tense. Przemek and I had to approach it as if we might get into the final, as our teachers hoped we might, and this meant rigorous endurance training. When you prepare for any final you perform five dances one after the other, with a ten-minute break in-between. Then you repeat this five times. Each dance is just over two minutes, and in Poland the order is always the same: the Samba, Cha Cha Cha, Rumba, Paso Doble and finally the Jive, which is the most energetic dance of them all. The idea is that if you can perform all of the dances five times over in training, making twenty-five dances in total, then if you get to the final it should feel easy to perform them just the once. The better your fitness and stamina on the day, the better your technique will be too, and so the higher your chances are of winning.

I was mentally and physically tired as we prepared for the championships, and I think my Mum and Dad went through the mill too. Two days before the competition I left my dance shoes on the bus on my way home from training in Warsaw. Mum made frantic phone calls to the bus company and I was panicking like mad. Not only were the shoes new and expensive, but I needed to wear them in before the competition. Thankfully, the bus driver found them on a seat and Dad went to collect them from the bus station.

That was one panic over, but on the way to pick up my dress, en route to the competition, we had another drama when Dad's ten-year-old Fiat broke down.

'This is turning into a disaster,' I thought. 'This is jinxed.' My stomach was churning with nervous energy and I was feeling completely stressed out.

Dad managed to crank the car back into life and when we eventually arrived at the dressmaker's house I breathed a sigh of relief. 'Please no more panics,' I thought.

I'd been measured for the dress and I'd been to a couple of fittings so I was cautiously optimistic. Thankfully, trying on the finished costume for the first time was a fantastic and unforgettable experience. It was a tiny little creation with a cut-away waist and hundreds of gold sequins shimmering all over it. Mum and Dad gasped when they saw me in it. 'You look lovely!' Mum said, beaming.

'Thank you,' I smiled. I felt lovely, and I wanted to do them proud. I knew the dress had cost a fortune – much more than a month's wages for my dad – and I told them over and over again how much I appreciated what they had done for me.

Our accommodation that night was a hostel with a shared bathroom down the hallway, and I went in there to cover myself in fake tan. I'm not sure what I did wrong, but the tan went all streaky and looked a terrible mess.

'For God's sake, how many things can go wrong!' I cursed as I did my best to patch it up.

On the morning of the competition it took me hours to do my hair and makeup. My sister Monika had taught me all she knew, but I was still learning. I plastered my face in thick foundation and dark, dramatic eye make-up. That was the fashion back then, and I completed the look by decorating my hair – which at the time was slicked into a short black bob – with a wide sequinned band to match my dress.

The final drama came when Przemek and I realised that one of us had forgotten the record book you are meant to take to every competition. You are supposed to have it stamped before each competition, and we feared we might be disqualified before a friendly official let it pass.

I was a nervous wreck, but once we'd cleared that final hurdle I caught a look at myself in the mirror and took a deep breath. I loved my dress and I felt a surge of excitement. I couldn't wait to start dancing; at last that was all that was on my mind.

Mum and Dad sat in the audience, near my teacher, and I smiled over as Dad got his video camera out and prepared to film me on the dance floor.

I have very little memory of the intricacies of the actual dances we performed, or of the physical effort we put into every one, but I can remember the excitement I felt as we got through the first round, then the second, and just kept going all the way. Finally, about ten hours after we'd done our first dance, the compere announced the names of the six couples in the final. 'Przemek Lowicki and Aleksandra Grabowska,' he called ceremoniously over the microphone. My heart skipped a beat and I gasped.

I couldn't believe we'd made the final six couples. When we took to the floor for the final the adrenaline was rushing through every part of my body and I felt flooded with nervous excitement. It was a surreal experience, because it somehow felt like I just blinked and then it was all over.

Przemek and me were standing on the podium, on the highest point in the middle, surrounded by the runners up. We had won, and I could scarcely believe it when we were presented with the big silver trophy and crowned the youth champions of Poland. It was simply amazing. My mum and dad were cheering and clapping and I felt like I was living in a dream that had somehow come true. Everybody wanted to congratulate us. I was surrounded by lights and sequins and smiling faces. It was a moment I will never, ever forget.

I was totally exhausted afterwards, and ravenous too. I had barely felt like eating all day but now I was eating bread and meat and cheese and whatever other snacks my parents had brought.

I collapsed into bed, totally spent but feeling euphoric.

The next morning, when I woke up in the hostel, it was a different story. The excitement and satisfaction of winning came back to me, but then I immediately felt unsettled.

What would happen next? My mind was jumping around, trying to piece my thoughts together and make sense of them. I was the youth champion of Poland. This was an amazing achievement and I felt proud, but I was scared. This was a stepping stone to greater things, but there was a wall in front of me.

It was like waking from a dream and realising things aren't quite what they seem. My dream had come true, but the reality was this title would heap more pressure on me to go to the next level with Przemek.

I looked around the room. It was sparse and functional and grey, and it was a stark reminder of my circumstances. Getting to this competition had cleaned my parents out. When I look back now I don't like the fact that my story keeps coming back to money, but unfortunately that was exactly how it was. There are no state hand-outs or benefits in Poland,

and if you earned a low wage you just had to make do. There was no safety net at all for a family like ours, so the reality was that I had no choice but to keep thinking about where the funds were coming from.

All the way home from that competition my emotions swung from joy to despair. The title had brought me happiness laced with a whole heap of worry.

5

Przemek and I continued to compete but I felt increasingly uneasy. As the weeks went by I had a very strong feeling that I was on borrowed time. Przemek and I would be expected to go to the next level, which was the Polish Amateur Championships. There was no way I could turn up in the same gold dress at another big competition, and I couldn't expect to get another costume so soon. It felt like a hopeless situation, and I soon began to think about exactly how I was going to tell Przemek it was over, and that I really could not carry on.

I had started at a good senior school in Nasielsk, the town where I was born, when I was fifteen. It was a vocational business school and, like all the other pupils, I was being prepared to take an office job when I left at the age of eighteen. My mum had left her old office job in that town by now, but I'd think about how she had commuted for years and worked long hours. 'That will be me,' I thought. 'I will have to stop dancing and I will have to do the same job as my mum did.' I began to imagine that the commute I made home from school on the bus would soon become my daily commute back from work. I'd earn a living and I'd be able to put food on the table, which was essential. Dancing wasn't essential. That was the plain truth.

Sometimes I'd look at my parents and feel despondent and upset. They worked so hard, and they were tired. I wished they had a better life and I wanted more from my life, but there was no point in being angry or resentful. There was nothing I could do to change my circumstances.

I limped on for a while. Przemek and I were asked to take part in the World Youth Championships in Vienna, which was an honour and very exciting, but my memories of the event are dominated by thoughts of how tough it was for my parents. As contestants, Przemek and I had a lovely hotel room provided. His parents checked into the same hotel as us but my mum and dad had to stay with friends as there was no way they could afford the hotel bill.

Przemek and I did reasonably well, finishing about fourteenth, and I enjoyed the competition itself; whatever was on my mind, I always lost myself on the dance floor and loved every moment.

Afterwards my parents and I wandered around the markets in Vienna in the snow. It was November and we drank hot punch to stay warm. I looked at Mum and Dad, wrapped up against the cold in thick coats and hats and gloves, and I felt a huge surge of love for them. They had done so much for me, and the last thing I wanted to do was exploit their good nature or make life harder for them in any way at all.

We went to a few other competitions in Austria, Germany, Lithuania and Slovakia, driven across the border either by Przemek's parents or by one of our coaches. I remember Lithuania was really poor, worse than Poland. There were holes on the dance floor at one competition, the local women looked worn down as they carried their bags of shopping and it was dark and cold.

Przemek and I did well every time, usually progressing to the quarter-finals or the semis or even the finals, and our coaches told us they wanted us to take part in the British Open Championships in Blackpool.

'Blackpool?' I blinked, thrilled at the idea. I could already see the glitter balls and sequins and hear the big band music I'd seen on TV. It made my heart thump.

Blackpool was and still is the Mecca of the ballroom dancing world, and the British Open is the biggest competition in the world.

Przemek and I knew we would not come away with a trophy, but we felt confident we had the potential to do well and survive several rounds. It would also be a fantastic opportunity to dance on the same floor with some of the greats I'd seen on television over the years. All the pros I admired would be there: Carmen Vincelj, Bryan Watson, Allan Tornsberg, Paul Killick and Hanna Karttunen, Karina Smirnoff and Louis Van Amstel... these were my childhood heroes, and I would finally see them in the flesh and step onto the same dance floor they had danced on. It was amazing.

Inevitably, money was still on my mind and as well as feeling excited about Blackpool I was fretting about the travel arrangements and the cost of the trip right from the moment it was mentioned. 'We'll do our best,' Mum and Dad said. They smiled, but I could see in their faces that they were digging deep.

'I don't have to go,' I said.

'Ola, you go. We have saved some more. You must go.'

When I looked at them I thought to myself: 'This will be the last time. Blackpool will be my finale.'

The plan was for Przemek and I to travel by car and ferry from Warsaw to England with our coach. We'd spend a few days training at the famous Semley Dance Academy in Norbury, near Croydon, where many of the top dancers in the world practised, before taking part in the All England Dance Competition in Brentwood, Essex. From there we would travel up north to Blackpool, actual Blackpool! Przemek's parents would fly over and meet us there, but sadly my mum and dad could not afford to travel to England.

I was shaking with excitement when we set off. I had no idea at the time that the car and ferry journey would be very long – over a thousand miles long – but I wouldn't have cared anyhow. I loved travelling abroad, Przemek and I had photographs taken of us smiling on the ferry, and I thought it was very funny when we crossed the Channel and suddenly had to drive on the left-hand side of the road.

'This is what I want to do,' I thought. 'This is how I want to live my life.'

I couldn't wait to dance at Semley, let alone Blackpool. I stayed in a room in Norbury with about six other young female dancers, and we were all packed in with sleeping bags on the floor. The cramped conditions didn't bother me in the slightest; in fact, I gave more thought to the fact the electric sockets were different to the ones in Poland as they had strange on-off switches, and that the hot and cold water came from two taps instead of one mixer tap like we had at home.

'How can I wash my face? I laughed as I tried to run my hands between the hot and cold.

It made me tingle to step into the legendary Semley studio for the first time and Przemek and I trained very hard, loving every minute. I was also very excited to go to the All England Dance Competition. It was a well-known and respected competition and still is, and it was valuable experience for us to have on our way to Blackpool. It had been a long and tiring trip and I was quite exhausted, but when I put on my dance shoes I felt completely energised and threw myself into every routine with passion.

I drank in every moment. I can remember looking around the dance hall in Brentwood and feeling dazzled by the lights and the soaking up the music and the atmosphere. When I danced all my worries about the future were forgotten and I was totally focused on my moves. Przemek and I did reasonably well and I was feeling good. I felt I was in the right place, and this was my destiny.

'I don't want this to end,' I thought.

When the music stopped and the lights went out at the end of the night, logic told me it had to end, yet something deep inside, some sixth sense, told me not to give up, not yet.

I felt this very powerfully at that All England competition. It was like I had an angel on one shoulder saying: 'Ola, keep following your dreams. Work hard and be true to yourself, and all your wishes will come true.' On the other shoulder there was a devil saying: 'How can you do this? It's not fair to Przemek. It's not fair to your parents. This is not your destiny, Ola. You are a poor girl from a poor family. It's time to get real. It's time to stop dreaming.'

I felt torn, and I wished I had a guardian angel who would swoop down and sort it all out for me, but that wasn't going to happen, was it? Just like my parents, all I could do was my best.

There was definitely something in the air, and unbeknown to me I was admired across the dance floor at that competition, by an English dancer I'd never met or ever heard of before. He had a string of titles to his name and had won a lot of some major titles, all over the world. Never in a million years would I have thought he'd have looked twice at me.

Apparently his mum had pointed me out to him. When he watched me he loved the way I danced and thought I was a natural, raw talent.

'Wow,' he said to himself. 'She's mesmerising. I love the way she moves!'

It didn't enter his head to pursue me as a partner, as he already had a very good partner he was doing extremely well with, but those were his thoughts. He was twenty years old and very ambitious, but I had absolutely no idea about any of this.

Blackpool was a fabulous experience. Stepping out onto the famous ballroom at the Winter Gardens was totally thrilling for me. I was still only sixteen years old and I was on this floor with hundreds and hundreds of dancers, many of whom were the best in the world. I was awestruck.

In the early rounds there were so many dancers all around that you almost had to step over people to get a look at the great names. Carmen Vincelj and Bryan Watson were dancing together and I was absolutely thrilled when I spotted them. I'd only ever seen them on Mum and Dad's tiny little TV, on the foreign satellite channels I'd tuned into ever since I was a little girl. Now they were before my eyes – on a floor I was going to dance on – and I was loving every moment of being in the midst of such talent and excitement.

I admired so many of the other contestants I saw that day, but one in particular caught my eye. He was tall and very good looking with slicked-back black hair and piercing blue eyes, and he was dressed in an incredibly well-cut grey suit. His dancing was amazing, which was hardly surprising, as I found out he was ranked as one of the best dancers in the world in his age group. His partner was Polish, and when I watched them dance together I was filled with just one thought: 'I want to have a partner like that one day.'

At one point during the competition I actually got introduced to this tall, dark stranger, very fleetingly.

'Hello!' he smiled. It was busy, chaotic even. He smiled, and then he was gone. All of the dancers were quite distracted, thinking of nothing but their next dance, and where they had to be next. The brief meeting stuck in my mind, though. I thought this guy would be incredible. I would really like a partner like him one day, I thought, but he was well out of my league. A girl could dream, though, couldn't she?

6

P rzemek and I did reasonably well in Blackpool. I don't think we got our best scores ever, but we did ourselves proud and thoroughly enjoyed the experience. Quite soon after this one of our coaches started to talk about the upcoming Polish Amateur Championships. Przemek was keen to take part, and this was expected of us after winning the Polish Youth Championships. There was a long list of other competitions Przemek wanted to enter too, but once I'd come down from the excitement of Blackpool all my old negative, fearful thoughts returned to the forefront of my mind. This was impossible. My family simply didn't have the money for me to keep doing this. I would be seventeen later this year and I was going to have to get a job; it was as simple as that. I would be an adult soon and I couldn't expect my parents to keep supporting me once I had finished school.

Within weeks of going to Blackpool I finally made up my mind to stop dancing with Przemek. It wasn't fair to hold him back, and I thought he would be better off with a new partner. The fact I could not go to the Polish Amateur Championships in my old gold dress put the top hat on my decision. The costume had cost my parents so much money – my dad had literally grafted for a month to pay for it – and I'd had a lot of use out of it, but I simply couldn't get away with wearing it again. I'd stood on the winning podium at the Polish Youth Championships in it and had my photograph taken holding the winning trophy. Everybody would know I was in the same old dress. I couldn't face it and it was unacceptable in the dance world.

I phoned Przemek with a heavy heart. It was a cold day in the summer of 1999. I didn't discuss it with anybody, because I'd made up my mind and it felt exactly the right thing to do.

'I'm very sorry, I can't be your partner any more,' I told him.

'I know it's been a struggle…' he started.

'I know you understand,' I interrupted, not wanting to pick over the whys and wherefores.

'I do, but…'

'I'm sorry Przemek. I've made up my mind and I'm not going to change it. I don't want to hold you back. You are one of the best boys in Poland and you will find a new partner who won't hold you back.'

He sounded gutted and I was too. Przemek didn't make it any harder for me than it already was, and he didn't protest. He had seen the writing on the wall for a long time as he'd watched me and my parents struggle to pay for my dancing, and he must have known how hard it was for me to make this call.

We wished each other good luck, and I put the phone down and stared at the receiver. I didn't cry, though I was very upset. I was trying to be strong, trying to tell myself I'd done the right and decent thing. I shouldn't have regrets. We'd had a great run together and all good things must come to an end. Nobody could take away my skills and I'd had some amazing experiences.

I took a deep breath. Life had to go on. I would study hard, finish school and start saving up for driving lessons as soon as I got an office job. I could look forward to that.

Mum and Dad were very kind and supportive and said lots of positive things about the future, but I didn't feel they truly understood how I felt, because how could they? I had one friend who did appreciate how tough my decision was, because she competed at swimming at a very high level and knew what it was like to be driven by a passion, but fundamentally it was a lonely time for me. I'd devoted so many years to my dancing and my whole world was wrapped up in training and competing.

I did carry on dancing after the split from Przemek, going to some training sessions and practising with another guy, but it wasn't the same. I still loved to dance, but my focus and goals had been taken away, and that was very hard. The other boys I danced with were not as talented as Przemek and I sensed very strongly that I was on a downward spiral towards stopping dancing altogether. I was clinging on though, not wanting to let go despite the fact my dancing career was now going nowhere.

Looking back, I went through a patch where everything looked grey in my life. I'd still watch the dancing shows on TV, but the excitement I used to feel was tainted. The sense of wonderment I used to have, feeling that I could reach out and touch that life, and that it was actually attainable to me, was gone. I'd had a taste of that life in Blackpool and I really had reached out and touched it, but where had it got me? Ultimately, it had brought me nothing but disappointment.

Now, watching a big competition was like having a recurring dream that starts off really well but then turns bad, and the worst thing is that you know it turns bad. It means that even when you are in the good part, you can't enjoy the colour and the glamour like you did the first time, because you know what's coming. The lights will dim, the sequins will lose their sparkle, and the world you wanted to be in – the world you actually did step into – has faded and is slowly turning to dust.

'How are you?' Dad would ask from time to time. 'Are you happy with your decision, Ola?'

'Of course,' I'd say. 'I'm fine. You don't need to worry about me!'

Dad was always going on about politics. He was, and still is, very angry about corrupt politicians and the Communist regime he'd spent so many years living under. One day, when he asked me how I was, a reply sprang immediately into my head.

'I feel like a wall has been built in front of me.'

Of course I couldn't say this out loud; Dad would have been devastated. But that is what I wanted to say because that is exactly how I felt. I'd lived more than half my life after the fall of the Berlin Wall, but the sad fact was that the closer I came to achieving my ambition to travel the world as a dancer, the more I was restrained by the Communist legacy my family had been left with. The wall may have been demolished, but a huge, insurmountable brick wall was standing in my way, because we didn't have the money to get over it or around it in any way. I was trapped behind it, and now I always would be, because dancing had been my passport to the rest of the world.

I was at dance practice one day when my dad called the studio in Warsaw.

'Someone is trying to call you from the UK,' he said.

'Who?'

My ears pricked up.

'She's a Polish girl. She said she wants to speak to you, something about a partner. She phoned the house. I've given her your mobile number.'

'Right, did she say anything else?'

'No. She's ringing you any minute.'

I put my mobile down and it immediately rang again. To my amazement, the girl explained that she was the dance partner of the English dancer I'd seen and admired in Blackpool a few months earlier. His name was James Jordan, and it seemed that each of them had decided to look for another partner, in order for them both to progress further.

'James would like to come to Poland and have a trial with you,' the girl explained.

'OK, that would be great,' I said. I was in total shock and couldn't believe my luck. I wanted to scream 'Oh my God!' and punch the air but of course I didn't. 'I'd like that,' I said calmly. 'How has this come about?'

The girl explained that James had seen me dance in Brentwood and been very impressed. I was surprised by this, because when we'd met very briefly in Blackpool I had no indication that James had ever seen me before in his life, though I guess he was so caught up in the competition there was no time for small talk. I was told that James had spent many months having trials with forty or fifty different girls but had not found a suitable match, and that was why he wanted to fly to Poland to try out with me.

I could not have been happier. I went straight home, not even finishing the practice session I'd planned. On the bus home I was brimming with excitement. I couldn't get my head around the fact this amazing dancer, who was not only very talented but also very gorgeous to look at, was going to come all this way to try out with me. I didn't seem real at all. He'd seemed so out of my league, and I was bowled over by the fact he'd been impressed by me at Brentwood. It was a lot to take in.

I rushed in the apartment and told Mum and Dad the news. They were really pleased for me, because they could see how excited I was, but seeing them suddenly reminded me about our circumstances. I was potentially opening up a whole new world of financial struggle if this partnership worked out. It had been such a fantastic surprise to even get the call that I'd not given this a second thought until now. Having a trial with James Jordan had eclipsed everything. It was too big an offer to turn down. Fortunately for me, my parents were in complete agreement that I absolutely had to take the opportunity.

'But how will we manage if it comes to anything?'

'One step at a time Ola. Have the trial and then we just have to take it from there.'

The arrangements were made swiftly, via James's current partner. I booked the dance studio at my old school across the road and Dad agreed to collect James from the airport in Warsaw the following Saturday. As well as being James's dance partner, the girl who had phoned me was also his girlfriend. This was part of the reason they wanted to find separate new partners, as it wasn't really working out for them being in a couple and being in a dance partnership. Immediately after the trial with me, James was going to take a short internal flight to where his girlfriend lived on the other side of Poland.

It didn't bother me that he had a girlfriend; in fact, I don't think I even thought about this at all. I was four and a half years younger than James and never considered for one moment that he could possibly be interested in a girl like me, not in that way. He was spoken for and was very renowned in the dance world, and I felt young and inexperienced by comparison. Nevertheless, when I saw James walk through arrivals at the airport my heart skipped a beat.

'Oh my God!' I thought. 'This gorgeous thing had flown in to dance with me! How lucky am I?'

James was dressed in very tight jeans, a white tee-shirt and a puffy black sleeveless jacket. His jet black hair was long, his eyes piercing blue and he looked incredibly handsome.

'Wow!' I thought. 'He's actually here!'

I was trying to act all cool and calm, but apparently my dad could tell how bowled over I was. When he called my mum to tell her we'd collected James at the airport he told her: 'This is the start of something. She'll definitely dance with him…'

James didn't speak a word of Polish and I had precious little English, so we communicated by smiles and nods on the car journey to our apartment. We were both used to being around foreigners because of dancing so it wasn't particularly awkward, just frustrating.

Przemek had been to one of the best schools in Warsaw and spoke perfect English, and so I'd been able to rely on him in the past if need be. I'd been taught English for two years at school but my language skills were shocking and I couldn't say anything. I really wished I could; there were so many questions I wanted to ask James. I would have loved to talk to him about all the competitions he had been in, what his favourite dance was and why, what his goals and ambitions were for the future and exactly how he lived in England.

My cousin came over, as she spoke a bit of English, and that was helpful. Mum gave James some soup and some pierogi, which is a type of filled dumpling she often made. He seemed to enjoy it, and then we went over to the studio at the school. Mum and Dad sat down in the corner, we put on the music and then James took me in his arms.

I'll never forget that first dance. I felt completely at ease right from the start, and I know now that James felt the same. In fact, after just three steps he had made his mind up that he wanted me to be his next dance partner. We did a back basic, which is when the man takes a step forward and the woman steps back, then a hip twist and a simple fan position to start. James says he could feel me oozing through the music, and I know what he means. It felt just right and very comfortable, like we were made to dance together. I felt connected to James and the music and so I relaxed into it very easily.

We did the Rumba and the Cha Cha Cha and James says I felt all s[...] and fluid and womanly in his arms, rather than stiff and hard like some of the other girls he had tried out with. It was an amazing, surreal experience. James looked great and he danced brilliantly. I couldn't believe my own luck, and even if nothing came of this I felt so fortunate to have had this experience and to have caught the eye of a dancer like him.

We danced for about an hour in total before walking back to the apartment, where my cousin was waiting for us. We all squashed around the small table in the lounge, and it was only at that point that I realised I was wearing a thin pink tee-shirt with no bra. I had big breasts even at that age, but back then I was so innocent I often went braless without giving it a second thought, as young girls do. All my attention was focused on the dancing and getting my steps right. In fact, though we laugh about it now, James says that my lack of a bra was also the last thing on his mind. He noticed of course – what man wouldn't? – but like me, what interested him the most at that moment was how I danced and how we interacted. He had spent thousands of pounds searching for a new partner, and my dancing and compatibility with him was all that mattered.

'Can you move to England?' he asked, smiling.

My cousin translated James's words, though I could tell what he was saying.

'Yes,' I blurted out immediately. It was a no-brainer. I had absolutely no hesitation in replying.

My dad spluttered. 'Hang on, not so fast. What do you mean?'

James explained that he trained regularly at the Semley studio in Norbury, where I'd practised before Brentwood and Blackpool earlier that year. He described to my parents how, being in South London, the studio was about thirty miles west of where James lived with his parents in the Medway area of Kent.

'I'd like Ola to train with me in Norbury,' he said. 'The best dancers in the world train there and it's a hub for the best Ballroom and Latin teachers in Europe. Lots of champions have come out of Semley. Can she move over? I could help her find a place to rent nearby, so we could train every day.'

My stomach was doing cartwheels. I simply couldn't believe this was happening to me. James had walked into my life and completely turned it on its head. I could pursue my dream of having a dancing career after all, and James was so talented that we might really go far. I was so excited and so sure this was the right thing that I would have walked out of the apartment and got on a plane to England with James that night if it were possible.

Inevitably, it wasn't that simple. I was still only seventeen and my parents were not at all sure about sending me to England on my own, or how they could fund it. They started asking all sorts of questions about how I would manage, and of course they wanted to find out more about this tall dark stranger who had walked into our lives and set the cat amongst the pigeons.

It wasn't easy speaking through my cousin, but we managed to work out that James lived with his mum and dad, Sharon and Allan, in a place called Strood in Kent. Allan was a site manager at a local power station, and James also worked there to fund his dancing. Sharon worked in a bank and James had one sister, Kelly, who was just a year older than him.

James seemed very polite and friendly, his family sounded nice and hard-working, and he was clearly incredibly dedicated and serious about his dancing. There was just one little question mark hanging over his reputation. Before James had arrived in Poland my parents had naturally asked some of the coaches they knew if they could tell them anything about him. One or two had mentioned that James had a bit of reputation for having an 'eye for the girls' when he was single. It seemed that before he was with his girlfriend James was quite a 'player'. I had heard the same thing myself when I asked around at my dance school in Warsaw. I wasn't surprised because he was so good-looking and, in any case, what was the harm in someone like him playing the field when he was young, free and single and surrounded by pretty girls? Besides, James was a potential dance partner, not a potential new boyfriend. I really hoped his history wouldn't worry my parents unnecessarily when they came to make the final decision on letting me go.

We talked for a long time around the table. Unfortunately, when James eventually explained that it was time he left to catch his internal flight to meet his girlfriend, we all suddenly realised we'd left it far too late to get him to the airport on time. James had missed his flight, so my parents offered to put him up for the night. He accepted, and made arrangements to catch another flight early the next morning. Mum said he should sleep in my room, and so I had to share the pull-out bed in the lounge with my mum while my dad slept in my sister's old room. With the apartment being so tiny it was quite a crush.

'Mind your head,' I tried to explain when James went to the toilet. The room was so small that men of his height had to open the door a bit before they stood up, or they'd bang their head as they tilted forward.

'Ouch!' I heard him say as we all heard the bang from the kitchen table just feet away.

I wasn't worried about James staying in the apartment. Even though it was nothing fancy by any stretch, my mum always kept the place shining like a new pin. She was still as proud of it then as she was when they first moved in seventeen years earlier, and she was pleased to be able to offer our guest a room for the night.

My bedroom was so small that there was next to nothing in there besides the bed and the wardrobe, a small desk and a fairly recent picture of me on the wall, smiling in the gold dress. I didn't care about James being in my room. I had nothing to hide, though I had no idea at the time that he was quite shocked that we lived in such cramped conditions.

I would learn later that James had lived in a variety of houses of all sizes, including a huge five-bedroom property his dad built himself and a poky, two-up two-down council house, after his family ran into financial trouble in the early 1990s. Mind you, even that was about three or four times bigger than our apartment, which had a floor space of just forty-six square metres.

James says it was an eye-opener for him to see how I lived, and he remembers my bed being hard with dimply covers and a stiff mattress. He was under no illusion that my family would find it a struggle to fund my trip to England, and that there was a lot for them to discuss before they agreed to let me go, but this didn't faze him. He was full of ambition and drive, and he had a positive, can-do attitude.

I could see he had set his heart on having me as his dance partner, and I could also tell that he was not the sort of person to take no for an answer. He had a spark in his eyes and he spoke with passion. Though I couldn't speak English I'd had lessons in school and I felt I understood a lot of what James was saying because he spoke with such enthusiasm and was very expressive, using his hands to help him get his point across.

James's girlfriend was not happy he had missed his flight and she phoned the apartment late at night to find out what was happening. I picked up the phone and immediately went to my bedroom and handed it to James, waking him up.

'Where are you?' James's girlfriend asked him.

'In Ola's bed,' he replied innocently, half-asleep.

'What?' his girlfriend said, sounding alarmed.

'Don't worry, she's not in here with me or anything like that!'

Having spoken to me just a split second before, James's girlfriend was understandably confused.

'Then how come she gave you the phone straight away if she is not in the bedroom with you?'

'Believe me, if you saw the size of the apartment you would understand!' James laughed.

He left the next morning and got on a rickety old propeller plan to Szczecin, which is about an hour's flight to the north west of Warsaw, towards the Baltic Sea.

As soon as he'd gone I started nagging Mum and Dad.

'You've got to let me do this,' I said. 'It's an opportunity I might not get again.'

If I went, I'd be flying by myself, for the first time. Mum and Dad both had to work and would not even be able to take me over to England to check out the location or settle me in. None of these things bothered me.

'You're very young,' Mum said.

'I know, but opportunities like this don't come up every day.'

While James was a well-known 'name' in the dancing world, having either reached the finals or won every major competition he'd gone in for, I was an unknown. The youth title I'd won with Przemek was a feather in my cap but it didn't compare with the huge collection of trophies James had amassed.

'I'm lucky he's prepared to take a chance on me,' I said, 'and he knows what he's doing. He's tried out with forty-odd girls! We have something that could really work.'

Mum and Dad called a family meeting with my Dad's parents and my aunts and uncles. It was held at Grandad's house. I wasn't allowed to listen, but I can remember them all sitting around the table looking serious as they prepared to discuss my fate. I waited anxiously in another room, terrified that they might say no. I'd have been absolutely devastated and I was pacing the floor, praying for a positive outcome. Eventually I was called into the room. My heart was beating fast and I held my breath as Dad spoke.

'We have decided you can go to England, Ola,' he said.

My heart exploded. I was absolutely thrilled to bits.

Dad had a mixed expression on his face. I could tell he was delighted to deliver the news I wanted to hear, but at the same time he was a little bit sad and concerned, as any parent would be in the circumstances. I had a close bond with my family and we all knew we would miss each other so much, but Mum and Dad loved me enough to let me go. It was a huge moment in my life.

I started smiling and laughing and thanking everybody. Mum started explaining that one of the deciding factors was that I had an aunt in Covent Garden, so at least there was a relative nearby if I got into difficulty. My safety and wellbeing was what concerned my parents the most, so having my aunt there was very reassuring to them.

'Thank you!' I beamed. 'Thank you! Thank you!' My heart was absolutely thumping. I felt on top of the world.

From that point on everything moved very quickly. James was ecstatic when I phoned to say I was allowed to come over, and he immediately started to look for a flat for me to rent in Norbury. My parents used what few savings they had to buy me a one-way plane ticket to London, and they said they could afford to give me the equivalent of £300 cash to take with me. It was a huge amount of money to them, and it wiped their savings out completely. After that money ran out I would be on my own, so I would need to find some sort of work to support myself. None of us knew how long the money would last as we had no idea how much rent I would have to pay, or how much money I would need for food and basic bills. All of this was for me to work out when I arrived in the UK. James knew that my parents couldn't afford to send me any more money, and that they were relying on him to find me affordable accommodation and help me find work.

'Don't worry,' he said. 'She's going to be brilliant. We'll make it work. It will all be worth it!'

James said that he would pay for the practice sessions out of the money he earned working with his dad at the power station. 'We're a team,' he said optimistically, 'I'll do what it takes.'

I wasn't nervous or daunted in any way when I thought about flying to England on my own. Poland would always be there for me, so what did I have to lose? The answer was nothing, and I had everything to gain. I couldn't wait to get to Norbury and start dancing every day with James, and I'd have boarded a plane to London the very next morning if it were possible.

In the end, my flight was booked for two weeks' time and I was buzzing every day as I prepared to leave. I didn't discuss my decision with anyone outside the family. I told my friends what I was doing, of course, but I didn't feel the need to talk it through with them because I was absolutely confident I was doing the right thing, and nothing anybody said would have changed my mind. The boyfriend I'd had – the one who said his ambition was to have three kids and a dog – heard about my plans and came up to me in the street one day.

'You'll waste your life,' he said.

I shrugged off his remark. He was just jealous, I thought. I believed very strongly that I'd be wasting my life if I stayed in Poland and didn't follow my heart. If anything, his pessimistic remark made me more determined to leave the country and strive to succeed at the highest level possible.

I took myself to the local hairdressers and decided to have my long bob cut short, right up to my cheekbones. I also asked the hairdresser to shave it up the back.

'Are you sure?'

I nodded. The style was very severe, especially as my hair was still dyed jet black.

'I don't know when I'll get it cut again,' I explained. 'I need a cut that will last.'

My sister was delighted I had such a fantastic opportunity and she supported my decision to leave, though she was worried about how I'd look after myself and manage on my own. She was still very protective of me, and she took me out and bought me a black coat with buttons down the front to keep me warm. I bought myself a few English books, including a yellow dictionary, and I decided what I would take in my one small bag: one pair of black shoes that matched everything, one jumper, a pink shirt, a pair of black trousers, my practice skirts and leggings and my old dancing costumes and dance shoes.

Meanwhile James found a room for me to rent in Norbury, in a big house where a lot of dancers stayed. Everything was in place, and all that remained was for my parents to take me to the airport.

Saying goodbye was bittersweet. I knew I would miss them, but I couldn't wait to get going.

'Take care, Ola,' they both said, hugging me goodbye and telling me they loved me, and to let them know when I arrived safely. The plan was for James and my aunt from Covent Garden to meet me at the airport and take me to my room.

'Everything will be fine!' I smiled. 'Thank you for everything! See you soon.'

The truth was I had no idea how long I would be away. I wanted to cry and laugh all at the same time, and I was full of nerves and excitement. I had never flown in my life before, so even boarding the plane was an adventure to me. As I buckled my seat belt on the flight I had a very real sense that life was never going to be the same again. I wasn't nervous at all about flying on my own; it was just another step towards my goal, another step in my adventure.

When I came through arrivals and saw James, I felt really excited. He was wearing green combat trousers, a white tee-shirt with capped sleeves and the black sleeveless bomber jacket he'd had on in Poland. I thought he looked gorgeous.

'Welcome!' he smiled.

He looked very charming and friendly and I had absolutely no worries that I was putting a lot of trust in him, and had changed my life so dramatically to train with him.

I think the fact I'd been in the dancing world for so many years already had made me grow up fast in many respects. I was used to dancing with older partners, travelling to new places and meeting people from different walks of life. It was what you had to do to if you wanted to rise through the ranks as a dancer.

James showed me and my aunt to his little black Citroen Saxo GTR and we set off to Norbury.

'This is it,' I thought, as I looked out of the window at unfamiliar buildings and billboards daubed with slogans I couldn't understand. It was a dull, cool day in early April 2000 and most of the landscape looked as grey and nondescript as it was back home, but nevertheless I felt like I had landed in paradise. I'd got over the wall. 'I'm on my way,' I thought. 'Bring it on!'

7

I looked wide-eyed around the room in the house in Norbury that
James had found for me to rent. It was small and clean, with a pull-
out bed, a TV and a cupboard.

'Thank you,' I said in my heavily accented voice.

My aunt checked the room out too and said she thought it seemed
OK. The rent was £280 a month, so that meant I'd be left with just £20
to live on.

'Don't worry,' James said. 'I'll help you find a job.'

I nodded. I probably looked like a rabbit caught in the headlights but
I wasn't scared, just a little awestruck. I trusted James completely. He
was like a knight in shining armour to me. He'd swooped into my life
and brought me to a whole new world. He carried himself with great
confidence and I felt happy to let him take control.

'We're a team,' he repeated. 'I'm working. I will help you. Don't worry
about anything.'

I smiled. I had a good feeling about this, which was amazing
considering I was already very nearly flat broke and had no plan B.

The studio was very close by, and James took me there later. I was
glad I'd been to Semley before, because everything else around me was
so unfamiliar. I'd switched on the TV in my little room and not been
able to understand a word. Strangers had spoken to me in the corridor
and I just nodded blankly. The streets smelled different to the streets at
home. I couldn't put my finger on it; perhaps it was the diesel fumes of
the buses or the London taxis that I wasn't familiar with? Even crossing
the road felt alien to me, as I automatically looked the wrong way to see
if any cars were coming.

Once I was in the dance studio with James I felt more at home. This was
an environment I was very comfortable in, and I was looking forward to

getting started. The evening practice sessions were typically two hours long – something I was well used to – and about thirty couples would share the floor, each paying £8 for the night.

As soon as James and I started to dance I felt myself relax. It was just like at the try-out. We clicked again immediately, and it felt like we'd been dancing together for years. I looked at James and felt secure and happy. I could see he was respected amongst the other dancers, and it was also very obvious how incredibly passionate he was about practising and perfecting every step. That was how we had to be if we were going to make it, and I was prepared to give one hundred per cent too.

From that day on we got into a routine whereby James would drive to the sessions every evening after finishing his job at the power station. I learned that he had been working for his dad, who was an engineer and the power station supervisor, for a few years. James had left school at seventeen, worked for a company that made medical air filters for about a year, changing the filters on the machines, and then left because it was difficult to take all the time off he needed for competitions. After that he started working for his dad, making the tea for the men on the site, and then he did lots of manual jobs all around the power station. He had no desire to be an engineer or pursue a career in the power industry, but the job was flexible and fitted around his dancing, which was his priority.

'The dancing comes first, second and third,' he said.

Despite having been the number one male ballroom dancer in the UK for several years, James had never received financial help or sponsorship of any kind. I started to see that in many ways he was in the same boat as me, having had to self-fund his dancing, with the help of his family, all the way through. The only difference was that the UK was a richer country than Poland, so James and his parents had always been able to earn more money than my mum and dad to keep the dancing going.

In some other countries, like Denmark, the top-level dancers are paid up to £30,000 a year by the Dance Association so they don't have to have a separate job and can devote all their time to training and competing.

Brits and Polish people have never had that luxury, but at least this meant that James could identify with my situation, and he never once made me feel bad or embarrassed about my lack of funds.

I learned very quickly that James never saw money as anything other than a means of financing his dancing. Money for money's sake meant nothing to him; it was a currency to be exchanged for lessons and practice, or dance shoes and competition fees. Paying my share was never an issue, because as far as he was concerned we were in this together and my progress was bound up with his. However, James did understand that I wanted and needed to support myself as best I could outside of the dancing, and that I was prepared to roll up my sleeves and do whatever it took to support our joint goal.

'I've found you a job,' James said chirpily one day, not long after I had arrived.

I frowned.

'Pardon?' I said, struggling to understand his Kent accent.

'Job. Work. For you,' James said patiently, realising he'd spoken too quickly for me.

He was very used to talking to foreigners because of all the international dancers he'd met and worked with, and he knew how to make himself understood, but he forgot himself sometimes.

'OK,' I smiled, realising what he was telling me. 'Thank you.'

If I'd spoken better English I would have added: 'Thank God for that. I've been living on the cheapest burgers from McDonalds and I've only got £4.50 left to my name!'

I'd been in lots of the shops and cafes and local businesses asking for work but had got nowhere. I was prepared to clean, wash dishes or wait on tables, but my English was virtually non-existent so nobody was interested in taking me on.

Later that day, James took me to a boutique hotel near my rented room, which was also used by a lot of dancers. The owner was prepared to pay me £4 an hour to serve the breakfasts and do a bit of cleaning from 7 a.m. to 1 p.m. He seemed like a decent family man and I accepted the job, thinking to myself this could work well. I would be able to sleep after work then go to practise with James in the evening. I took the job gratefully, and started work the next morning.

In the meantime, James was still living with his parents in Strood and working from 6.30 a.m. to 4 p.m., at the Kingsnorth Power Station on the Isle of Grain. As he had no qualifications in engineering or mechanics he was still basically a handyman, even though he'd been there for a few years by now. He was driving trucks, making deliveries to different sites, doing some basic welding, cleaning furnaces or dangling two hundred feet in the air stripping metalwork. Thankfully his pay had risen to a generous £400 a week despite the menial nature of the work, which meant James could easily afford to pay for all of our practice sessions at Semley and as many lessons with the best teachers as we could afford.

He'd drive straight to Norbury after work every night and we'd go in the studio, sometimes dancing until midnight. Then he'd drop me back at my room before driving back to Kent in his Citroen Saxo.

'Are you OK Ola?' he asked me every day.

'Yes, I think,' I said. 'Thank you, James.'

I had started to watch EastEnders and other soaps and TV shows whenever I was in my room, and I was slowly picking up some words and phrases. James was very patient with me and helped with my English a lot, but it was still really hard for me at first. I'd look through my books to try to help myself, as there was no way I could afford proper language lessons. It was a frustrating and slow process, and I had to push myself every day.

Despite this, I always felt comfortable in James's company and our dancing was going well. Both of us could sense that our partnership was working, and that our initial reaction to each other had not been wrong. Every night I enjoyed the moment we stepped onto the dance floor. Though it wasn't always easy to communicate with words, when we danced it was as if we completely understood one another. I'd follow James easily, and it felt like we were bringing out the best in one another.

I phoned home to tell my parents about the job and they seemed pleased. I bought a BT phonecard and went to a phone box in the street as that was the cheapest way to call abroad, but it still cost about £5 an hour to call Poland. That was more than I was earning so it wasn't something I could do very often. Hearing Mum and Dad's voices was always good. I did miss home a lot and had some bouts of feeling homesick, but my drive to succeed as a dancer eclipsed everything. I didn't long to go back. I knew I would see my family again before too long, and I told myself that all this effort would all be worth it. James and I would do well. We had the potential to be winners together, and all my energy went into making this happen.

Our plan now was that we would spend five or six months practising hard together until, hopefully, we felt ready to enter competitions as a partnership. I had no idea how things would work out in the long run, but I had faith in James and his commitment to me and our dancing. I could tell he liked a challenge, he liked to be in charge and he did not take no for an answer when he believed in something. I admired all of those qualities in him.

I couldn't afford to pay my rent after the first month so I looked for another room. I wasn't unhappy about having to move out of the first place as it turned out my landlord was also a drug dealer, which I didn't like at all. After that I stayed in several different rooms, taking whatever was cheap and available and, most importantly, local to the studio. Living like this was tough, but I had to watch every penny and I had no choice. It was unsettling and I was on my own a lot of the time, but when I look back I don't remember getting downhearted or lonely. I have never minded my own company and I'm not afraid of hard work, so I just got on with it, almost without question. Some days were absolutely horrible and stressful, but I gritted my teeth and pushed on, day after day. I guess that's how you are in your teens. Life was an adventure and I had an optimistic outlook, because why wouldn't I? Dancing motivated me and I loved it with a passion, so it would have taken a lot for me to become demoralised.

The only time I ever remember questioning what I was doing alone in the UK was when James cancelled practice, which he did on a handful of occasions. I didn't fully realise at the time, but he was having problems in his relationship with his girlfriend, and as the weeks and months went on it became apparent to me that this was turning into a painful break-up for him.

I had got myself a cheap mobile phone and if ever he couldn't make it, James would call me and explain that he simply couldn't get to practice. He would always be very apologetic and sounded very disappointed.

'I'm sorry,' he said one time. His voice was cracking and I could tell he was trying not to sob.

Other times he turned up looking upset, tried to hold it together but then he started crying in the studio. I was kind to him, of course, and always told him not to worry about me, and that it was not the end of the world if we missed a session. I felt uneasy about the future though when this happened, because I needed James to be rock solid if we were going to make it.

'What if James can't carry on dancing with me?' I fretted privately.

I was scared that James might pull away because of his personal problems, and then what?

'Don't think about it, Ola,' I told myself. 'Keep going. All you can do is your best. Work hard, do your best.'

I heard my parents' voices in my head; their powerful work ethic ran through my blood. I would not be defeated. I would carry on, and I would not give anyone in Poland – and especially my old boyfriend who had been so rude about my opportunity – the chance of saying: 'I told you so.'

8

One day the owner of the hotel where I did the breakfasts and the cleaning offered me a deal.

'You can stay in a room in my hotel for free and I will give you £30 a week. What do you say?'

At this time I was earning £60 a week from him, so it seemed like a good offer to me. I'd effectively be paying just £120 a month rent in total, which was a lot less than I'd paid anywhere else. It was a good deal for him too as he'd be paying me £30 less and he had plenty of spare rooms.

'Yes, I agree,' I told him. 'Thank you.'

I moved in as soon as I could, and I also picked up some extra work cleaning the dance studio a few days a week. This meant I was often scrubbing floors and polishing mirrors from 4 a.m. to 6 a.m. before doing the breakfasts and other jobs in the hotel from 7 a.m. to 1 p.m., or sometimes 2 p.m. if there were extra chores to do. After that I'd sleep and go to practice, dancing with James for three or four hours, right up until the studio closed at midnight. It was an exhausting routine but I could manage it, or at least I could to begin with.

'Ola, I need your help! There is more work to do.'

It was the hotel boss, and he was telling me, not asking me, that I was obliged to do yet more jobs.

'Really? I have worked seven hours for you already today.'

The boss had started to get me to do extra cleaning and change and iron the sheets, and it was very hard to say no. I was trapped because I needed the job and of course the boss also provided the roof over my head. My natural instinct is to avoid a conflict if at all possible, and so I'd just think to myself: 'Oh never mind, why not just do it? It's only a bit of cleaning.'

Thankfully, his wife was a very kind Indian lady and she'd slip me an extra £20 whenever she knew I'd done more work, but as the weeks went on the boss started to ask me to do even more and more, and the unpaid hours were adding up fast.

'But I cannot do more,' I said many times. 'I have to sleep. I am tired now.'

'You have to do more! You are staying in my hotel and you have to help me!'

I was starting to get headaches and I didn't feel very good in my skin. There was another reason for this, besides the tiredness and lack of sleep. I still couldn't afford to eat well and I was living on a lot of cheap junk food and ready meals.

I had gained five kilos – about eleven pounds – since I arrived in the UK, though I didn't realise this until one of the coaches at the studio made a remark about it. He was a teacher I knew who travelled to Poland from time to time to coach Polish dancers.

'Ooh, you've been eating well Ola,' he said, eyeing me up and down in my leggings and tee-shirt.

My English was still poor but I couldn't fail to understand what he was saying as he looked at my curvy body. I ran my hands over my hips, feeling self-conscious.

'What?' I spluttered, not able to find the words to respond.

Nobody had ever commented on my weight like this before and I really didn't know how to handle it. I felt embarrassed, and I also felt a bit foolish to have not realised I'd been gaining such a noticeable amount of weight. I had been in England for a few months by this time and in hindsight my weight must have been creeping up slowly ever since I stepped off the plane. I was seventeen going on eighteen, so I was at the stage where my body had been naturally changing too. I was filling out and developing a different body shape as I matured. This had been happening since I was about sixteen, but I'd been oblivious to any weight gain, until now.

I ran to the toilets to gather my thoughts.

'What can I do?' I thought, feeling horrified as I looked at myself in the mirror in the toilets.

My belly was rounded and I looked bloated and puffy all over. I couldn't believe I hadn't noticed this myself. I had always been the petite one of the family, and that's how I always viewed myself, right up until this remark was made. It's a day I won't forget, because in my mind it marks the start of a long and continuing battle to control my weight.

I didn't know what to do to lose the weight. I'd never had to think about what I was eating in my life before. I had avoided eating too much of the fried, stodgy foods my mum and others cooked all the time in Poland, but this had nothing to do with consciously watching my weight. As I was dancing all the time, I didn't want to feel stuffed with heavy food and I didn't like to feel really full, so I simply never ate huge portions. I hadn't considered that a burger or a ready meal I picked up from a takeaway or the corner shop in Norbury would make me fat, because junk food didn't fill me up in the way a plateful of home-cooked Polish food did, and it didn't make me feel stuffed or too heavy to dance. I'd been eating whatever I could afford, whenever I felt hungry, and not giving it a second thought. After all, that was how I had been brought up. Food was fuel and you filled your body at regular intervals, making the most of what was available. You consumed what was on the plate in front of you, just in case the next day there was a shortage.

I was completely clueless about nutrition, dieting or counting calories. All I knew was that I had to do it. My looks mattered a great deal. I was under no illusion that young dancers like me were meant to have amazing-looking bodies, and it was no secret that the girls with the best figures, who looked the most dazzling on the dance floor even before they took a step, were at an advantage. Dancing is a spectacle, a show. You are there to entertain and captivate the audience and the judges, and the better you look physically, the better chance you have of progressing to the top of the profession.

James had never mentioned my weight, thank goodness, but I was worried about what he thought. I hated the idea that he might be looking at me differently now I'd put on weight and was more curvaceous than when first met. He was lithe and toned and had a washboard stomach, despite the fact he was often the one who would suggest we picked up a burger or a pizza. We both remember that at the time you could buy a meal from McDonalds for £2.88, and that is often what we did, because it was cheap and convenient and we needed every penny to pay for our dancing.

When I weighed myself I discovered I was over nine stone. I'm only five foot three and I was used to being around eight stone. That was a healthy weight for me, and one that suited me. I didn't want to be super-skinny and I'm not suggesting that nine stone is an outrageous weight by any means. I wasn't fat, but for a short, seventeen year old dancer like me, being over nine stone was just too heavy. To shine on the dance floor, particularly in a little dress, I needed to feel great about myself and one hundred per cent confident in my appearance, but suddenly I didn't.

I decided exercising more was the answer because I wasn't over-eating. I can see now that it was the quality and type of food I was eating and not the quantity that was the problem, but I didn't understand that then, and even if I did I couldn't have afforded to buy the fresh fish and chicken or fruit and vegetables I should have been eating.

I couldn't afford to join a gym either, so I took up running. I usually ran with one of James's dancer friends, Neil Jones, before and after my hotel jobs. It would be dark in the morning and it wasn't great running along the pavements of Norbury, but I persevered. I pushed myself, in fact, running for miles until I was red in the face, sweating and seriously out of breath. Neil seemed to get progressively fitter and trimmer and at first I thought I must be doing really well too, because I was exhausting myself and burning up a lot of energy. The results didn't come though, and to my dismay my weight stayed the same, and I continued to feel bloated and puffed up.

'It is not fair!' I said. 'Why can I not lose this weight?'

James and I were working very hard in the dance studio every night too, so it didn't make sense that I wasn't losing weight. Every day I was exercising for anything between two and five hours, but nothing made a difference to my shape or weight. I'd started to talk openly to James about the problem by this time, as we were getting to know one another well, but unfortunately he could not come up with any answers. This was unknown territory to him; in fact, he would complain that he could not put on an ounce even if he wanted to.

I kept up the running and I decided to eat less, to see if that worked. I wasn't very happy about this because it wasn't as if I was eating huge quantities to begin with, and I enjoyed my food. I also got tired when I ran or practised with very little fuel in my body, and I think this was why I was suffering from headaches, and continued to do so for months on end. I found it difficult feeling hungry, and I had no real plan when it came to my diet. I'd deny myself a biscuit, say, but then have a shop-bought sandwich or ready meal for my dinner, because I needed something quick and cheap to eat.

Life was a struggle, not just physically but emotionally too. Sometimes when I phoned my mum I cried because I felt homesick when I heard her voice. Strangely, I can't remember this, but my mum does. She says she would ask me if I was sure I was doing the right thing.

'Yes,' I'd always say. 'I know it will be worth it.'

Mum and Dad would never have told me what to do or encouraged me to go home. They wanted me to follow my heart, but they always kept close tabs on me, making sure I knew that I didn't have to stay in England if I didn't want to, and that they would support me in whatever decision I made.

My sister came to visit me after a few months, and she was very shocked by the way I was living.

'I don't know how you can do it, Ola,' Monika said, looking around my shabby little room. I know I couldn't.'

'Really?' I said, surprised at just how shocked she was.

I honestly didn't think my situation was that unbearable, despite my occasional tears.

'You're stronger and braver than me,' she said.

I'd never considered myself to be strong and brave, but I guess Monika had a point. The dancing had given me drive and determination.

I wanted to be number one in the world, and if I had to put up with a few hardships along the way, so what?

My sister hardly had any money with her, but she spent almost all of it on buying me food and toiletries. She kept back just £20 for herself, as she wanted to buy some duty free perfume at the airport on the way home. To this day she feels guilty about that.

'What was I thinking?' she says. 'You were living in poverty and there was me thinking about buying perfume! I wish I could turn back the clock and give you back that £20.' She cried when she got on the plane home, and she told my mum how sad it was that I was living like that.

I have told her not to feel guilty. At the time it never even crossed my mind that I could make better use of the £20 than she could. I was getting by, just, and I was dancing every day with James. That was all I really cared about. The experience was priceless.

9

In the summer of 2000, James and I decided to enter our first competition together – the British Closed in Bournemouth. This is an annual competition open to dancers living in the UK, and it's useful in terms of showing you how you rank in the country. It's not a massive competition like some of those held at Blackpool, for example, but it was a very good starting point for us.

James and I had been training together for three or four months by now, and things were going very well in the studio. As well as taking part in the practice sessions where you shared the floor with lots of other dancers, we were having about four private lessons a week, which cost around £60 each.

A lovely man called Greg DeWet ran the Semley studio with a wonderful lady called Linda Ungaretti. Greg is now in his sixties and Linda is sadly no longer with us, but in their heyday the two of them were the life and soul of Semley. Greg was in charge of playing the music and was also a costumier. He was always very kind to me and James and knew we didn't have much money, so he'd sometimes let us into a practice session without charging us, and he also took us out to dinner from time to time, which was a treat we really appreciated.

'Would you like me to make you a dress?' Greg offered when he heard we were going to Bournemouth.

My eyes lit up. I had been thinking that I would have to wear my old gold dress, though I really wanted something new, to make me feel at my best and to give me a boost to my confidence.

'Yes!' I smiled. 'Thank you!'

James paid Greg about £200 for a pair of trousers and £150 for a competition shirt for himself, and Greg said he would keep the cost to below £400 for my dress, which was not a lot of money for a custom-made Latin dress, even then. I couldn't keep up with the whole conversation between Greg and James when this was being discussed, but I understood how much money we needed to find, and I obviously looked concerned.

'Ola, I will get the money,' James said. 'Don't worry.'

'Thank you, but...'

'It's not a problem. This is what I go to work for.'

I knew James's parents were very good to him and that they didn't charge him rent or housekeeping, so he could put all his earnings into our dancing. He had told me many times that I didn't have to worry about money, and that he would pay for everything he could afford, but this was a lot of cash to find.

'Ola, I've got the money,' he said. 'If I didn't have it I wouldn't offer to pay.'

I had met James's parents several times by now, as they often came to watch us dance. They reminded me of my parents, because they would look on proudly and offer words of encouragement, and they clearly enjoyed seeing their son doing what he loved to do. It was always a pleasure to see them when they came to Norbury, because they were so positive and supportive, and they accepted and welcomed me very warmly, right from the start.

Before James was earning money for himself his parents spent thousands of pounds every year supporting his dancing. Even now he was working, if he needed to find extra cash for clothes or competitions, James knew he could always rely on them to help out if need be. They always did this willingly, knowing how hard James was prepared to work and how much he wanted to progress and achieve with his dancing. They believed in his talent one hundred per cent, and they completely understood that in the dance world you have to accept the concept of deferred gratification. You don't win prize money or payment of any kind for taking part in competitions, even the biggest ones in the world. First and foremost you compete for the pure love of dancing. The financial benefits hopefully follow later, when the higher you climb in the world rankings and the greater your reputation as a dancer becomes, the better the chances you have of sustaining a career as a dancer by doing shows and teaching, at home and abroad. Allan and Sharon accepted this willingly and were happy to do whatever it took to help their son fulfil his ambitions – just like my parents did.

Greg made me a simple black dress with a slash up one thigh and a few stones on the top to make it sparkle, and in the days leading up to the competition I got to work on my false tan, an essential part of every dancer's preparation, men included. Of course, we didn't have the luxury of spray tans back then. Instead I applied five layers of fake tan cream to achieve the very dark tanned looked that was the fashion at the time. It was a boring, messy process and I ended up with black palms that had to be scrubbed and scrubbed afterwards – once it was so bad I even had to use bleach provided by James's dad Allan to get it off.

The day before the competition James drove us to Bournemouth in the Saxo and I was feeling very nervous all the way there. As well as James's parents, his gran and grandad, some aunts and uncles and a couple of his close friends, David and Martin, were also coming to watch us, none of whom I'd met before.

I wanted to make a good impression on everyone. I wanted to do James proud in front of his friends and family, and of course I wanted to impress the judges and the various dancers and coaches who I knew on the circuit. The dance world is very close-knit, and you saw the same faces all the time at competitions. I knew there would be people I'd met in and around Poland, and I wanted to prove to everyone that I'd made the right move and my partnership with James was working out.

James was equally keen for us to prove ourselves. When he asked me to come to the UK he'd been told by several people that he had made the wrong decision, because I wasn't a 'name', and he could do better. In fact, one of his coaches even dropped him when James took me as his partner, warning him he was messing up his chances of success.

'I know I am right,' James told the coach confidently. 'And when I make up my mind, I don't change it. Ola will be incredible, you wait and see.'

On the morning of the competition I spent ages applying heavy make-up with dramatic, dark eyeliner, which was also the style then, and I slicked back my black bob, which was still severe and very short, setting it hard with half a can of hairspray. Most dancers opted for a slicked-back look or wore their hair in tight buns or plaited styles, set in place with loads of grips and decorative stones and clips. You needed to make sure your hairstyle would stay in place all day, and so loose curls or high maintenance styles didn't work.

James dyed his naturally mousy brown hair jet black regularly, and he also slapped on the fake tan with abandon, as the Latin look was all the rage for the male dancers. This complemented my look, and all of James's family and friends who came to support us were very kind when we were finally ready, telling us we looked great together. James's dad added the finishing touch by pinning our competition number onto James's back. This had become something of a family ritual. Allan had made laminated number cards, as James didn't like it when the paper numbers got a bit sweaty and torn as the day wore on. James was also very fussy about having the number pinned in precisely the right place on his back: not too high that it looked wedged between his shoulder blades, and not too low that it made the number dip into the small of his back.

Despite all of our fastidious preparations, when we stepped onto the dance floor for the first heat I suddenly felt totally unprepared. It was like we'd only just met and had rushed into things, and I felt horribly uncomfortable in my dress. I hadn't lost any weight and I felt I was too big and could have looked so much better if I was several pounds – if not a stone — lighter. Years later James joked that I had looked like a Teletubby with a Star Trek hairstyle, but thank goodness he didn't come out with that on the day. My confidence was frail enough.

To my relief, when the big band music started up and we began to dance I lost myself in the moment. I focused totally on my dancing and I found my confidence and drive, which I know now is what always happened when I began to dance. It was like I was transported to another place. All my worries and fears disappeared, and all I could think about was the dance, and how much I enjoyed it.

Our practice served us well. James and I passed through all the heats with ease, and at the end of a very long day we secured fourth place.

'Not bad,' I said.

'Not brilliant,' James said.

I think we had both secretly hoped we could do better than that, and we were a bit disappointed. To put things in perspective however, this result ranked us amongst the very top couples in the country, but that wasn't good enough for us. James and I both wanted to win, and we didn't just want to be number one in the UK, we wanted to be champions of the world.

Returning to Norbury was a bit of an anti-climax. It had been exciting to go away to Bournemouth and compete, and I had enjoyed being with James and his family and seeing another part of the country. We'd stayed in adjoining rooms in a guest house, but now I was on my own again in my little room, working hard with my various jobs and living each day for James's arrival in the evening. Then we would rehearse the same dances again and again, perfecting our steps in the five Latin dances you are required to do for competitions: the Cha Cha Cha, Samba, Rumba, Paso Doble and finally the Jive. Although we were both trained in Ballroom we'd chosen to specialise in Latin, as it was more passionate and expressive and we enjoyed it so much more.

One good thing was that my English was improving quite quickly now, so much so that my boss had started to ask me to answer the phone on reception, and take bookings. I didn't like doing this and I still don't really enjoy speaking English on the phone, as I find it more difficult than speaking face-to-face and taking cues from body language and facial expressions.

'E'd loch tae book a dooble room fur thes weekend,' a gruff voice said.

'Sorry, can you please say again?'

I could feel myself starting to panic, as I couldn't understand a single word.

'E'd loch tae book a dooble room fur thes weekend,' the man repeated, beginning to sound agitated.

'Sorry, I get help.'

I was in quite a flap as I nervously explained to my boss that there was someone on the phone, who didn't seem to be speaking normal English. The boss sighed, took the phone off me and made the booking without any problem at all, speaking English the whole time. I looked at him in surprise and confusion.

'He was a Glaswegian,' my boss said when he put the phone down.

'Pardon? What is this?'

'Scottish. He was from Scotland. They talk with a strong accent, especially when they are from Glasgow. You will learn!'

He laughed kindly. My boss wasn't all bad and could be generous-hearted at times, but I was still being called upon to work a lot of hours over and above what we'd agreed. I was starting to think about looking for a new place to live before too long, and then something happened that brought this about quicker than I'd anticipated.

James and I had decided to enter another competition, and I explained in advance to my boss that I would not be able to work on that particular day. He agreed to this, saying I would have to make the hours up. However, when I tried to leave early on the morning of the competition he blocked my way, putting his foot down aggressively in front of the hotel entrance door.

'What are you doing?' I asked, shocked.

'You're not going anywhere!' he shouted. 'I need you!'

'No!' I screamed, feeling panicked. I wasn't scared of my boss, but I desperately didn't want to miss the competition. 'I have to go! I need to leave now. I already told you!'

'No!' he yelled back, 'I need you here!'

He stamped his foot and I managed to slip past him and run to where I'd arranged to meet James. When I told him what had happened he flipped, and marched straight round to the hotel, fuming.

My boss also ran a coach business, and when James arrived he was standing in the street up the side of the hotel. There were about a hundred passengers on the pavement waiting to board his coach, and the worst of it was that we knew most of them, as they were dancers on the way to the same competition as us.

'Who do you think you are, threatening a young girl like that?' James ranted.

'And, first and foremost, Ola has moved to England to dance, not to clean your hotel! You knew that when you employed her.'

The boss's wife was there too, and she started waving her arms around and shouting at James to stop making trouble.

'I'm not the one making trouble,' James screamed. 'I'm not the one who's upset a young girl. How dare he!'

James forced my boss to apologise in front of the other dancers waiting to board the coach, and he made him promise faithfully to never, ever talk to me like that again, or to put me in any situation that made me upset or panicked.

James and I then went to the competition, and once I got back I smoothed things over with the boss. I agreed to continue serving the breakfasts from 7 a.m. but said I would not be doing any extra hours, and would finish work at 2 p.m. on the dot every day. There was no argument about this, but as soon as I could I found another room to rent, in a house shared by a group of German girls.

I was glad to move out of the hotel, but the new place was really horrible. There was no bed in my room, just a mattress on the floor, and the whole house was freezing cold.

'I'm cold, can I turn on the heating?' I asked, shivering.

'No,' the girls said. 'It's too expensive.'

I was trying to apply my false tan, but when I put the cream on it just sat on my skin and stayed wet. In the end I had to use my hairdryer to get it to dry, which took ages. By the time I was finished I was really fed up and miserable. To make matters worse, I was paying £300 a month to live like this, and I had quickly found out that the rent for the whole house was only £600. This meant the three German girls were only paying £100 each, even though I had the tiniest room. It wasn't fair, but what could I do? I was sick of moving around, and I wasn't confident I'd find anywhere better for that money, so I just put up with it and kept myself to myself. I didn't want any more trouble.

James and I were getting to know each really quite well by now, and I was starting to express myself much more freely than I had at the beginning. For instance, in the September, when I'd been in England for around five months, I told James on the phone: 'I can't train, birthday.'

'What do you mean Ola?' James said, annoyed. 'You can't just cancel practice because it's somebody's birthday.'

I wasn't sure exactly what he was saying so I just repeated: 'It's birthday.'

James didn't hide the anger in his voice.

'Ola. Listen to me. Practice is important. Whose birthday is it?'

He knew I didn't have any close friends so he was confused about why I was prioritising someone's birthday over training.

'It's birthday. My birthday.'

'Oh! I see…'

James could have kicked himself. Not only was it my birthday, it was my eighteenth. My aunt from Covent Garden was coming down see me. She was bringing a cake so we could have a little celebration, because she knew that I would be on my own and that I probably wouldn't have any presents, as it was too expensive for my parents to send stuff over.

'Of course you don't have to train on your eighteenth!' James said. 'Happy birthday Ola!'

Occasionally, James and I would have a little bust-up in the dance studio about a step that went wrong, or a certain move that one of us made. For instance, I found it very easy to pick up a new routine, while James tended to take a bit longer for something to click. Once he'd got it he was brilliant, but sometimes I'd get impatient with him along the way.

'No, James! It's like this!' I'd say, unable to see how he couldn't get it right first time.

Usually he was fine with me being a bit bossy on the dance floor; he understood that I simply wanted our routine to be perfect, just as he did. In the same way I accepted that if I made a mistake, it was natural for James to get angry and let off steam.

'Ola, what are you doing?' he'd snap.

'I'm sorry.'

'You should be!' he'd then tease, immediately softening.

Neither of us took criticism personally. If we'd had words in the studio it would all be forgotten immediately afterwards. 'Arguments are bound to happen,' James would say. 'After all, we're trying to be the best in the world!'

Very early on he taught me a phrase that we have stuck by ever since those early days.

'What happens on the dance floor stays on the dance floor,' James said, and this has always worked for us. In time we added to this, agreeing that whatever happened outside the dance floor stayed outside.

This didn't always happen back then. James had continued to have problems with his girlfriend and one evening, the night before another competition, he turned up to practice looking very upset indeed, worse than I'd ever seen him. He had finally broken up with his girlfriend, and his eyes were red from crying. I told him to take a break if he needed to, but he wanted to practise. We also did the competition the next day, and did very well. After that James went away on holiday for a week with his friend David, and when he came back he had obviously been doing some thinking.

'It must be really hard for you, Ola,' he said. 'I'm sorry I've not really thought about what life is like for you.'

James told me that he had been so caught up with his own problems that he had failed to see how tough it must have been for me, living alone in a series of grotty rooms.

I shrugged. 'It's OK. You work hard too.'

'It's not the same. I live with my parents, I am in my own country. I'm older than you. I think you have done amazingly well, and I have been the one coming to practice in tears! I'm really sorry.'

I laughed it off. 'James, it is fine! I am fine.'

When what he had said sunk in, I was grateful to James for being so honest and caring. I didn't need him to acknowledge the sacrifices I'd made. He had given me an amazing opportunity and I was happy to make them. I knew what I was doing, but it was still nice that he had taken the time to talk to me like this, and it marked a change in our relationship. We understood each other better still, and that could only be good news for our dancing partnership.

I admired the fact James had carried on with the competition when he was going through a bad time, though this didn't surprise me. James's determination was phenomenal; I'd seen that in his eyes the very first time I met him. He was not a man who gave up; he was a fighter, and we had that in common. Nothing was going to knock us off course, and now we had no distractions. The world was our oyster.

10

'W'ould you like to come to my parents' house for a meal?' James asked one day.

'Yes, thank you. That would be nice!'

Even though I'd met Sharon and Allan, and also James's big sister Kelly, lots of times by now I had never been to Kent, and I was interested to see where James lived, and pleased he wanted to invite me. Kent was just the name of a place to me. I knew nothing about the Medway area where he grew up and still lived, and I didn't know much about his background at all. By contrast, James knew a lot about me, having stayed with my parents in Poland, and having been involved with my various landlords and rented rooms. I felt he knew more about me than I knew about him, so I was looking forward to seeing more of his world.

Around this time, James and I were planning to take part in two important open competitions that were coming up, where we felt we stood a very good chance of doing well. We'd recently taken part in a competition in Holland and were pleased with our position, and we'd also started to travel to Germany for lessons with a top teacher, Holger Nitsche. Our partnership was working. We felt optimistic about the future and our plan was to keep competing, keep improving our position and ultimately, one day, take the big crowns, both in the UK and internationally.

On the way to his parents' house, James told me stories about his childhood and upbringing. We'd reached a point where he was actively teaching me English, and I can remember that as we headed out of London and into Kent he suddenly pointed and started telling me that the black and white animals in the fields were called cows.

'Cows?' I said, confused.

'There, Ola. Look. Those things that go "mooooo".'

'Ah! I understand. Cow. Mooooo.'

'Good! Cows go "mooooo". Well done Ola!'

I think I was getting the general gist of most things he said, although I still had moments when I completely misunderstood or lost the thread of a conversation, and I occasionally got upset about this and cried in frustration.

'Keep watching EastEnders!' James would joke. 'Mind you, you'll end up sounding like a Cockney barrow boy…'

'What?'

He patiently explained what a Cockney and a barrow boy were.

'I see,' I said. 'My mum and dad had a market stall when they were young.'

'Did they?'

'Yes, but not fruit and veg. Clothes. They sold clothes but it did not go very well.'

It was nice to share information about our lives. James asked me questions about my childhood and I explained to him how Mum and Dad hardly had any money for treats or hobbies, and that we only went on one proper big holiday, the one to Leba, when I was eight. I could see that James found this quite sad, though he wasn't surprised. He'd seen how we lived in Poland and he knew how tough it was.

By contrast, I learned that James and his family went on foreign holidays almost every year throughout his childhood, and they always had lots of fun, eating out in restaurants every night and doing things like jet skiing and scuba diving. His dad was always game for a laugh and would enter things like Tarzan contests in the holiday resort and win every time. James told funny stories about how Allan once wanted to win a pedalo competition so badly that he made James jump into the sea halfway through the race, as he was slowing their pedalo down. On another occasion, in Greece, Allan asked James's grandad to photograph the moment when he did a spectacular dive off the top of a very high cliff. Allan completed the dive, only for Grandad to say: 'Sorry, I left the lens cap on. Can you do it again?' Allan did dive again, even though he'd used up almost every bit of courage the first time around. It sounded like they had a laugh a minute, and it also sounded a world away from the upbringing I had.

'My childhood was very happy,' I said, 'but not so funny!'

James also told me his parents were both very hard-working and family orientated, and they had brought him and his sister up with a strong work ethic. James had three paper rounds at the age of eleven, and whenever he wanted any extra pocket money his dad would tell him: 'Go and clean one of the neighbour's cars and earn it,' because he believed in teaching his kids the value of money and the rewards you can gain from an honest day's work. I knew my parents would have totally agreed with this attitude, but I was starting to think that there might not be as many similarities between our families as I'd first thought. The holidays James described made me realise he'd had a far more comfortable upbringing than mine. It sounded privileged even, and I really wasn't sure what to expect as we approached Strood. When I saw the family home I was bowled over.

'Wow!' I thought, eyes widening as Sharon and Allan welcomed me inside.

Sharon explained that the house was a former show home. It was decorated beautifully, and everything about it was absolutely perfect. Looking back it was actually a fairly regular four-bedroom detached home on a pleasant but ordinary road, but I'd never seen anything like it in my life. I had only been inside bedsits and grotty hotel rooms and hostels during my time in England, and this was a palace by comparison.

'It is so lovely,' I said. 'It is a very beautiful home.'

'We like it,' Allan said modestly.

James could tell I was impressed. He'd been to my family apartment in Poland after all, and the difference in living standards was glaring. My parents' apartment and this house were worlds apart. James tuned into my thoughts.

'In England this is how people can live when they work hard,' James said. 'We are just a normal family like yours, Ola. We aren't rich!'

'Oh,' I said, still taking everything in.

James's parents made me very welcome and gave me my own bedroom to stay in for the weekend, which was warm, very comfortable and luxurious compared with what I was used to. They couldn't have been more hospitable.

James's grandparents came round for dinner and Sharon cooked a lovely roast. I really enjoyed it, especially the roast parsnips and Yorkshire pudding, which I'd never had before. Unfortunately, halfway through the meal James asked me a question about something he planned to do or say that I disagreed with.

'No James, you can't!' I said.

There was a sharp intake of breath all around the table. Grandma in particular gasped in horror. 'Oooh!' she said, looking at me sideways.

'But you can't,' I repeated.

James was lost for words, and I didn't know why.

'What is wrong with saying that, James? You can't!'

James had to quietly explain that the way I pronounced 'can't' in my strong Polish accent sounded like a very impolite word.

'Well what does it mean, this 'cunt' word?'

That was the end of that conversation. I was very embarrassed when James managed to explain things later, but of course we laughed about if for years afterwards.

The next morning I was alarmed to discover that Sharon had cooked a full dinner for breakfast.

'What is this?' I asked James in confusion. 'It is breakfast time, but this is dinner?'

'Surely you have heard of the famous full English breakfast, Ola?'

At the hotel we served some sausages and bacon, or maybe poached eggs on toast, but not the full works like this. Sharon had really gone to town, serving up not just sausages and bacon but beans and grilled tomatoes, fried bread, black pudding and mushrooms and a choice of eggs. The plates were groaning, and there were stacks of toast and butter, pots of jam, fresh orange juice and steaming mugs of tea.

'Yes, James. I know about English breakfast, but I didn't know it could be like this! It is so big! It's a whole dinner. It's so strange.'

'No. Ola, it is strange to have cold ham and cottage cheese and gherkins. This is normal. You Poles are the strange ones. Continental breakfasts! Tsk! They are weird!'

Once I'd worked out what James was saying I smiled, because I realised he was teasing me. It was a good moment. Getting jokes and understanding sarcasm or any kind of gentle humour is difficult for foreigners – perhaps more so for Polish people, as we don't tend to joke nearly as much as Brits – but I was starting to 'get' James. He was a joker and a wind-up merchant, and he often said things in a deadpan way that he wasn't serious about at all.

The more I was getting to know James, the more I liked him as my friend. I still fancied him too, because he was very handsome and always looked great, but romance honestly didn't enter my head. There was no way James was going to be interested in a girl like me; I didn't think along those lines at all.

11

James's mum and dad got out their photo albums, as they did on many subsequent visits, and they started to tell me all sorts of stories from the family history, and about James's childhood.

I learned that James was born in April 1978 in a place called Gillingham, one of the Medway towns. His first memories were of living in a small three-bedroom house in a cul-de-sac in Walderslade, also in Kent.

Allan and Sharon were childhood sweethearts, and in their teens and early twenties they used to practise ballroom dancing at the renowned Peggy Spencer dance school in Penge in south east London. Peggy Spencer was a very famous teacher and choreographer, and she was also a judge on the BBC's original Come Dancing show, which ran from 1949–1998, so I was very interested to hear about this. I didn't remember watching Come Dancing as a child – we couldn't get it on our TV in Poland – but I knew all about it. I'd heard coaches and dancers talk about it very fondly, and of course it was filmed at the legendary Tower Ballroom in Blackpool, which gave it great kudos.

Allan and Sharon explained to me that they used to enter amateur competitions together, purely for the love of dancing. They won lots of medals but never had designs on competing at a serious level. They simply enjoyed themselves and liked the social side of dancing with the friends they made at Peggy Spencer's, and they carried on their hobby until their mid-twenties, only stopping when Sharon was expecting Kelly.

'You should see them jive,' James said, smiling proudly at his parents as I listened to their story. 'They're brilliant. They can steal the show at any party, even today!'

When James was a boy Allan was forever doing home improvements, but James was never interested in getting his hands dirty doing DIY with his dad. Instead, he'd be out climbing trees, or tearing around the cul-de-sac on his BMX Boxer bike, roller skates or skateboard.

'He was very active and very coordinated, even as a small child,' Sharon recalled. 'I suppose it's no surprise he was good at dancing. You should have seen how he moved on that skateboard, Ola!'

James and Kelly had all the toys and gadgets they could wish for. They wouldn't necessarily get the latest model, but their parents did all they could to ensure they never went without, and they were forever encouraging them to try out new sports and hobbies, like gymnastics or football. James even tried his hand at maypole dancing one time.

'What is maypole dancing?' I asked.

It took a while for James to explain what this was, and I really couldn't imagine him in the knee-length shorts and braces, decked with ribbons and bells, that he was describing.

'You are having a joke with me James,' I laughed. 'Bells and ribbons? Dancing round a pole? I don't believe you!'

'No, honestly Ola. I danced around a maypole with ribbons. It's an English tradition, on May Day. You dance around in circles and make a sort of plait down the pole with the ribbons, as you weave in and out of other dancers...'

It sounded so unbelievable I needed a lot of convincing and had to see the photograph before I believed it.

Allan encouraged James to take up judo when he was in primary school, as he thought he'd be very good at it, which he was. However, he didn't bank on how James would use his judo skills. One day a boy James really disliked at school jumped on his back and started hitting him, and James saw red and swung into action.

'This boy was horrible, and he was dating a girl I fancied,' James explained, 'so when he started hitting me I went mad and I did a bit of judo on him.'

'What did you do?' I asked.

'I threw him off my back and he landed on his head and arm. He was concussed and he broke his arm.'

Allan told James off for using his judo in that way, and James was hauled before the strict nun who was headmistress at his catholic school, St Thomas More in Walderslade. James was reprimanded very sternly and had to apologise to the boy, and he naturally thought that was the end of the matter.

'In my book you say sorry and move on,' James said. 'I thought it was dealt with, but it wasn't.'

Two days later, out of nowhere, the headmistress picked James out in assembly and announced to the whole school: 'This boy has hurt another child!'

James was mortified and couldn't understand why the incident was being dragged up again, or why he was being named and shamed in front of the entire school. Allan found out through Kelly what had happened, and he went mad and stormed up to the school to complain.

'That was typical Dad,' James said. 'He was very strict, and so was Mum, but they were always very fair. They would fight tooth and nail to protect me and Kelly if they felt it was justified, and they also brought us up with a strong sense of right and wrong.'

While James was still at primary school his parents started searching for a plot of land on which to build their own home, which had been their ambition for many years. They eventually bought several acres of woodland in Walderslade, and Allan slowly set about building the house.

'When I say "build" I really mean it,' James said, taking out an entire photo album dedicated to 'before' and 'after' pictures of the land and the building work. 'Dad cut down trees, he laid the foundations and constructed every part of the house himself. It took about four years to complete the work. It was a labour of love, and the results were awesome.'

I looked at the final picture wide-eyed. The house really was incredibly impressive. It was built in a Tudor style and was absolutely enormous, more like the size of a spacious hotel than a house. There were five enormous bedrooms and every room was huge. James told me the house was five hundred square metres, which didn't mean a lot to me until I recalled the size of my parents' apartment: forty-six square metres.

There was a gym, a giant study and a wine cellar, but James's favourite room was the purpose-built games room, where a table tennis table took pride of place. The family had lived in a caravan on the land for the four years while the building work was taking place, and on the day they finally moved in Allan turned to Sharon, breathed a deep sigh of satisfaction and said: 'We've made it!'

It was such a fantastic achievement for them, a moment they had looked forward to for so long and would never forget.

Sadly, James's face fell when he turned over the last page of the photo album.

'It was such a shame,' he said, shaking his head.

James went on to explain that the house was built in the late 1980s, when the UK was in recession and interest rates were going through the roof. Allan's kitchen-fitting and plumbing businesses collapsed as demand for new installations slumped and, after clinging on for as long as he possibly could, he ultimately had no choice but to put both businesses into liquidation. He then struggled like mad to keep the family afloat, but it was no good. Interest rates soared to sixteen per cent, he couldn't meet the extortionately high mortgage payments on the newly built house, and it was in massive negative equity. Allan eventually had to declare himself personally bankrupt, and the family home was repossessed. James recalled his mum explaining how she cried when she came out of the court on the day of Allan's bankruptcy.

'I came home from school and saw the bailiffs on the drive,' James said, tears pricking his eyes. 'I was twelve years old. They took my dad's keys and drove our cars away, and my dad's van. I'll never forget it, Ola. I wanted to cry, but I tried to stay strong for my dad. It must have been so terrible for him but he didn't crumble, not in front of me, at least. I know he was trying to stay strong for the rest of us, and he did a great job.'

James remembers that his school had been planning to purchase a table tennis table for the pupils to use, and so he suggested to his dad that he could sell them his table from their games room.

'Dad agreed. We were on the list for a council house and there was no way we could take the table with us, so I sold it to the school.'

James paused before finishing the story, clearly moved.

'Then I tried to give the money to my dad,' he said, his voice cracking, 'but he wouldn't take it.'

James was clearly affected by this, even after so many years. I felt so sorry for him. I couldn't imagine what it was like to be in that position. Allan and Sharon would have been in their forties when they lost the house, with two children to support. They thought they'd made it, but they lost everything, and all within a year. It was utterly heartbreaking.

The council put the family in a two-up two-down house in a rough area nearby. James remembers his dad taking the lounge carpet from the big house and using it to carpet every room in the rented council house.

'Do you know what Ola?' Sharon said, coming in on the end of the story. 'James and Kelly never once complained. They just got on with it and made the best of what we had. I was so proud of them.'

I admired the family's honesty. Many people would not have wanted to share such a story, but Allan and Sharon were very open and didn't mind at all.

I thought it was remarkable that they had managed to recover so well and so quickly, and that they owned the lovely home they had now. James told me that Allan and Sharon had achieved this with sheer hard work. Allan got his job at the power station and he worked every hour possible, seven days a week, which he still did. Meanwhile, Sharon worked full-time in her bank job.

I thought again about how James's parents must have struggled exactly like mine had when I was growing up and my dancing was taking off and becoming more and more expensive to sustain.

'Did it affect your dancing?' I asked James. 'How did the family find the money for you to carry on?'

James knew that I'd all but given up on my dream when he came on the scene because of the lack of money, but he said that, unlike me, he never had to face the possibility of giving up dancing and finding an alternative career.

'I can't remember a single time when Mum and Dad didn't take me to my classes or find the money, even through the bankruptcy,' James said. 'They supported me come what may, and even when times were really tough they always worked as hard as they possibly could to make sure Kelly and I didn't miss out on anything.'

I thought what a shame it was that my parents were of the same mind, but that their hopes and dreams were capped so harshly by the state of the Polish economy.

12

James was nine years old when he went to his first dance class, which was held on a Saturday morning in Walderslade town hall. Kelly had started classes there a short while before him, and Allan and Sharon decided they should send James along too, as they thought he might enjoy ballroom and Latin dancing just like they had. James wasn't particularly keen but he was prepared to give it a go because a friend of his also attended, and he thought if nothing else they could have a laugh together.

The teacher was called Ernie Yard and was a builder by trade, and right from the start James enjoyed the classes and looked forward to them every week.

'It was great fun, I loved it. We did have a laugh, and I really enjoyed learning the dances. I also liked being in the spotlight. As a boy I was a rare commodity. There were very few boys, and all the girls wanted a male partner. I had my pick of the girls, so what was not to like?'

James had a twinkle in his eye when he told me this, and I laughed.

'What did the boys at school think?' I asked, as I'd met male dancers over the years who'd been teased about their dancing.

'I tried to keep it quiet because it was kind of frowned on, but of course it eventually got out. One or two of the lads took the mickey when they found out I was doing the Samba on a Saturday morning instead of playing football like them, but by that point I loved it so I really didn't care. They called me names like 'woolly woofter' and said things like "where are your tights?" but I shrugged it off.

'"I'm copping a hold of a lot more girls than you are!" I'd retaliate.'

Having said that, James admitted that at this young age he was very shy around girls and would often go bright red when they had to get close on the dance floor. Despite this he was having a great time and before long he was socialising more with the kids he danced with than with the kids at school.

'I was starting to live and breathe dancing, and so I didn't give a stuff what anybody else thought,' James said.

I smiled when he said this, because I could identify completely with that.

By all accounts Kelly was a very good dancer, much better than James to begin with. She started to compete and won lots of trophies, but then she got really tall. This made it difficult to find a suitable partner, so Allan and Sharon suggested she could dance with James. Neither Kelly nor James thought this was a good idea. Kelly wanted her own boy partner, and James thought it would be a bit weird to dance a sexy Rumba, for instance, with his sister.

By the time she was fifteen – and five foot nine tall – Kelly decided to quit. By now James had realised that he not only loved dancing, but also could be 'quite good' at it. He'd entered and won a string of local competitions, and then he started having lessons at the Margaret Preedy Dance Studios in Maidstone, where he could train several nights a week as well as on a Saturday. As he progressed, Allan and Sharon paid for him to have occasional lessons with some top teachers in London, and James soon began to think about entering some of the national open circuit competitions alongside the country's top dancers.

'I knew I'd get knocked out in the first round,' he said, 'but when you're dancing alongside the best, and training with the best, you get as good as the best. That was my motto. I was thinking big, and I wanted to be a champion.'

When James was sixteen his dad contacted a couple he knew from his own dancing days, Alan and Hazel Fletcher. They were teaching now, and they had a reputation for being excellent coaches, so Allan asked if they could give James lessons.

Unfortunately, Alan and Hazel didn't teach juniors, but they offered a suggestion.

'One of our former students is a pro dancer and he's just started teaching,' they said. 'His name is Richard Porter. Why not give him a call?'

James's dad did call Richard, and James quickly began having lessons with Richard in Woldingham in Surrey, while at the same time entering some open circuit competitions. At sixteen, as he'd anticipated, he did always go out in the first round, but after just one year with Richard everything changed. James entered the Closed British Championships at Blackpool, open only to couples living in the UK, and made the final six in the country. This was the first time he had broken into a final.

'Richard Porter was AMAZING,' James enthused. 'Not only was he an incredible teacher and mentor, but he knew all about my parents' bankruptcy. Right from the start he agreed to give me one free lesson for every one we paid for, which was a massive help, as the lessons were £60 each. He said he did it because he saw potential in me, and the more he saw me improve, the more free lessons he gave me. I owe Richard so much. There's no way I would have progressed so quickly without his help.'

After leaving school and starting work, James spent all his wages on lessons and costumes, just as he did when we met. He began travelling to France and Germany to compete and he entered all the major UK competitions, including the British Open Youth Championships in Blackpool, the UK Open Championships in Bournemouth and the International Championships at the Royal Albert Hall. He made the final of every competition he entered in his Under-21 age group.

When I'd spotted him at Blackpool and thought, 'I want a partner like him one day!' it was James's last Under-21 competition before he would have to move up to the adult category.

I found out, eventually, that James was a very naughty boy when he was in his teens and travelling all around for competitions. He became really good friends with Richard, who was not much older than him. They were both young, free and single, hot-blooded and game for a laugh. James didn't tell me what they used to get up to until many years later, but I knew it had something to do with chasing the girls.

'You wouldn't want to know, Ola,' he laughed at the time.

I frowned. I knew by now that he'd been in a relationship with almost every dance partner he'd had through his late teens and early twenties, and of course he also had a reputation as a player.

'What did you and Richard do, James?'

'It's nothing nasty!' he teased. 'You don't need to worry Ola!'

'Then tell me.'

'No.'

'Why not?'

'Because what happens in Blackpool stays in Blackpool.'

'Oh James!'

13

'How do you feel?' James asked.

'Nervous,' I said.

'I know that, but do you feel comfortable in the dress?'

'Oh, yes! Of course. I love it!'

James and I were competing in a major competition held at the Lakeside Complex in Frimley Green, Surrey – by far the biggest competition we'd entered since our very first competition, Bournemouth, when we came fourth. That had been a great result, but of course we wanted to do better still.

James had saved up £850 to buy me a beautiful lilac dress from one of the best dancers in the world at the time – a lovely lady called Beata. A lot of dancers sell their dresses, and particularly the top dancers, as they can't be seen in the same dress twice. This meant up-and-coming dancers like me could have a dress that probably cost thousands of pounds new for a greatly reduced price. It was still a lot of money to James, though, and I was very grateful indeed.

'It's perfect,' I told him. 'I love it!'

The dress had a silver clasp that held it together across the front, and it fitted me really well and was quite a showstopper. James and I decided that I'd wear my old black dress with the slit for the early rounds, which I did, and change into the lilac dress for the semi-final, which would hopefully make a really big impression.

As I put it on in the changing room I felt a wave of confidence ripple through me. The dress was pitted with sparkling Swarovski stones and beautifully designed, with a silver bra top, a short skirt at the front and a train at the back. It made me feel so much better than the black dress, and when I stepped onto the dance floor in it later in the day I felt really positive and at my best.

We were performing the Paso Doble, which we'd practised hundreds and hundreds of times. The dance would end dramatically with James sliding on his knees towards me, while I would throw my arms wide and hold the final pose.

We both loved the Paso Doble; it was passionate and feisty, and when we performed the dance I really imagined James was the matador and I was the bullfighter's cape, which is how you are taught to interpret the Paso, as it's based on the music and ceremony performed at the start of Spanish bullfights.

As always, our routine lasted just over two minutes, and I stayed confident with every step. It was going extremely well, and now James was preparing to fall to his knees and slide towards me for our big finale. I flung my arms wide in triumph and jubilation, but as I did so I felt the silver clasp on the front of my dress pop open. I held my pose for the briefest moment before clasping my bare breasts. Then I gasped in panic as the awful truth hit me. My boobs were on display for all to see, and my little hands weren't big enough to cover them up, try as I might. I was aware of people staring from the audience, from the judges' stand and from, well, all around me. People were laughing and clapping and I was mortified.

There were hundreds and hundreds of people there that day, including James's parents, and I had flashed my bare boobs to them all. I ran off the dance floor in a blur, still trying and failing to cover myself with my little hands.

'Oh my God James!' I gasped. 'I'm so sorry!'

'Don't worry, that was brilliant Ola!' he said.

'James!'

'I'm joking. I don't think you need to worry. I don't think as many people as you think saw it. It won't affect our marks. Well, it might do – we might get a few more!'

'James!'

We didn't make the final, but James was right. We actually did extremely well that day and received a lot of positive feedback and compliments, and the focus was on our dancing and not my faux pas. Even so, it took me a while to get over the embarrassment. I was still only eighteen years old and, despite being a dancer who had to flaunt her body in little dresses, and having a good-looking guy like James touching my body every day, I was still shy about my figure.

My weight didn't help when it came to me feeling self-conscious. I was still heavier than I wanted to be, but whatever I ate and however much I exercised and practised I still stayed closer to nine stone than eight. I wondered if it might be a phase, as I was still growing and full of teenage hormones. I really hoped so.

I went home to Poland for my first Christmas, having not seen my parents for eight months. They sent me the money for the flight, and I was really looking forward to seeing them. I'd missed them a lot and it was lovely to see their smiling faces when they greeted me, but when I saw the apartment, exactly as I had left it, I knew in my heart that I'd done the right thing in leaving. It was comforting in a way to know that nothing had changed, and I enjoyed speaking my own language and taking part in the Christmas traditions I'd grown up with, but I felt very strongly this was my past. I wanted change, and I knew then that would never go back to my old life. Of course, I had no idea how long I would be James's dance partner, but I wanted to see how far we could go. He had been very kind to me, and I felt more settled in England after meeting his family and being welcomed into his home. James had even done me a little Christmas stocking, filled with things like make-up brushes and sweets, after I told him I'd never had one before, as it's not a Polish tradition.

I can remember Mum and Dad asking me lots of questions.

'Are you sure you don't want to come home, Ola?' was the main one. Of course they had heard from my sister how poor my living conditions were, and they knew I'd been homesick at the start.

'Are you sure you want to carry on? Do you think it is the right thing to do?'

As always they didn't force their opinions on me, they simply made it very clear that they would support me in whatever I wanted to do, and that my home was always there for me if I wanted to return.

I explained that James and I were going to compete in the British Open Championships at Blackpool in 2001, which they understood was the biggest and best competition in the world. This time I would be competing at amateur level rather than youth, as now James was twenty-two and too old for youth competitions, which stop at twenty-one in the UK.

'We are both so proud,' my dad said.

'Thank you. I couldn't have even got this far without your help.'

Mum cooked all my old favourites, like kotlet schabowy with potatoes and vegetables, though she understood that I wanted to watch my weight.

'You are beautiful,' she said, 'but you are wise. We should all eat to live, not live to eat!'

I appreciated that she understood about my weight, though I was also acutely aware that I was living in a totally different world now, and there were lots of details I didn't share with her. She would have been so worried if I told her I'd put on weight because I could only afford junk food, so I didn't enlighten her. I kept other details of my life to myself too, like the fact I was tired out from serving early morning breakfasts, or that my rented room was cold and bare and the German girls I lived with were ripping me off. What was the point in telling her that? In any case, I wasn't even that bothered about my situation. It's only in hindsight that can see how bad it was, because at the time the way I was living and working was a very necessary means to an end.

James and I competed together in Blackpool for the first time in May 2001. By now James had upgraded his Citroen Saxo GTR to a Citroen Saxo VTS, which was his pride and joy, and we drove all the way from Kent in it. As we approached Blackpool and the Tower came into view I felt a rush of adrenaline. So much had changed in the two years since I'd competed here with Przemek. James had been my fantasy partner then, someone I admired from the side of the dance floor. Now we were a strong partnership, and we both felt ready for the challenge. Greg DeWet had put some music on a CD for us and we'd been using that to practise and James had bought me another dress, this time a fitted, black, long-sleeved lace number. The skirt was knee-length, boned and lined with satin, and I loved it.

We stayed at a B&B on Albert Road, a couple of roads down from the Winter Gardens where the competition took place, and I was very excited as we got ourselves ready. The Winter Gardens was such an amazing venue: huge, with high ceilings, pillars around the dance floor, balconies and a big staircase. When it was built in 1896 it was the largest ballroom in the world, and you could really sense the history all around.

I got goosebumps when I heard the orchestra play that day, and I felt incredibly proud to be dancing with James in such a prestigious venue. He looked amazing, with his jet black hair, golden tan (applied painstakingly from a bottle, just like mine) and his immaculate tailored trousers, tight shirt and our laminated competition number on his back.

We'd done everything we could in terms of preparation, even grazing on pasta during the day to make sure we had enough energy to see us through each round, and when the music started I was brimming with hope and determination. This was a day to remember, a day we'd been planning for a whole year.

After a gruelling day, we finished in the top twenty-four, which was not a bad result for us. Of course, we'd have liked to finish higher, but again we had to put things in perspective. This was our first Blackpool together and we had beaten hundreds and hundreds of couples, from all over the world.

'We have done well,' I said to James.

'We have,' he conceded.

Neither of us said it, but we were both thinking the same thing.

'We want to do even better. We need to keep practising and keep competing. We can do it if we keep working hard.'

14

'Ola, I've been asked if I'd like to teach in Hong Kong,' James said. 'Hong Kong?'

This took me by surprise. I had heard that Ballroom and Latin dancing was popular in Hong Kong, but I didn't know much more than that. James explained that he'd been approached by another dancer, a guy called Christian Bradbury, who was already teaching out there and having a fabulous time.

'He says there's a great ex-pat community of teachers and the Chinese absolutely love their Ballroom and Latin dancing, so there's loads of work available. It would only be for a few weeks. I think I should do it.'

It did sound like a good opportunity. My only reservation was that it would interrupt our daily practice. James and I were getting better and we wanted to improve and win some of the top titles, and we could only do this if we kept practising every day as we had been doing. On the plus side, the money was really good in Hong Kong and this would be really useful to help us pay for better costumes and lessons and take part in more competitions.

Funding our dancing was still a big issue for us. We witnessed all the time how other couples who were doing better than us in competitions had had lessons with every judge on the panel. It was no surprise to us that their results were better; we knew all too well this was the way the politics of the ballroom dancing world worked. We had no desire to buy our way to the top in any way, but we did want to compete on a level playing field. We wanted to be able to be taught by the best, we wanted to be able to dress in beautiful costumes that would put us on an equal footing with more privileged dancers, and we wanted to be able to travel to competitions and lessons without cutting corners, staying in the cheapest B&B every time, or taking ferries and driving into Europe for days on end, as we had done when we went to Holland, for example. It would have been so much better if we could have taken a budget flight for a few pounds more and arrived fresher at the competition, and the same went for the lessons we had with Holger Nitsche in Germany.

Christian explained that a young, talented and good-looking British dancer like James could work all day long if he wanted to. As well as teaching classes, there was a lot of work available accompanying students to tea dances and dinner dances, which were extremely popular. The set-up Christian described was intriguing and completely alien to James and me; we'd never heard anything like it before. It seemed that Hong Kong was teeming with wealthy students – typically mature ladies – who had a great passion for ballroom dancing. They not only wanted to improve their technique, but also enjoyed winning amateur medals by taking part in ProAm competitions, where an amateur partners a professional. These well-to-do ladies normally had a lot of time on their hands as their husbands worked long hours, or they were retired or widowed or divorced and liked nothing better than to spend their days indulging their hobby. Many were also very successful in their own right, having had high-flying careers, and they now wanted to treat themselves and do something they loved. As well as taking several private classes a day with their chosen coach, many of these ladies also attended the popular tea and dinner dances or both, where they danced for pleasure with their teacher. It was all very sociable. Dancers and students dined together, all in the company of the student's like-minded friends, and in the plush surroundings of some of Hong Kong's fanciest hotel and club ballrooms in the bustling centre of the city.

'Sounds a bit funny,' I said to James when he first explained all this.

'I know what you mean. It's certainly not something I'm used to, but I still think I should give it a go. It's a new experience, why not?'

I agreed and James said he would get our flights organised.

'Our flights? I was thinking you would go alone?'

'Alone? Why would I want to do that? We're are a team, Ola. When I'm not working, we can practise, or you may even be able to teach a bit too.'

'I thought it was all ladies who wanted a partner?'

'It mainly is, but you might get a bit of work or you can help me, and it will be better than staying in Norbury on your own. Like I say, it's only for a few weeks. Let's do it!'

Before the Hong Kong opportunity came up we already had a trip booked to Canada, to compete in the Canadian Open. As we'd got good results in all the competitions we'd taken part in together we'd been officially invited to enter this one. This meant we had our flights paid for and got to stay in a nice hotel for a change. Of course, this was also an opportunity not to be missed, so we went to the competition, had a great time and, to our delight, actually ended up winning the Canadian Open. We were absolutely ecstatic. This was our first big international win together and we were both on cloud nine, not least because we also really enjoyed seeing a new country and staying in a lovely hotel. It was a fantastic experience, and immediately afterwards we flew to Hong Kong rather than returning to the UK, as that was the most efficient way of getting there.

'I have a great feeling about this trip,' James said when we sat on the plane bound for Hong Kong, still buzzing from our success in Canada.

'Me too!' I said.

I've always loved travelling and I felt really excited. James and I were embarking on an adventure together and life felt good. I shared James's gut feeling this was going to be a good trip and I was intrigued to see what Hong Kong would be like and was really looking forward to getting there.

Our route was via Dubai and the first leg went well. Then, as we neared the airport in Hong Kong, the pilot announced that there was a typhoon, which might make it difficult to land.

'Ooooh,' I said, looking out of the window as we began our descent in lashing rain. 'This is dramatic!'

James looked at me like I was mad.

'Dramatic? It's terrifying Ola!'

We could see the runway now, but just before we touched down the pilot pulled back.

'I'm afraid we'll have to try that again,' he announced.

This performance was repeated several times before the pilot said that if we couldn't land safely in Hong Kong we would have to have a stopover in Manila.

'Just go direct to Manila, now!' James shouted as the pilot announced he was making one last attempt. 'Don't bother trying again! Just go! I've never been to the Philippines!'

I was surprised that James was so worried; I just thought it was all another part of the adventure and kept very calm.

In the end we did go to Manila and in total it took us forty-eight hours to get from Canada to Hong Kong. We were exhausted when we finally checked into the Southfield Pacific Hotel, which would be our home for the next few weeks. Being in Hong Kong was like stepping into a whole new world. My immediate impression was that in one way it did remind me of Eastern Europe, in that everything was concrete and built-up. There were no ancient buildings, historic landmarks or pretty open parklands like I was used to seeing around parts of London and Kent, and in Blackpool, for that matter. The vibe was completely different to anything I had ever experienced before, though. The buildings were lit -up and technicoloured, the city was alive 24/7 and it was hard to tell what time of day it was as nothing ever seemed to stop. My eyes were everywhere, taking it all in. I loved it.

Our hotel was right in the centre of Hong Kong, in the Causeway Bay district, a short underground ride from where James would be working in the dance studio run by Christian, and close to the Li Hua restaurant, which had a large dance floor and a live band for the tea and dinner dances.

James began working the very next day while I busied myself by going to the gym and taking myself out for runs. I also made sure James had the clothes he needed, and that the hotel room was tidy and all the little jobs were done. It was a bit odd. I felt like I imagined a housewife might feel, looking forward to her husband coming in from work, and that was the highlight of the day.

I couldn't wait to find out exactly how the tea and dinner dances played out; it sounded like such a curious arrangement. James explained how it worked. He said he would sit at a table with whichever student was paying him for lessons. They would eat together, have a drink and a chat and then take to the floor. There was no formal teaching going on; this was just for pleasure, because the students loved to dance and could afford to indulge their passion in this way.

'I feel like a gigolo!' James laughed when I asked him how his very first dinner dance went.

'But you don't mean?' I gasped

'Ola – no! There are plenty of student–dancer relationships going on, so I hear. I would never, ever do that! I'm there to teach them, and I want to do it well. As if I'm interested in anything else!'

I laughed, and I felt my heart pound. I was more relieved than I possibly should have been. Of course James was not my boyfriend, but this conversation had made me realise I had strong feelings for him. I was not in love with him or jealous or anything like that, but we'd become very close and I felt protective of him, like any really good friend would. I certainly would not have liked to think of him being one of 'those' boys who would sleep with a wealthy student.

It was well known that some of the ladies showered their partners with extremely extravagant gifts like sports cars and expensive watches and jewellery too, which inevitably raised questions about exactly what the deal was between them. James was most definitely not like that. He had been a bit of a lad when he was younger, but that was in the past now and of course he treated his students with the utmost respect.

Once James had found his feet and got to know a few of the students he invited me to join them at some dinner dances so I could see for myself what it was like. I was pleasantly surprised. The ladies welcomed me warmly and told me how wonderful James was as a dancer. I always had a lovely time, chatting and enjoying some good food, then watching James with his students on the dance floor.

Through this I ended up being asked to work at a few dinner dances, guiding gentlemen students around the dance floor as they grappled with the Waltz or the Foxtrot. They were all middle-aged and very polite and appreciative, and I enjoyed dancing with them. The surroundings were plush and very civilised, with fresh flowers in the centre of the tables, beautiful palms decorating the edges of the dance floor and a good live band playing the music.

After the dinner dances James was always invited out to a bar or club with the other male dancers and I went too. I loved the nightlife, and we always had the best time ever, having a drink and a dance, trying out new clubs and bars and just having fun and letting our hair down.

As well as going to the gym and running I started doing yoga classes, including hot yoga.

I was around eight and a half stone now and still felt too heavy. Of course, I wasn't practising with James for hours every day as we normally did and I was concerned about putting on even more weight. With time on my hands, I began to worry about this and think very seriously about how to slim down.

Ideally I wanted to lose a stone. I figured the hot yoga especially might help me sweat off a bit of weight and I started having saunas too, even though the weather was very warm and humid all the time. I'd weigh myself straight afterwards and think I'd done well, as I was always a little bit lighter. Of course, all I was really losing was water, so when I got weighed before a sauna or hot yoga I'd be back to eight and a half stone.

When I look back at this now I can see how uneducated I was about controlling my weight. I didn't have a clue what I was doing, and I was clutching at straws.

Not long after arriving in Hong Kong I can remember thinking that it was time to take drastic action. I'd tried cutting back on food, I was exercising every day and I'd tried sweating the weight off at hot yoga and in saunas. Nothing had worked so I figured there was only one thing for it: I had to go on a proper, intensive diet and cut down even more on what

I was eating. I had the time to do it, and this was finally it. I was going to lose the weight. My goal was to be seven and a half stone by the time I went back to the UK, and I was absolutely determined to succeed.

I bought a pile of diet books and read them for hours on end in the hotel room on my own while James was at work. The concept of counting calories was an eye-opener to me. I still knew next to nothing about nutrition and metabolism, but by reading the books from cover to cover I was starting to understand that if I counted every calorie and put fewer into my body, whilst also continuing to exercise at the same level, I would lose weight. It wasn't exactly rocket science, was it? Nevertheless, I knew it would be hard. By now I had accepted that I was the sort of person who gained weight easily. I'd seen how James could eat whatever he wanted and never put on an ounce, while I was the opposite. I had curves, and food just seemed to go straight to my hips and thighs and, well, just everywhere. I'd look at a slice of pizza or a bowl of pasta and imagine it was a pile of stodge and fat that would travel straight to my hips or tummy, making me instantly fatter. This was exactly what seemed to happen to me; food just stuck to me and made me expand instead of being burned off in the normal way. It didn't seem fair, but that was just the way I was built. My genes wanted me to be a plump and curvaceous not skinny and sleek. Worse still, not only did I gain weight easily, but it was hard for me to lose weight. I'd proved that in the UK, as my efforts to cut down on my food and increase my exercise hadn't worked.

There was no point in dwelling on these negatives; it was time to be positive. I simply had to accept that I would have to eat even fewer calories if I wanted to lose weight.

'The lower the calories, the more weight I'll lose and the quicker I'll lose it,' I thought as I jotted down notes from the diet books and began to calculate exactly how few calories I reckoned I could get away with consuming to function and not get ill. I'd read that the recommended daily intake for the average inactive woman is between 1,600 and 2,000 calories, but eventually I wrote down the figure 600 and underlined it.

'I'm going to go for it. I'm not going to fail this time. I'm going to stick to 600 calories a day and I'm also going to go running more.'

I knew this extreme dieting would be hard but I was determined to do it. I told myself my career depended on it, and that my life would be so much better if I was thinner. I pictured myself on the dance floor with James at the next competition. I'd be thin and I'd feel so fabulous, and our results would be better than ever, because we'd look so stunning and I would have so much more confidence.

I began to read food packets meticulously, avoid high-calorie foods and skip meals. At first I didn't really discuss this with James, other than to say I was 'on a diet'. He accepted this readily. He'd sat there with a burger while I had a salad on many occasions in the past. What he didn't know was that I was now avoiding breakfast completely and starving myself until I cracked every day. I was also an expert on scanning absolutely everything on my plate and doing mental calculations. In short, I became completely obsessive about counting calories, and it dominated my every waking thought.

'I can eat half a piece of the grilled chicken. Can't touch the bread. Avoid the salad dressing. Eat the salad. Beansprouts are fine. If I do that I'll be able to have a few spoons of soup later...'

That's how my mind worked every time I saw a plate of food in front of me, and I became such and expert that I could take one look at any piece of food or meal and instantly calculate its calorific content.

'Do you want to come out for cocktails with me and the boys, Ola?' James asked one night.

'I'm not sure...'

'Why? I know you're the only girl in the group but so what? It's a great bar, you loved it last time.'

I really wasn't bothered about being the only girl in the group. I was used to mixing with boys, and older boys at that. Dancing from a young age had meant that I hadn't grown up with a clique of girlfriends the same age as me. I was never one of those girls who had a best friend or a tight group of school friends. I had spent most of my time with male and female dancers of all different ages, and I was very used to being independent and spending time on my own.

'Look, don't worry about me, I'm just happy staying in tonight, that's all,' I said. James looked at me aghast. He hates being on his own. Though we hadn't been in Hong Kong for very long he knew how much I enjoyed going to the clubs and bars in the city.

'I'm on a diet, anyway,' I added, by way of explanation. 'A proper diet, this time.'

'What's that got to do with it? We're not eating, just having a few drinks.'

'Exactly. Did you know that an average glass of wine has more than a hundred calories in it? And a cocktail? Well, a mojito has about two hundred and fifty calories.'

This was alien territory for James, who had never counted a calorie in his life.

'Ola! You're allowed to have a drink!'

'Yes, but I'd prefer to save my calories for food.'

James was bemused. He was out drinking every night with the boys and never gave it a second thought. I never drank very much in any case, which confused James even more.

'One cocktail won't hurt,' he said. 'You don't have to keep up with us!'

I didn't want to explain that that would be nearly half my daily calorie intake so I just tried to make light of it.

'I would be the size of a house if I kept up with you, James. You go, I'm happy staying in.'

James shrugged and shook his head. He was gaining an insight into the mindset of a weight-conscious and extremely driven nineteen-year-old girl, and I think it was quite an eye-opener to him.

James and I were sharing a hotel room to keep costs down, which didn't bother either of us. We'd done this many times when we travelled to competitions. Dancers are used to sharing changing rooms and seeing each other in various states of undress, and you get to know your partner's body and personal habits very intimately when you are dancing cheek to cheek all the time, and going on the road together. James inevitably started to notice that I was losing weight, and he paid me compliments and said I looked good. I was really pleased about this. I valued James's opinion, and it was also flattering as he looked so good and was in perfect shape. I wanted to lose weight for both of us, so we'd do better in competitions, and when I started to see results I was even more determined.

It really was tough living on so few calories. I'd have moments of weakness when I really felt like cracking and having something forbidden, like sweets or chips or a big sandwich, but I never did. I weighed myself every day and the pounds were slipping away, and this is what kept me going. I'd envisage the display on the scales dropping lower and lower.

'Keep going,' I told myself. 'You've come this far. You can do it.'

I felt weak sometimes and there were days when I struggled through a gym session or a run, lacking in energy. I'd get headaches too sometimes, but I'd tell myself it was like being on a detox, and this is how it felt to be burning off unwanted fat and losing weight. I really wasn't worried and I felt I had everything under control and knew exactly what I was doing.

I might have set a very tough daily target for myself in terms of calories, but it wasn't as if I was aiming for dangerously low weight, was it? That is what I told myself. I just wanted to have the perfect dancer's body, because how can you become the world's top Latin dancer if your body isn't in perfect, super-slim shape?

Our stay in Hong Kong was extended to six weeks as things were going very well for James on the work front. As the weeks went on and I got thinner and thinner James began to ask questions about my diet and was forever asking me if I was OK and checking that I wasn't overdoing things.

'James, I'm fine!' I always said. 'I know what I'm doing.'

I'd drink mineral water when we went out and lived on nothing but salads and soups, but I told him I was perfectly happy and that I was not doing anything unhealthy, so he had no need to worry.

I guess deep down I knew that such extreme dieting couldn't be good for me and I wasn't particularly proud of how I was losing weight, but nothing was going to stop me now. Obsessively counting calories had become second nature. I did it subconsciously, and even if I saw a poster advertising a snack or saw someone eating something in the street I'd work out exactly how many calories were in the food. My goal was in sight and I was going to hit it, come what may.

It's only with hindsight that I can see how very dangerous this plan was. Even though I have been watching my weight all my life since then I would never dream of going to such extremes again, and I certainly would never advise anybody to go on such a drastic diet. I was young and naïve and very foolish.

'Do you fancy going to the cinema?' Christian asked me one night.

I smiled. It was an unexpected invitation and I was pleased to accept it. Unbeknown to me Christian had cleared this with James beforehand, asking if it was OK to take me on a date, as he didn't want to step on James's toes.

'Of course mate,' James had said flippantly. 'She's my dance partner, not my girlfriend!'

Christian and I had a lovely evening at the cinema. I wasn't looking for a boyfriend but it was nice to be taken out, and to just do something different. Christian dropped me back at the hotel at the end of the evening, and when I got to the room James was there.

'Where were you?' he demanded, eyes blazing.

I was taken aback because James looked really angry and he'd never spoken to me in that way before. It was like he was telling me off for coming in late, and I couldn't believe it. Who did he think he was, especially after all the times he'd been out until the early hours!

'James!' I spluttered, 'I was at the cinema. You know I was at the cinema, with Christian…'

As soon as I said Christian's name James completely snapped. He was standing beside his bed, and he was suddenly in such a temper that he flipped it up with both his hands. The bed wasn't very heavy and, to the shock and surprise of both of us, it crashed down right in front of me, making me jump. We both stared at each other and then at the bed, which was messed up and wedged at an angle between us.

'You idiot, James!' I shouted. 'I don't want to go on any other date!'

'What?'

I had worked out that James was jealous, and in the heat of the moment I let him know I wasn't interested in dating another boy. James meant more to me than anybody. I didn't want to make him upset or jealous, because I had feelings for him.

Until now I hadn't even acknowledged to myself how I truly felt about James. I guess I'd been in a certain amount of denial, not wanting to make a fool of myself or get my hopes up that he might be interested in me in that way. Now James's behaviour had changed things. What he had just done had shown me that he had did have feelings for me, feelings that he'd kept under wraps.

'I said I don't want to go on dates with other boys!' I repeated. 'That is what this is about, isn't it?'

'Is it?'

'Yes, James, you fool! You're an absolute idiot! It's you I like!

I saw his expression soften and James put his hands to his mouth as he took this information in.

'I like you too, Ola. I have the same feelings.'

We gazed at each other, and then we looked again at the bed between us. It needed re-making, but we both had the same thought, at the same time: 'We can make it afterwards…'

15

When we got back to the UK we went straight back to our old routine, with me living in the rented room in Norbury and James living back home with his mum and dad in Strood, and commuting nightly from the power station to the dance studio. We'd become so close in Hong Kong, and it felt like a part of me was missing when James wasn't around.

We muddled through with our old living and working arrangements for a while, but everything was different now we were dating. I stayed at James's parents' house quite a lot – always in the spare room, as that was Allan and Sharon's rule – and James and I would go out clubbing locally, which was fun. We loved spending time together and I felt happier than I ever had done in England before.

My weight contributed to my good mood. I had lost more than a stone in Hong Kong and was delighted with my new look. I was also very proud of myself for achieving my goal. It had been incredibly tough, but totally worth it.

I was really skinny, to the point where nearly everyone I met made a comment about my size and said how different I looked. I felt fantastic. I was less than seven and a half stone, and when I was on the dance floor with James I felt amazing.

'This is how I have to stay,' I thought. 'This is how I have to be.'

I felt so much more confident than when I was heavier, and I was optimistic that losing the weight really would help James and me do better in competitions.

We continued to practise hard and compete in all the major championships, and at the first few competitions we did after coming back from Hong Kong several people went up to James and said: 'Who's your new partner?'

He didn't tell me this until years later, but apparently I'd lost so much weight I looked like a completely different person. I certainly felt like different person, and I had the confidence to wear the skimpiest costumes ever, and some amazing dresses with cut-out sides that really showed off my new figure.

Maintaining my weight was my next battle. Not being a naturally skinny person I had to keep watching everything I was eating, and I mean everything. I didn't want to lose any more weight so I was eating more than 600 calories a day, but I didn't want to put on a single ounce and so I was still obsessive about counting every calorie I consumed, every single day.

'Do you really think you should be eating that?' James would often say to me.

He knew how much I wanted to stay slim and I'd asked him to help me by speaking out if he thought I was indulging in something I might later regret. He often did it with a raised eyebrow and a little smile on his face, to make light of it so I didn't feel bad. I really appreciated his help but if he spoke to me in this way when other people were around I could feel them bristling and swapping glances. They clearly thought James had a nerve, telling me what to eat like that, but this wasn't how it was at all. We'd talked about my weight many times, and he was simply helping me stay on track.

By this point he knew all about my 600 calories-a-day plan and I was very open about my diet. I kept buying more diet books and I read everything I could about nutrition and metabolism. I began trying out everything from the Atkins diet to detox cleanses, blood type diets – you name it, I did it. Whatever I tried I found that basic calorie-counting combined with burning off calories with exercise was my winning formula. I was not one of those people who could eat whatever they liked provided they gave up certain food groups or avoided sugar or wheat or anything like that. With me, the only diet that worked was keeping my calorie intake low, and so that is what I tried to do, and it worked. As long as I kept my calories down my weight didn't change, and if I had the occasional blow-out and had a weekend where I ordered pizza, had a few drinks or ate cake and ice cream, say, I put on a few pounds. I would then have to eat less the next week to make up for the blip. It harsh and I had moments when I felt it was so unfair to have a metabolism like that, but that was my reality.

James started to stay over in my rented room in Norbury occasionally, but it was grottier than ever. The German girls were unpleasant to me and James and I both hated it there. Before long James asked me if I'd like to move into his parents' house. He'd discussed it with Allan and Sharon and they said they were happy for me to have their spare room, the one I used whenever I visited.

'Are you sure?' I said, delighted by the invitation.

'Yes. Mum and Dad are great like that. They understand it'll help us out. It's no problem, they say it'll be a pleasure to have you. What d'you think?'

I was very happy. 'Yes!' I smiled. 'I'd love to! Thank you, James.'

It seemed like the ideal set-up for the time being, and I couldn't get out of my rented room quick enough. I left my job at the hotel too, because it would have been impossible to get there so early in the morning, and it made sense for James and me to drive to Norbury together in the evenings when he was home from work.

I felt more settled than I had since leaving Poland, and I would look at James and feel my heart swell. I was falling in love with him.

We talked about returning to Hong Kong for a month or so at a time, whenever we could manage it, in order to earn more money for our dancing. I wanted to be with James even though I knew that meant I'd be a bit bored and lonely again while he was out at work, and in any case I didn't have much to do in Strood all day. I can remember waiting for James to come in from the power station, covered in grease and dirt. He'd shower and we'd drive to Norbury; that's what I lived for.

When we told one of our teachers at Semley our plans about going in and out of Hong Kong we were met with derision.

115

'I don't think that's a good idea,' he snorted. 'You need to be here, practising regularly together. If you don't practise every day, you'll get nowhere.'

'In an ideal world we would be here every day,' James said, getting annoyed but biting his tongue. 'But the fact is, if we don't go to Hong Kong we can't afford to pay for all the lessons we want. It's Catch 22. If we stay here we have the time to practise but no money – if we go there we have the money but no time.'

We spent some of the money we'd made in Hong Kong on upgrading the old Saxo to a second-hand Saab. This also provoked criticism from one of the teachers, who took one look at the car and sniffed: 'How can you afford that! You should be putting every penny into your dancing.'

James shrugged this off in his typical self-assured manner, and I did too. A little bit of James's natural self-confidence was slowly rubbing off on me, and I was beginning to feel more sure of myself than I had done ever since my arrival in England. Even though I was brave and determined when it came to pursuing my career, I was shy by nature and my instinct was typically to comply and avoid conflict wherever possible. By contrast, if anyone challenged James he would always stick up for himself and stand his ground, which I admired. This also made me feel secure, because James was on my side and I knew that he would always protect and defend me as best he could.

I'd passed my driving test just before I left Poland but I wasn't a confident driver, had no experience and of course had never driven on the left before. James offered to give me driving lessons in the Saab, which seemed like a good idea, as then we'd be able to share the driving to Norbury, and on our long trips to competitions.

Unfortunately, the first time I got behind the wheel we were in rush hour traffic in South London. Each time I tried to change gear I struggled and every time, without fail, I looked down at the gearstick to see what I was doing wrong.

'Keep your eyes on the road!' James shouted, alarmed that I was looking at the gearstick instead of out of the windscreen.

'But I can't put the car in gear!'

'I know that but you need to keep your eyes on the road Ola! Why are you looking down?'

'Because I have put my foot on the clutch and it hasn't gone into gear. I want to see what is happening...'

'Stop! Oh my God, now you've just crossed lanes on a roundabout. Ola, I think we need to... what was that?'

James turned round to see one of the hubcaps rolling down the street. I'd clipped the curb and knocked it off.

'Pull over Ola! That's it, I've had enough!'

We repeated this charade several times and every time James was tearing his hair out, shouting at me to watch the road, stop cutting people up on roundabouts or telling me I was going to pop a tyre if I hit the curb one more time.

Despite this, James and I were getting on better than ever and it was working out really well living with his parents. They were very generous with both of us and the only thing we would have changed was the sleeping arrangements. Despite the fact James was now heading towards his mid-twenties and we were very much a couple, his mum and dad still didn't let us share a bedroom. Whenever we thought we could get away with it James and I would sneak into each other's room at night. We did get away with this for ages, but then one morning the cleaner saw me coming out of James's bedroom in my nightie. Unbelievably, she grassed us up and we both got a telling off from Sharon! I guess mums never stop being mums: it took James until he was twenty-five to sit his parents down and confess to them that he'd had a tattoo done in Hong Kong, in the image of a panther on top of his arm. Sharon had a right go at him, but Allan was relieved. 'I thought you were going to tell us Ola was pregnant!' he snorted.

James and I continued to drive to competitions abroad as well as in the UK and we also had more lessons with Holger Nitsche in Germany. We were making very good progress, and in-between the competitions we returned to Hong Kong for weeks and sometimes months at a time. Our plan was to break into the top twelve amateurs in the world, and then hopefully the top six and maybe even higher. We had no real timetable for this. We loved flying in and out of Hong Kong, we loved competing and we both wanted to continue with this lifestyle for as long as we were enjoying ourselves, and for as long as we were making progress with our dancing.

Whenever we were in Hong Kong James worked as much as he possibly could. He enjoyed the work, and every hour James taught would earn us enough money to pay for a lesson for ourselves with a world-class teacher, or to put towards new costumes or travel expenses for the next big competition.

Looking back, the schedule was insane. James taught four lessons from 10 a.m. to 2.30 p.m., then had less than half an hour to get himself to the afternoon tea dance. After that he would squeeze in another two lessons between 6 p.m. and 8 p.m. before going straight to the dinner dance, which ran from around 8.30 p.m. until late. Then he'd go out to clubs and bars with the boys. I was always invited and I often went and had a great time, though I never drank like the boys did and I'd usually go home earlier than James. He and the boys would often stay out partying until 4, 5 or even 6 a.m. James would then grab a few hours' sleep before starting a fourteen-hour day of teaching and doing the tea and dinner dances.

'I don't know how you do it!' I'd say.

I'd be flat out asleep when James came in in the early hours, usually only waking up when he was getting ready for work in the morning

'You're only young once!' James would say.

He looked incredibly fresh on just a few hours of sleep and I admired his stamina and his outlook. When he rushed out the door to go to his morning classes I'd feel inspired by his energy, and I always tried to make the most of my day.

I had a great lifestyle, going to the gym and to yoga and occasionally helping James out at work. My diet was still strict, but now I was slim it was much easier to simply maintain my weight rather than trying to lose weight. Also, it was completely second nature to me to only eat healthy foods and stick to a low-calorie diet. I knew exactly what I was doing and so I just got on with it, choosing healthy vegetable soups and sticking to grilled chicken and salad if we went out. I didn't have to think twice about avoiding anything with sauces, for example, or processed foods that I knew might contain hidden fats and sugars. I was an expert in calorie-counting and I just had to be disciplined, every day.

Eventually, James and I did the Internationals at the Royal Albert Hall, and we managed to break into the top twelve in the world as amateurs. This was our best result to date and we were still very ambitious. We wanted to get into the top six in the world, if not higher. We'd set the stakes high, even though we knew this was going to be difficult to achieve while we were flying in and out of Hong Kong and missing so much practice together whenever we did so.

It was tough, but whenever we took to the dance floor at a competition we remembered why we did it. Hearing the big band music striking up, having the spotlight on us and the glitter balls twinkling above as we launched into a sensuous Rumba or a an energetic Jive was what it was all about. My heart sang and I lapped up every moment. The triumphs felt more powerful now we were a couple, too. We'd look into each others' eyes and didn't even have to say anything to know what the other was thinking. We'd won together, so we got double the pleasure, seeing how the other reacted.

16

'Why did you hit me?' the angry man shouted in my face.

I was in a club with James and about eight other male dancers when all of a sudden this complete stranger had pinched my bum. I'm not a flirt and I don't like that kind of thing, so my gut reaction was to turn round and slap him, which is exactly what I'd just done. James was on the other side of the club with some of the boys getting the drinks in when this happened, and I'd been standing with Christian, minding my own business and waiting for the others to join us.

After shouting at me this guy then grabbed both my arms and started shaking me really hard, demanding to know again why I'd slapped his face like that. He was absolutely livid.

'Why? Why did you do that?'

It was frightening, and people were staring as I struggled and asked him to stop.

'Get off me!' I said. 'You know why I slapped you!'

Seconds later James thundered over and punched the guy square in the face, knocking him to the ground. Security came over, picked the guy up, and the next thing we knew they had hauled him away and kicked him out of the club. He carried on shouting and was clearly very angry, but I was relieved he'd been dealt with.

I don't like fighting but I was very glad James had got involved, because the guy had been shaking me really hard, hurting my arms as he gripped me. It was a horrible, scary experience.

'Thank you, James,' I said. 'I'm so glad you were there.'

'So am I. Some people are just so out of order…'

We got back to enjoying our evening and as the night wore on, when everyone had had a few drinks, Christian said he had something he felt he ought to tell us.

'What, mate?' James asked.

'Well, it's like this… actually, perhaps I'd better not say it.'

'What? You've got to tell us now!'

'OK, but you might not like it. The thing is, you know the guy who pinched your bum Ola?'

'Yeeees,'

'Well, it wasn't the guy you slapped.'

'Not him?'

'No.'

'I'm confused. Who pinched my bum if he didn't?'

Christian grimaced.

'Er, actually it was me. I was just mucking around, I didn't expect you to react the way you did, or him for that matter.'

I gasped and James looked like he'd seen a ghost.

'Oh my God, you mean that poor guy was slapped, punched and thrown out of the club for no reason?'

'In a word, yes.'

James and I were mortified, but the others in the group fell about laughing and never let us forget that night.

Unfortunately, that wasn't the only night when we found ourselves in the centre of a drama. It seemed that whenever I went on a night out with the boys something unexpected happened, often with me right in the thick of it. For instance, one time James and I and a group of several dancers were all standing outside a kebab shop when one of Hong Kong's notorious triad gangs appeared. There are lots of these gangs in Hong Kong and we knew to stay out of their way, as they can be violent and menacing, and they carry weapons.

'You white piece of trash!' one of them suddenly said to me.

I ignored it, thinking that was the best thing to do, but one of James's friends heard what was said and started swearing and lashing out at the gang member. Within seconds about thirty triads appeared, all spoiling for a fight, and then out of nowhere about fifty police officers with batons and shields appeared.

It was complete pandemonium, like something out of a movie. James managed to send me back to the hotel in a taxi and then returned to make sure our friend was OK. He wasn't; he was completely surrounded and was trying to jump over the triads and police to get away from the melee. Then one triad pulled a knife on our friend, so James weighed in and hit the knife out of the triad's hand before he did any damage with it. James slashed his finger as he punched the blade away, but thank God he and our friend managed to escape into the night.

'I'm so sorry,' I said later. I was waiting in our hotel room, worried sick and feeling guilty that the insult thrown at me had kicked all this off.

'It's not your fault, Ola,' James said as I helped clean up his cut.

'Maybe not, but why do things happen to us like this? It's crazy. I just want a quiet time. It is just as well you are so brave, James.'

As I spoke, a giant cockroach ran across the tiled floor of our hotel room. James screamed like a girl and jumped on a chair, pulling his knees to his chest, while I rolled my eyes, grabbed it and threw the critter out of the window.

'As I was saying, it is just as well you are so brave, James!'

I'm happy to say I wasn't to blame for every drama. We were in another club when a guy dressed in a white vest and a bandana kept jumping on the stage and making a nuisance of himself. The bouncers must have thrown him off the stage six times before he eventually stopped. James and I were up dancing, minding our own business, and once the guy had disappeared we didn't give him a second thought.

Back at the hotel, much later that night, our phone rang.

'It's reception, there is a man to see you.'

James went downstairs, and there was this guy, still in his vest and bandana.

'I come to your room,' he said forcefully, eyeing James up and down.

James was absolutely horrified when he realised what the guy was after.

'I don't think so, mate.'

'Yes, I come to your room, for sex!'

James went mad and complained to the hotel management. The man knew which room we were in and we were worried he'd come knocking on our door.

'You'll have to move us,' James said.

They did, and we were upgraded to a suite, but better still we never saw the man again.

'That was horrible, Ola,' James said, once it was all sorted out. 'Why are some people so rude?'

There was no answer to that. Hong Kong definitely seemed to attract more than its fair share of weird, wild and sometimes very scary and menacing characters. One time we were in a nightclub when a load of deadly snakes were thrown on the dance floor, apparently in some triad feud. Another night we saw a Western guy being tended to in the street by a police officer. The man had blood pumping from his neck where he'd been stabbed, and on a different occasion there was a fatal shooting near our apartment.

'It's a hit,' we were told. 'You can pay 5,000 HK$ to have someone taken out in this city.'

On rare days off James and I went wakeboarding, taking a taxi to a beautiful rural spot the outskirts on the city. James had tried every type of water sport on his family holidays abroad, while I'd never wakeboarded before in my life. I picked it up quickly. I think having a strong core and good balance from dancing helped and I absolutely loved it. It was great to be out of the bustle of the city, we'd spend hours on the water, and afterwards we'd have some food and chill out.

I'd be shattered and very hungry after hours and hours of wakeboarding, but despite this I still stuck rigidly to my diet. I can remember fretting over whether or not I should have a bowl of soup at the end of a long day on the water, because I was worried about the calories.

'Just have it!' James would say, but I'd shrug and agonise over the decision.

'My metabolism is a nightmare,' I complained, 'it's just not worth it.' Then I'd either eat half the bowl or nothing at all.

When we flew back to the UK, or whenever a good opportunity presented itself because we were doing a competition or having lesson in Europe, I'd go and visit my parents in Poland. James would usually come with me and we always really enjoyed ourselves. We'd take a few presents for my mum and dad, electrical goods and the things that they couldn't get hold of, and they'd always make a big fuss and be so pleased to see us. Mum would cook a lovely meal, Dad would be all smiles and I'd tell them every time how grateful I was for everything they had done for me. I'd translate for James and he would show them pictures of us at competitions, or at the dinner dances, explaining all about Hong Kong, and how the city never stopped and was so vibrant and colourful and loud and fast-paced.

'It looks so exciting, Ola! What a life you are leading!' they said.

'I wouldn't be doing this without you,' I always replied.

On every visit, at some point, James would normally end up asking me if everything was alright between me and my parents.

'Of course. Why do you ask?'

'You sound angry, you have a serious look on your face and you are waving your hands around all over the place.'

I'd laugh.

'It's just how we talk. Even when we're not being serious at all we are like that! You don't need to worry.'

We always enjoyed being back in the UK too. We got on so well with James's mum and dad and they never once complained about us coming and going. They could not have done more to accommodate us and welcome us back every time. We missed them when we were away, and I enjoyed being back in Kent, having a break from the bright lights of Hong Kong and spending every day dancing with James. He'd given up the power station job as we'd gone more and more often to Hong Kong and so when we were in England we had loads of time to practise at Semley and compete.

Eventually we decided it was time we got a little place of our own. James's parents had been very kind, but as soon as we could afford it we decided that we wanted to stand on our own feet. We'd been saving up hard, and in time we managed to buy a little three-bedroom end of terrace house in Iwade, not far from Strood. We didn't have a lot of money after the sale had gone through, but we slowly began to furnish and decorate it, looking forward to having our own base whenever we were back from Hong Kong. We didn't get very far at all before we ran out of money. The TV was on a paper box and we had one sofa and no other furniture, but at least it was a start. Once we'd earned more money in Hong Kong we could do it up properly. That was the plan.

17

In May 2003 we competed together at Blackpool. It was an amazing competition and we absolutely loved taking part. I had a beautiful dress and we got a great result, finishing in the final twelve, just as we had at the Internationals the previous October. Once again this meant we were in the top twelve amateurs in the world. This was fantastic, of course, especially as we hadn't been training full-time. Our coach said our performance was amazing and we felt proud of ourselves. However, the truth was we hadn't progressed. We wanted to be in the top six.

'Where do we go from here?' James said.

'I don't know.'

'We're at a crossroads.'

'What do you mean?'

'I think we need to think very carefully about what we do next. I have a flourishing business in Hong Kong. We're doing a lot of travelling. Is this what we want? Is it worth travelling in and out all the time if we're not getting any higher in the world rankings?'

I didn't know the answer. James was right. We needed to think very carefully about the future. Maybe it was time to stay in Kent and focus one hundred per cent on the dancing, or maybe we should move full-time to Hong Kong, take a sabbatical from the competitions and take the pressure off ourselves.

'It feels like we're in a Catch 22 situation,' James said.

I nodded in agreement. We'd talked about this many times. Hong Kong earned us the money we needed to keep competing at a high level, but by spending so much time out there we were not practising as much as we wanted to.

'You're right James, but what should we do?'

'I don't know Ola, but it's time we made some big decisions.'

We booked a holiday to Skiathos, where we could chill out and decide what to do next. This felt exactly the right thing to do. I'd never been to a Greek island before and this was my first proper beach holiday. I was bowled over by the scenery and I loved bathing in the sea. I couldn't believe how warm it was compared with the sea in Poland, and I relaxed more than I had in a long time. James's gran and grandad were also on holiday in the same resort for part of the time, and it was lovely to spend time with them too.

Despite the dilemma hanging over us about how to proceed without dancing competitions I felt absolutely great. I was madly in love with James and I knew that whatever happened, as long as I was with him I'd be happy. We went wakeboarding and sunbathed every day, just enjoying being together. We talked for hours too, mulling over our life and our plans, and we started to discuss how our priorities had changed since we'd fallen in love. Dancing was still a huge part of our lives, but we both had a new love too; each other. Maybe it was time to put ourselves before the dancing? Maybe we should just move to Hong Kong and enjoy life and put competing on hold for a while?

'Do you know what I think, Ola?' James said decisively as we sat on the beach one day.

'What?'

'I reckon a sabbatical is the answer. That is what we should do. Let's take a complete break from competing and move to Hong Kong,' he said. 'You only live once. We're young enough to do it and we can come back to competitions when we're ready.'

Everything James said made sense, and I felt relieved to hear him say it. By now it was more than three years since I'd left Poland, yet I was still only twenty years old, soon to be twenty-one, and James was just twenty-five. We could easily take a year or two out of competing. With a bit of luck the break would do us good and we could come back fresher and keener, and with some money behind us. We needed to shake things up, and it felt like exactly the right time to do it.

'Why not?' I said. 'I agree with you James. Let's do it. Let's go and live in Hong Kong!'

James gave me a big smile and kissed me. I could feel the tension melt from my shoulders. This was the right decision, I was sure.

'We'll rent a flat this time,' James said. 'We'll go wakeboarding on our days off. We'll have a ball.'

Of course, there was going to be the issue of work for me. While James would be working really hard I'd go back to spending a lot of time alone during the day.

James read my mind.

'Ola, if you want to dance with someone else, you know I would support you, don't you?'

The idea of finding a new dance partner had never crossed my mind, but I was very touched that James had made the suggestion.

'No, James, I don't want to! I don't want to dance with anyone else but you. You are my partner. It wouldn't be the same.'

James was equally touched by what I said.

He was quiet for a while and I could tell he was deep in thought.

'Ola,' he said eventually, taking a deep breath, 'do you think we should get married first?'

'Married?'

'Yes, married! Shall we get married before we go and live in Hong Kong? Why don't we get married as soon as we can?'

I laughed. We'd talked about marriage before, especially around the time when we were buying the house in Iwade and had inevitably discussed our hopes and plans for the future. We were very serious about each other and we had told each other we wanted to spend our lives together, but until now marriage had been something that I imagined might happen way off in the future. I was shocked that James was suddenly talking about getting married now, but also very pleased. I loved James to pieces and I wanted to be his wife, so why not now? That was my reaction as I sat in the sunshine taking it all in.

'Marriage? Well, James… are you serious?'

Outside Grandma's house. You can see the reins used
to hold me in the pram when I tried to escape!

Me, modelling new clothes Dad brought home from
Germany and learning to pose for the camera.

Visiting Father Christmas. Nobody was going
to take my bag of oranges off me!

My Holy Communion. Mum tried to convince me that my short
Holy Communion dress was special, but really I wore it because
it was cheaper than a long one. She added the long sleeves,
made from a pair of tights, so I wouldn't be cold.

Dancing with my first serious dance partner, Krzysztof
Ostrowski. This is the outfit my parents bought from my dance teacher.
Dad made me a matching skirt so I had two costumes. I am also
wearing my prized first pair of Supadance shoes.

Me and my sister Monika. I was just
a one-year-old and she was nine.

Przemek Lowicki and me winning the
Polish Youth Championships in 1998.

This is the gold dress my dad spent a month's wages on. It is the one I was wearing when James spotted me for the first time in Brentwood, Essex.

My first competition with James, the British Closed in Bournemouth.
I'm wearing the black dress Greg DeWet from Semley made for me.

Wearing the lilac dress I popped out of at a big competition in Surrey. Here I am posing in my tatty rented bedroom. You can see the mattress on the floor.

At a house party with James. I had
already started to put on weight.

Getting to know James's family. (L–R) James, James's grandma,
his mum Sharon, me, his dad Allan and sister Kelly.

Our holiday to Skiathos, when
we decided to get married.

Another competition. We could afford better costumes and
more fake tan once we started going out to Hong Kong!

James and me loved up on
a night out in Hong Kong.

Me and James
in New York.

Putting on a show
in Hong Kong.

Our wedding day, 12th October 2003. Our sisters were
bridesmaids and my niece was a flower girl. This was the
first time our two sets of parents had met each other.

Here I am as the new Mrs Jordan!
You can see how happy we both are.

Posing in my red catsuit. I wore this when I danced with Chris Hollins. I had no idea how much controversy my catsuits would cause over the years.

Me and some of the other pro dancers dressed in sexy
Santa outfits with Brucie at the Strictly wrap party.

Meeting one of my heroes,
Robbie Williams, backstage on Strictly.

In fancy dress on a night out with
dancers on the Strictly Pro Tour.

Me with my leg in a brace after
my accident on The Jump.

Me and Chris with
the glitterball trophy.

'Think about it,' he said. 'We know we'll get married some time, so why not now?'

I laughed because his words echoed my thoughts.

'James, have you just proposed to me?'

'Well, yes, I suppose I have...'

I told him I wanted to marry him, and I could not have felt happier. We kept the news to ourselves for a while as we worked out exactly what to do next. Neither of us wanted to tie the knot in Hong Kong as we wanted a wedding that both our families could share with us, and our friends.

We decided it made sense to get married in Kent. We could fly my parents over for the wedding, and afterwards we could go to Hong Kong as a married couple, to start the next chapter in our life together. It felt completely right, and once we'd set the ball rolling we wanted to get married as soon as we possibly could.

We both wanted a have a traditional wedding with all the trimmings, but we also wanted to keep it simple and not spend money we didn't have. Going into debt was never an option for either of us, ever. James had obviously lived through his parents' bankruptcy and I'd seen my parents making ends meet on a shoestring. We were in total agreement that we would have the best wedding we could afford, but that we would not spend a penny we didn't have.

Now it was just a question of making the arrangements.

'I can't wait!' I said.

'Me neither,' James said. 'Ola Jordan. It has a nice ring to it.'

When we were home from Skiathos James surprised me by producing a ring. It was a simple plain band he'd bought from a jeweller in Rochester, and he explained that he was going to buy a diamond in Hong Kong and have the jeweller make a proper engagement ring for me.

'Wow!' I said, giggling. 'Now you can get down on one knee and do this properly!'

He did, and we were both buzzing with happiness. I couldn't believe I was engaged to James; it seemed only five minutes ago that I'd eyed him across the dance floor in Blackpool and thought he was completely out of my league.

We sat James's mum and dad down and told them our plans and they were absolutely delighted, but I was scared about telling my mum and dad. I just wasn't sure how they'd react to their youngest daughter suddenly announcing she was getting married: it could come as a bit of a shock. I wasn't worried about how they felt about James. I'd been home at least twice a year, often with James, and I knew my parents liked him a lot, even though they still couldn't understand a word he said.

'Perhaps that's why they like you James,' I often teased.

James was very naughty sometimes in my parents' apartment. He'd lean across the table and say something like: 'Ola, I want to take you to bed,' very boldly, in front of Mum and Dad.

My dad would ask in Polish: 'What did James say, Ola?' and I'd have to make something up. 'Oh, James says he wants to taste the soup.'

'Of course!' Dad would smile, passing the bowl while James was trying his hardest not to laugh.

James said I should get my sister Monika to tell my parents the news, as at least then they would hear it face to face rather than down the phone. That's what I did, and I needn't have worried. Everybody in the family was delighted for me. My mum's only concern, in fact, was that she didn't want to let me down when they came over to Kent for the wedding.

'What do you mean?' I asked. 'How could you let me down?'

Mum was worried about having the right hat and outfit, and not being able to afford the best.

'Oh, Mum!' I said. 'You always look lovely. I just want you there.'

We got married on 12th October 2003 at Cooling Castle in Kent. We were offered either that date or 30th September, which was my twenty-first birthday, but I wanted my wedding day and birthday to be separate. James's mum and his sister Kelly helped me organise everything in a matter of weeks, and I couldn't have done it without them.

The day was perfect. James and I had everything we wanted despite having a low budget. I did my own make-up, bought my dress in Monsoon and we hunted around for the best value wedding car and photographer.

We had a video too, and whenever I watch it back the emotion of the day comes back to me. I remember looking at James and seeing his Adam's apple move as we stood together waiting to say our vows, because he was gulping with nerves and emotion. When the vicar asked: 'Who gives away this bride?' I had to squeeze my dad's arm to prompt his response, as he didn't understand. This was a very funny moment, which lightened the tension in the room. As soon as I squeezed Dad's arm he said: 'I do,' in a really deep voice that boomed all around. It was like I'd press a button that triggered his speech, and to make it even funnier he didn't even know what he was saying. I joked afterwards that I could have been tricking him into agreeing to anything in that moment.

After the ceremony we had a carvery and when James and I had our first dance we kept it casual and intimate. It was our moment, not a time to show off.

'We want to see you dance!' our guests said later in the evening. We had a lot of people we cared about there, which was lovely. James's friends had become my friends and we had a lot of our mates from the world of dance there as well. It was too expensive for my whole family to come from Poland but my sister and one other relative flew over with my parents, and my aunt from Covent Garden also came.

We didn't want to disappoint anyone at the party, so in the end James and I did a Rumba to Michael Jackson. Our guests enjoyed it, but I was more interested in seeing them have a good time, and watching our parents taking a turn on the dance floor. They had all supported us so much, and both James and I were incredibly grateful to them for everything they had done. My dad was the life and soul of the party. He danced with every woman in the room, even James's eighty-year-old aunt, and the next day he was in agony because his bad knee was hurting so much but he had no regrets. Mum kept apologising because she didn't speak English but she enjoyed the whole experience nonetheless, and she sat there smiling and taking it all in, telling me how happy she was for me.

It was amazing to think how James's request to have a try-out with me just a few years before had led to this day. I felt like the luckiest girl in the world.

18

'Ola! Oh my God, Ola! You won't believe what's happened!'

It was James on the phone, and he was crying and gasping for breath.

'James, what is it?'

My heart leaped into my throat.

'Ola, I don't want to be here any more... I can't believe it. Oh my God...'

'James! Tell me what has happened? Are you safe?'

Shortly after the wedding I had gone to Poland to sort out my passport, as I needed to get it re-issued in my married name before flying to Hong Kong to start our new life there. Meanwhile James went direct to Hong Kong to find us an apartment to rent. Everything seemed to be going well. He had a couple of possibilities and was shopping around for the best deal, and in the meantime he was renting a place temporarily from one of his students.

'Ola, this is terrible,' he cried.

'What is? What's happened?'

I was panic-stricken. I heard James take a deep breath as he tried to calm himself down.

'I came home and the door had been kicked in,' he explained. 'The apartment has been robbed, Ola.'

'Oh my God James, no!'

I felt relieved he hadn't been hurt and was not in danger, but I could tell this was a serious situation, because James's voice was still trembling and he was clearly in shock.

'What was taken?'

'Everything, Ola.'

'What do you mean, everything?'

James needed a moment to compose himself because he was crying and gasping so much.

'The apartment was completely cleaned out. Our wedding certificate, laptop, all the cash I had, the watch my mum and dad bought me for my twenty-first, all my best clothes…'

'No! I can't believe it! Oh my God James, thank God you're alright.'

'I am, but I really don't want to be here. It is just so horrible Ola. Our whole life has gone. I have literally been left with the clothes on my back. There is not a stitch left.'

James had hidden several thousand pounds under the mattress as he hadn't had the chance to open a bank account yet. It was all our savings, just gone, in the blink of an eye. I didn't care about the cash itself, but when I thought how we'd budgeted so carefully for our wedding I felt a burst of anger. How could someone do this to us? A lot of our wedding photos were on the laptop, and that broke my heart. I had taken a copy of the wedding certificate as I needed it to get my passport, but how could our original have been taken? This was just absolutely terrible. I could scarcely take it in. It was like a scene in a film, something that wasn't real or was happening to somebody else. I wanted to hug James and be with him, but I was stuck in Poland indefinitely, waiting for my passport to be processed.

James ended up lodging with another student while the mess was sorted out. We had no insurance, and nobody was ever caught for the robbery. It was a terrible start, but once we'd got over the initial shock there was nothing we could do but try to put it behind us and move on.

By the time I arrived a few weeks later, James had found us a decent two-bed apartment in Causeway Bay, and we got a few pieces of furniture from Ikea. We couldn't afford much but we didn't care; we were together, and we were safe. That was all that mattered.

To cheer me up, James bought me a ginger cocker spaniel puppy as he thought the pup would be good company for me while he was out at work. We called him Rocky and I loved him to bits, but after ten days he was really sick. Rocky was crying and squealing and slipping all over the place when he tried to walk. James took him to the vet.

'The only humane thing to do is put him down,' he was told. 'This hasn't happened while you've had him. You've been sold a sick dog, he has had a disease from birth.'

I was distraught and cried my eyes out. James was upset too, and absolutely furious. He went back to the pet shop he'd bought the dog from in a blazing rage.

'I want a refund, on principle,' he shouted at the owner. 'It's disgraceful that you are selling sick puppies.'

'You want a refund, you show me the body,' the shopkeeper said.

With that James went mental and started shouting outside the shop to everyone who would listen: 'DO NOT BUY A DOG FROM THIS SHOP!'

The police were called but James continued to protest, shouting that he had the right to free speech.

I was utterly heartbroken and, even though I would never carry on the way James did, I was proud of him for making a stand against such cruelty.

We didn't get another puppy and my life returned to just how it had been when we'd been travelling in and out of Hong Kong. I ran to keep fit, I went to yoga and the gym, and I counted calories and watched my weight. I was as obsessive as ever. It didn't matter that we were taking a break from competing. I'd worked very hard to get slim before and I didn't want that work to be wasted. I'd gained a bit of weight, especially when we were in Skiathos and I let myself relax a little, so now I had my work cut out again. Even in my wedding dress, when everyone told me I was a beautiful bride, I didn't feel brilliant because I knew I'd put a few pounds on and I could feel it, especially on my hips and thighs.

I didn't want to just be slim, I wanted to be tiny and so once again I started surviving on a strict limit of 600 calories a day. I kept a little pocket book with me at all times and started noting down what I had eaten to make sure I didn't go over the limit. This was something I'd done last time and it had worked well, so I did it again.

'Are you sure this is safe?' James asked many times, although by his own admission he wasn't very clued up on diet and nutrition.

'It's fine,' I reassured him. 'I've done it before remember. I'm only five foot three. I'm a small woman, I can live on 600 calories.'

'Mmm, but is it healthy? Are you sure you're getting all the right minerals and vitamins?'

'Yes! I'm probably getting more than you,' I said, pointing out that I'd be eating a plate of boiled vegetables while he tucked into a greasy burger.

James knew how driven I was, and he could see there was no arguing with me. He was also very aware from past experience that I was at my happiest when I felt comfortable with my weight, and he came to the conclusion that I had to do what I felt was right, or I'd be miserable.

One of the inevitable side effects of this was that James went out more and more on his own with the boys, drinking, going to karaoke bars and clubs or playing pool until 5 or 6 a.m. while I stayed in watching TV.

I continued to be astonished by James's capacity to drink and stay out late yet still get up as fresh as a daisy the next morning.

'You're like a machine!' I'd joke.

'I'm young,' he'd say. 'I'm gonna do it while I can!'

He and the boys got up to all sorts of crazy things, and in hindsight James acknowledges that he behaved like a real idiot at times. All the boy dancers were earning really good money, and they'd regularly buy bottles of Jack Daniels for 1,000 HK$ – the equivalent of around £100 at the time – and then challenge each other to drink shot after shot until the bottle was gone.

One bar ran a regular competition, offering the prize of a tee-shirt and half-price drinks if you could down twenty-four different shots in ten minutes. James and his friends did it easily time and time again: in fact, one of the boys held the record at nineteen seconds.

Another bar, the 19th Floor was a favourite haunt. It had floor-to-ceiling windows that gave spectacular views across Hong Kong, and the boys thought it was funny to throw each other against them after a few drinks. The windows would bow, which was quite alarming, and the boys were always getting told off. In the end, the management put rails up to keep the boys away; they were such good customers I guess it was an investment worth making.

One night, James decided it would be a great idea to climb up some bamboo scaffolding outside one of the hotels. He was used to scaling heights from his time working at the power station, and he wanted to show off to his mates. The only problem was that he was so drunk when he reached the top that he couldn't get down, and he was one hundred feet in the air. Needless to say, he got a lot of stick from the boys when they had to climb up and help rescue him.

On many occasions James would literally crawl home on his hands and knees, arriving back at the apartment with rips in his clothing. I'd put him in the shower sometimes to sober him up.

'Sorry, Ola,' he'd giggle.

'I'm sorry for you,' I'd say. 'You'll be the one with the hangover tomorrow!'

In fact, he rarely did have a hangover, which astonished me, and even on two hours' sleep he'd look amazing. This didn't seem fair at all. Despite eating cleanly, exercising and taking saunas and yoga classes daily, in my opinion I looked awful. I still had weight to lose, but that wasn't the only problem. Suddenly my skin had started to look really unhealthy. James was really sweet and told me he was sure it was just a phase, but I wasn't convinced.

'I hope so,' I said, looking in the mirror and fretting. I began to develop a lot of spots, and they were red and angry. It looked like the beginning of acne to me, not a minor bad skin episode. I'd never suffered with spots before even when I was on my first extreme diet or when I'd tried all kinds of different diets. This was so strange. I never even had spots as a teenager. Surely it couldn't be acne?

I quickly became as obsessive about my skin as I was about my weight. I always cleansed and moisturised thoroughly, and I never failed to take my make-up off at night. I'd remove every last bit religiously, paranoid that if I missed anything at all my pores would be clogged up and I'd get more spots the next day. Because of my lifestyle in Hong Kong I didn't wear make-up every day and I wasn't using the fake tans and heavy competition make-up I had done in the past. If anything my skin should have been better, not worse, and it was difficult and very frustrating to try to work out where I was going wrong.

Every day I'd look in the mirror, my heart would sink and I'd start fretting and thinking of anything and everything I could possibly do to make my skin better.

I cleaned all my make-up brushes regularly and thoroughly, I washed the pillowcases all the time and I tried using different products on my skin, ones that were natural and gentle.

In the end, I went to the doctor and was given antibiotics, as she advised me that they were the only things that would work. The medication did work, for a short while, but then when I got to the end of the course of pills the spots came back again, and again. I couldn't keep taking antibiotics, so I got into a cycle of doing without for as long as I could, then only taking them again when the spots got really bad. By 'really bad' I mean I had dozens all over my face, but particularly on my cheeks. They looked like infected boils, and I was devastated.

'What is wrong with me?' I'd cry to James.

He didn't know what to say. He knew I'd tried everything and nothing was working to solve the problem long term.

'Ola, you are beautiful, spots or no spots,' he said one day.

I burst into tears.

James's work was going really well and he had taken on several students who were heavily involved in the world of ProAm dancing. Some of James's students were extremely good and very competitive, They travelled to competitions all over the USA, where ProAm is very popular, and of course when James became their teacher they asked him to accompany them.

I'd met all the ladies James taught by going along to the dinner dances from time to time. They were typically in their fifties and sixties and were incredibly fit for their age, and usually very charming too. I enjoyed their company, and it was nice for me to see James at work and spend time with him in the evening. When the ProAm competitions came up abroad the students invited me to go along too. They didn't have to, but money was no object to them and they were very welcoming and just wanted to include me. I thought this was very generous, though I was also a bit sceptical at first. As with the tea and dinner dance set-up, it was something I had to get my head around. It seemed a little odd for a middle-aged lady to take her dance teacher and his wife half way across the world for what was effectively a hobby, but this was what a lot of ladies did. James and I eventually went on a lot of these trips and the more I learned about the ProAm circuit the less odd it became, and I learned that it is an incredibly professional set-up.

One of James's students, Monica Wong, was particularly talented and dedicated, and she began to take us on some incredible trips. Though we'd travelled a lot in the past, James and I had seen very little of the world before this because all our trips had been on a tight budget. Now we really saw the world, and we saw it in style, always travelling first class or business class, staying in the best hotels and having plenty of time off between teaching and competitions to go sightseeing. We went all over the States, visiting LA, Vegas, New York, San Francisco, Miami and Florida. Monica paid for everything and we had time to chill out, meet up with friends who happened to be in the same place, go to all the top attractions and take loads of photos and just relax and have a lot of fun. It was absolutely brilliant. Sometimes we'd be away for five days and have four days to ourselves to do as we pleased. It cost about £30,000 on average for a student like Monica to take the three of us to a big competition like that, as only the best would do. It was incredibly glamorous and James and I would often find ourselves sitting in a luxury spa in a five-star hotel or standing somewhere iconic, like Times Square or on the Las Vegas Strip, saying to each other: 'Wow! I can't believe this is happening!'

Life was not just good, it was absolutely fantastic. We'd made exactly the right call when we decided to move to Hong Kong full-time. This experience was priceless and James and I could not have been happier.

19

'Ola, I'm dying!'

James staggered into the apartment, clutching his stomach and barely able to walk.

'James! What happened?'

'I don't know! The pain is excruciating! Oh my God!'

He was on the verge of collapse and I got hold of him and steered him to the bed. Every movement seemed to be agony for him, and his skin was pale and clammy.

'Seriously, I think I'm dying, Ola. This is hell. Arrhhhh!'

He gripped his stomach as a wave of pain shot through him.

James told me that he'd been at his friend's apartment after a night out when he started coughing and couldn't stop. He wasn't that alarmed at first, as at the time he was smoking at least a packet of cigarettes a day; it was a habit he'd had since he was a teenager. The coughing wouldn't stop, though, and then James coughed some blood up into his hands. He ran to his friend's toilet and coughed up more blood, and this carried on until he'd practically filled the toilet bowl with blood.

I took James to A&E. He insisted on walking from the taxi, but as soon as we got inside he collapsed on the floor. He was then put in a wheelchair and a nurse immediately started taking his blood pressure. She did it once and shook her head, then she got another machine and did it again but she still wasn't happy. 'It can't be that low,' she said. The nurse tried once again and her eyes widened in alarm. 'It is so low! It can't be.'

Then she turned to me.

'What religion is he?' the nurse asked.

I gasped in shock as I thought this meant James was about to die and they were going to call in a priest. I known now that they wanted to know his religion in case he needed a blood transfusion, but I wasn't thinking clearly at the time, and nor was James. He was so panicked by the nurse's question that he passed out, at which point about ten doctors and nurses descended on him, pushing me out of the way. All I could think about was a funeral. James might die, that's what I thought.

James was pumped with adrenaline while I stood on the sidelines in panic, feeling hopeless and afraid. James was my tall, strong husband, the man who always defended me. Now here he was, so weak he had passed out. It didn't seem real and I felt so scared.

The adrenaline kicked in and he was put on a bed with his feet raised in the air to keep the blood flowing to his head. Then he was given a shot of something that clearly agreed with him, because he suddenly came round and said he felt great. I don't know what the drug was and I didn't care. All I was bothered about was that my James had come back to me.

This sense of relief didn't last long, because the doctors then told me they thought James had a bleeding ulcer, which could be fatal. He needed an endoscopy there and then to investigate what was going on in his stomach. James was given local anaesthetic and a nurse strapped a big, plastic endoscopy tube to his mouth. I felt so sorry for him because he looked terrified, and now he was in absolute agony, clutching his stomach in pain.

'James, it will be OK,' I soothed, but I wasn't sure this was true. He looked absolutely terrible, and then the doctor began inserting the exploratory tube. James's eyes bulged and I could tell he was struggling to cope.

'Oh, James,' I gasped. I could see how uncomfortable this was for him but of course he couldn't speak. He was searching my eyes with his. 'OK, James, it will be over soon…'

I had no idea what to say because I was terrified too.

The endoscopy showed nothing, and the doctors were at a loss. They had given James a lot of painkillers, which had started to take effect, but they had no idea what had caused such excruciating pain in the first place.

'You can go home,' they said after hours and hours of tests, and when his pain had subsided a lot, 'but come back if the pain returns.'

James couldn't wait to get out of hospital, but at the same time he was worried about being discharged with no diagnosis.

Back at the apartment his pain came back almost immediately, dulled again and then returned with a vengeance, very nearly making him collapse again. He took to his bed and stayed there for days, doubled up in pain, trying to cope with the worst shots of agony that screwed up his insides, and panicking like mad about what was wrong.

'Go to the private hospital,' one of his wealthy students suggested. 'They will treat you well. They will give you better treatment.'

We did this, without thinking about the cost. James was then kept waiting for hour after hour on a private ward.

'I'm in pain!' he said.

'OK, we give you painkillers. For that there is an extra charge…'

James quickly discharged himself, having come to the conclusion that the care was no better than in the state hospital, but was going to cost an absolute fortune, which we didn't have.

After yet more days at home, trying but failing to cope with the pain, we went back to the first hospital. James was put on a ward that was grimmer than a prison. One of the other patients had soiled himself and the smell was like nothing on earth. Other patients were screaming out.

'This is hell,' James said, 'absolute hell, but I need to know what is wrong.'

The doctors checked him over once more, but again they could find nothing wrong and James was discharged. We were back in the apartment again, with James intermittently clutching his abdomen in agony, while I was tearing my hair out with worry, doing my best to look after him but worrying all the time about how serious this was, and whether he needed to see another doctor. We were in this state for a long time before James finally announced that he'd had enough. It had been about six weeks since he first fell ill, and looking back I'm surprised he didn't crack sooner.

'If I'm going to die, I want to die in the UK,' he said.

'James, don't say that!'

'I mean it. I'm booking us flights. I can't work anyway so I'm going to my GP back home, and what's more I'm paying for the best flights we can afford.'

'Why?'

'You never know, I might die, so we might as well fly business class.'

'Oh for heaven's sake!'

'Ola, I'm serious. Arrgggh!'

James was doubled up again and I couldn't argue. We'd exhausted the avenues of help available to us in Hong Kong and I didn't have a better idea so I paid for the upgraded flights and we flew to London, taking with us all the test results and paperwork we had collected.

James's GP in Kent checked him over, wasn't sure what the problem was and sent him to hospital for several tests on his intestines and pancreas. James was also checked for gallstones and ulcers.

'Tell me about your lifestyle,' the doctor said.

'I burn the candle at both ends massively, and have done for a long time,' James admitted. 'I drink too much, I smoke, I eat junk food, I work fourteen-hour days and I survive on an average of four hours sleep a night.'

'I see,' said the GP. 'When you say you drink too much, do you regularly exceed twenty-one units a week?'

'I would say I regularly exceed twenty-one units a day, doctor.'

The doctor suspected he had bleeding ulcers but when the test results came back they showed nothing. It didn't come as too much of a shock when the doctor eventually concluded that James's unhealthy lifestyle seemed to be the at the root of his problem.

'Stress and alcohol abuse can produce the symptoms you're displaying. All I can suggest is that you try to cut down on both. Let's start with that, and see how you go.'

James was chastened. 'My lifestyle has caught up with me in a big way,' he told our friends and family afterwards. 'I've been a silly boy, and it's time to change.'

Once we were back in Hong Kong, James cut down his lessons and his partying. Not only was this good for his health but we also spent more time together. We'd been living in Hong Kong permanently for about two years by now, and we began to talk about returning to the UK and competing together again before it was too late. We didn't make any decisions just yet, though. We were reluctant to leave Hong Kong as we had such a great lifestyle and were building up savings, but then again we didn't want to miss out on the chance to return to competing. Really, it was the same old dilemma that had plagued us for years.

Thankfully, James's health did improve once he slowed down a bit, and within a few months all of his stomach pains finally disappeared. As luck would have it, his student Monica Wong then offered him a very timely opportunity, which would further cut his working hours. Monica had started doing extremely well in the ProAm competitions she entered, so well in fact that she had become the best ProAm dancer in the world in her age category.

'James,' she said one day. 'I'd like you to teach me exclusively. Can you do it?'

'That's very flattering Monica,' he replied, 'but that would be just a few hours a day, and I can teach for a lot more than that if I want to.'

'I'll pay you for twelve hours a day,' Monica said, without hesitation, 'but I would only want three lessons on weekdays and four lessons on Saturday and Sunday.'

'Really?'

'Yes, really.'

James struck the deal, and it turned out to be a great decision. Monica and James got on really well and I began helping out at lessons too, acting as a third eye in the studio and giving James as well as Monica pointers on how they could improve. The three of us travelled together to more competitions in America, again all at Monica's expense. I'd tell her she didn't need to invite me along every time but she wouldn't hear of it, always saying that she liked to have her 'support team' around her.

As well as being good for James's health, his reduced working hours meant that the two of us could practise together again regularly. This was fantastic, and when we got back on the dance floor it was like we'd only stopped yesterday, even though we hadn't competed together for a couple of years by this point. I loved it, and I felt the same pulse-racing excitement I'd felt when I first started dancing with James. I lost myself on the dance floor when I was with him, just like I did in the early days.

'Ola, you look amazing,' he told me.

'Thanks,' I said, 'are you sure?'

I needed constant reassurance about my appearance. I was still getting outbreaks of spots, and my weight was an ongoing battle. I continued to obsess about every calorie, and I can remember that when I helped out with Monica's lessons at the weekends she would bring sandwiches, which I would never eat. I'd just pick out the chicken from the middle, provided it was plain and grilled. I'd do this even if I felt really hungry, because I knew that if I started eating bread I'd instantly put on weight that would take ages to shift off my bum or my hips.

Inevitably, the more we practised together the more James and I started talking about competing again, and we began to discuss where we would make our comeback. Blackpool was the obvious place and we were excited just thinking about it. We'd last competed there in 2003 as amateurs. Since then we'd turned professional, which meant taking exams to prove our skills. We were obliged to do this before we moved to Hong Kong, to demonstrate our worth as permanent residents and get the necessary paperwork. This meant that we would no longer be able to compete as amateurs and so we registered to compete at the British Open Rising Stars Latin competition. This was for professional dancers only and would take place in the famous Winter Gardens at Blackpool in May 2006, which was several months away. The Rising Stars is one category down from the 'open' professional competition and most professionals enter this competition as soon as they turn pro.

James and I practised as much as we possibly could. We wanted to make a big impression at our comeback and we wanted to see how far we could go. It was a big deal to us and we were determined to do our very best. We worked incredibly hard every day, and we even flew in our old coach, Holger Nitsche, from Germany to give us lessons. Maybe we would get into the semis or even the final? That was our dream. It was a very personal thing. We were pursuing this purely for the love of dance, and for the satisfaction we'd get from doing well at what was still our great passion in life. Nobody asked us to make a comeback and we didn't have to do it, but we wanted to because we loved dancing so much.

As the competition drew closer James and I started to feel that we might stand a real chance of doing well, and we believed our dream may come true. It was so exciting, and I was really enjoying myself.

When the day of the competition arrived I felt as excited as I had as a teenager, the first time I'd danced at the Winter Gardens with Przemek. There is something about Blackpool that never fails to make the hairs on the back of your neck stand up.

'Wow, you're back!' lots of other dancers said. 'And you're looking good!'

People didn't expect to see us back and it was great to get this reaction. James and I felt that we looked good and I think we had a new freshness about us. The break from competing had definitely done us good, and we had a much more relaxed attitude than before. Dancing was not the be all and end all as it had been in our early days. We had a great life in Hong Kong, and if we didn't win in Blackpool we still had that to go back to, so we had absolutely nothing to lose and everything to win. Above all, we were doing this competition for the love of dancing and we'd come back for ourselves and nobody else, to see how far we could go. This was a really refreshing position to be in.

We were both really fired up when the competition got under way, and we got through round after round with ease. We enjoyed every moment, and several hours later, to our absolute delight, we actually did get to the final. We hugged each other and had grins from ear to ear when our names were announced. It was a really special feeling to be dancing with James like this. We'd never competed as husband and wife, and I felt so proud to be there with him, looking and feeling so good. James said he felt the same as me, and I think we sparked off each other in a really positive way that day.

'You're going to win,' everyone was saying. 'You're smashing it!'

The final was electric; I got goosebumps when we stepped on the dance floor. James was the only Brit in the final, and we could feel the support from the home crowd, willing us to do well.

In the event, the couple who went on to win pulled something extra special out of the bag at the eleventh hour, and we came a close second. We were still absolutely thrilled; this was an amazing result for us after so long away from the competition circuit.

'We haven't lost it!' I laughed

'Far from it,' James said. 'We'll win next time, Ola.'

We'd got the bug again in a big way, and it seemed a certainty that we'd keep competing after this success. We'd thoroughly enjoyed ourselves, and we were on a real high for days and days afterwards

About a week after we returned to Hong Kong, James's mobile phone rang late at night. We'd been out to a club and were walking back to our apartment.

'Can you possibly call back in ten minutes?' I heard James say. 'We'll be in our apartment then.'

It was a BBC producer on the phone called Helen Bishop, and she wanted to talk to us both about a show. 'Would you consider doing Strictly Come Dancing?' she asked.

'What?' I said, horrified. The whole idea immediately shocked me, but James was more open-minded, and he was intrigued.

'Let's see what she says, come on!'

We dashed back to the apartment and Helen called back. James took the call again and I stood close to him, trying to hear what was being said. Helen explained that the BBC had had scouts at Blackpool, they liked the look of us and wanted us to come to London for discussions.

'Are you interested?'

'No!' I was mouthing, 'No, no, no!'

James and I knew Strictly was a very successful show – the first three series had already been aired – but the truth was we had never watched it in Hong Kong and didn't know much more than that. It was frowned upon by a lot of professional dancers, we knew that much, as we'd heard a few negative remarks being made by dancers we knew. 'Strictly isn't proper dancing,' I remembered one friend saying. 'All you're doing is dragging a celebrity around the dance floor…' It sounded like a nightmare to me.

James furrowed his brow as he continued the conversation.

He asked about how long you needed to be available in the UK and enquired about the pay. 'OK. I'll talk to Ola. We'll have to think about it.'

When James relayed all the details of the phone call I shook my head very firmly.

'I don't want to do it James, no way.'

'Why not?'

'I'm too nervous. You have to talk on camera. You have to teach on camera. I'm not sure my English is good enough. I'd be terrified!'

He disagreed with this and said that of course I could do it, if I put my mind to it. James had no worries at all about putting himself in the spotlight, but there were lots of other considerations to think about. Doing the show would amount to four months' solid work, from September to December. The combined pay on offer to both of us was less than James was currently earning on his own, so of course this was something we had to think hard about. More importantly, he was finally working civilised hours, thanks to Monica, whereas Strictly was practically a seven-days-a-week, non-stop commitment, involving long days training in the studio, the live show on the Saturday, and then starting all over again with the next lot of choreography on the Sunday. James clearly didn't need stress in his life, and of course it would mean we'd have to completely change our lifestyle and move back to the UK, at least temporarily.

We canvassed opinions from our family and friends and voiced all of our concerns. To our surprise, nobody could understand why we didn't just jump at the chance and their verdicts were unanimous.

'You have to do it!' they all said. 'It'll be brilliant!'

James's mum and dad were particularly enthusiastic, as they were massive fans of the show and understood much better than we did how high-profile and successful it was. In those days Bruce Forsyth was the main presenter, Tess Daly was his co-host and the panel was made up of Craig Revel Horwood, Arlene Phillips, Len Goodman and Bruno Tonioli. I had come across Len Goodman in the dancing world several times over the years and liked and respected him, and I knew Arlene had an amazing dancing career behind her, but I had barely heard of the others. I even had to have it spelled out to me what a legend Bruce was as I hadn't grown up watching him on big shows like The Generation Game and Play Your Cards Right, as James had.

The more I heard about what an important primetime show Strictly was, and how big its stars were, the more nervous I felt. However, I did have to admit that I was getting bored in Hong Kong by this time, and for me that was the best argument there was for potentially giving Strictly a go. We'd been living full-time in Hong Kong for two and a half years, and I'd started to get itchy feet. My lifestyle was great, but not particularly challenging. I was ready for a change, and to do something that would inspire me and allow me to push myself again. Strictly was certainly a challenge, and a very exciting one at that, but did I want such a dramatic change? It was terrifying, and I had sleepless nights thinking about it.

James asked Monica Wong what she thought. He valued her opinion, and as he was her exclusive coach he also wanted to involve her in the decision, as he was worried about letting her down.

'James,' she smiled wisely. 'You should take every opportunity that life throws at you. You never know where it will lead. Hong Kong will still be here – it's not moving anywhere! Go and do it, you have nothing to lose.'

When he heard this, James's mind was made up.

'Ola, it is four months out of our lives. If it doesn't work out we can come back,' he said.

I couldn't argue with that, and ultimately I didn't. I trusted James's opinion and I agreed with him, even though I had butterflies in my stomach every time I even thought about Strictly.

'The BBC don't know what's gonna hit them,' some of our dancer friends said kindly, but all the time I was thinking I don't know what's gonna hit me.

James and I flew to London later that summer and went into the Strictly offices at Television Centre in Shepherds Bush. I was scared to death and I can remember wondering if you could see my knees trembling beneath the little brown skirt I was wearing.

'You'll be fine,' James kept reassuring me, while I just looked at him and thought, 'How can you be so cool about this?'

James and I had to teach some of the production staff the Cha Cha Cha, and then we both had to speak in front of the camera. James was a complete natural and I was very proud of him. When it was my turn he could see how nervous and tongue-tied I was, so he started heckling me in a jokey way, to try to distract me and make me relax. It worked, and I joined in and argued back at him, all with a smile on my face.

'You're so funny together!' one of the production crew said.

'Are we?' we said, genuinely surprised.

We'd obviously made a good impression, as we were told in a phone call from Helen Bishop very shortly afterwards that we'd definitely got the jobs.

We accepted the offer straight away. We wouldn't have come to London if we were going to turn the jobs down at this stage, and now it was a question of making arrangements to start work in September.

'We're so happy you're on board,' Helen Bishop said, 'and the costume designers will call you in five minutes.'

I was a bit shell-shocked at the speed this was going. I still had my reservations but there was no going back now, and within a couple of weeks we were booking our flights and embarking on a whole new adventure.

'Whatever happens, we're in this together,' James said. 'It's four months of our lives. Let's see how it goes.'

I was getting excited now, as well as nervous. I smiled, and I heard Mum and Dad's voices again in my head. 'Work hard, do your best.'

I would never have done Strictly in a million years without James, but that was part of why I loved him. Life with him was an adventure, and whatever happened next, this was going to be an experience and a great big challenge.

20

'He's a DJ on the radio,' was all I was told before I was thrust into a room and introduced to DJ Spoony.

Having only been back in the UK for a matter of weeks before meeting my celebrity partner I had never heard Spoony's Weekend Breakfast show on Radio 1, so I was grateful to have it explained to me who he was.

I was nervous about meeting him, especially as there were cameras following our every move as they did in those days, but I needn't have worried. Spoony and I hit it off straight away, and I learned very quickly that he was a lovely, positive guy with a great big character.

'He's got energy,' I told James enthusiastically.

'That's good,' he said shrewdly. 'I think you're at your best when you can bounce off another person's energy.'

I'd never really thought about that before, but James was right: in many ways it was how we operated as a couple, as James's natural energy always inspired me and pulled me up.

As soon as I did a few practice steps with Spoony I could tell that he had potential. He obviously had an ear for music and could clearly hear the rhythm, which was a good start.

Our first steps together were captured on camera, which I found very nerve-racking. I'd never been on television in my life before, and here I was in a vest top and leggings, my hair scraped into a ponytail, being filmed for one of the biggest shows on national television. What's more, I was on my own, without James. For years now he had been my safety blanket when we were centre stage at competitions, but now I was on my own, as he was off meeting his celebrity in a different location.

I thought I'd find it hard being filmed all day long in training but to my surprise, after the first day, I was so absorbed in the teaching that the crew soon faded into the background and I started to forget they were there.

The arrangement was, and still is, that each professional dancer gets three weeks to work with their celebrity before the series starts. This means you can get to know your partner's strengths and weaknesses, find out if they have any tricks up their sleeve, whether they can do spins or pivots, what their posture or their 'ballroom frame' is like and what they feel comfortable with generally. Soon after you've been introduced to one another you are told which dance you'll be doing in the first week, so you have plenty of time to rehearse for that first number. Sometimes you're also told what you'll be doing in the second week, so you can get a head start on that dance too. All the training and practising takes place in a venue convenient to the celebrity, as often they are working on their day job at the same time, so the pro dancer is the one who does all the travelling and has to fit in around the celeb.

Once the show is on air the pace inevitably picks up. The pro dancers work on the choreography for the next dance on their own on the Sunday, teach their partner from Monday to Thursday, and on the Friday you are in the BBC studio in London. In those days the studio was at Wood Lane, but now it's in Elstree. Friday is the first time you get to see the other contestants dance and vice versa. There are three full rehearsals and this is the first time everyone is in the studio together. On Saturday there are two more run-throughs with the band before a full dress rehearsal. You also have a costume fitting and a spray tan, plus you practise walking down the stairs and have what is called a 'lighting block' to make sure you are going to be properly lit on stage. The professional dancers also rehearse the 'pro numbers', which are the set-piece dances that intersperse the competition. Two of the Saturday rehearsals are with the live band, and then you have a full dress run complete with hair and make-up. This means that when the show is live on air you are actually doing your routine for the fourth time that day.

Spoony lived in Islington, so that was where I had to go for the initial three weeks of training and then the daily practice in the run-up to the first live show. I'd got myself a little silver Peugeot 107, which I loved, and James and I were staying with his parents again, as we had decided to sell the house in Iwade when we relocated to Hong Kong. This meant my daily commute was from St Mary's Island in Kent to North London. Meanwhile, James was partnered with Casualty actress Georgina Bouzova and was travelling to Bristol every day in an old second-hand Jaguar we also bought.

'Where is Islington?' I asked James, getting out a map.

He helped me work out a route and I headed off into unknown territory. I was still a very inexperienced driver, and in the first couple of days I had two incidents to contend with. First of all the Peugeot broke down on my way through London in the morning rush hour. I knew James was already on his way to Bristol, so I called my father-in-law for help.

'Allan, the car's broken down,' I said, fretting. 'I don't know what is wrong!'

He asked me to describe what had happened just before I'd juddered to a halt, and then he got me to describe the warning light that had lit up on the dashboard.

'Ola, you've run out of petrol,' he said.

'Have I?'

'Yes you have! Honestly…'

He sent one of the lads from the power station out to rescue me with a can of petrol and I somehow got to the studio on time, albeit with my nerves a bit frayed.

Later that day I had trouble reversing out of the car park outside the studio in Islington. My foot was flat on the accelerator and I had the car in gear but I wasn't moving – the car was just stuck. I revved the engine and tried again and again before I remembered what James had told me.

'Always look in the direction you are travelling, Ola! Don't look at the gearstick!'

I twisted round and looked out of the back window, and that's when I realised why I was going nowhere. My little car was butted right up to another car and was simply pushing into it. Thankfully no harm was done, but I blushed with embarrassment.

'Oops!' I said to myself, manoeuvring out of the car park and driving off as quickly as I could, thanking my lucky stars that Spoony and the crew hadn't seen me.

Spoony and I had been given the Cha Cha Cha and we decided to perform it to Kiss by Prince. This had been our music suggestion, which the producers welcomed, and I was very happy with it. The only issue was that one producer, having seen my choreography, suggested we ended the routine with me planting a real kiss on Spoony's lips.

'Er, I don't think so,' James said when he got wind of this. 'The only man who kisses Ola is me!'

James said it in a fairly light-hearted way, but unbeknown to me he was actually jealous. He didn't tell me this until years later, and he only told Spoony very recently, but the truth was that James found it very difficult to see me dancing so intimately with another man. I'd come home from rehearsals talking enthusiastically about Spoony, and James would be biting his tongue and trying not to let me see how cut up he was feeling. James was not having a good time with his partner and he'd snap at me sometimes, saying things like 'Oh it's Spoony this and Spoony that!' I can remember James's mum saying to us: 'Don't you two argue under my roof! Do you hear me?'

Looking back, it was not easy for either of us to spend so much time apart. We weren't used to it, and making the adjustment was not easy as we had so many other pressures in our lives as we got to grips with our new jobs and lifestyle.

Before we'd signed our contract James had checked with the producers that I would have an input into my costume designs, because this was very important to me. I had a clear idea of what suited me, and I knew that anything full-length made me look frumpy, because of my height.

'No problem,' we'd been told, but then all of a sudden I received emails showing me the design for my first dress, despite the fact I'd had no discussion about it whatsoever. It was garish yellow and green and there was so much fabric I'd have been almost completely covered.

'Oh my God,' I said to James. 'I hate it. I don't want to wear that!'

'Then tell them.'

'I can't do that!'

'Well if you don't then I will…'

James rang the designer.

'I'm afraid there's a bit of a problem with the dress,' he said.

'What's the problem?'

'Well, there are two problems actually. The first is the colour and the second is the design.'

'I'm sorry, but it's too late now. We've already designed it. Ola will have to wear it.'

The designer wasn't moving and James was really annoyed.

'It's not that bad, is it?' I said, because I didn't want any trouble. 'Perhaps we should just leave it, James?'

'Ola, it's terrible! And what's more, we were told you would have a choice. It was part of the deal. This isn't on. I'm fighting it on principle if nothing else!'

James then called the producer, who immediately conceded that we'd been told we could choose my dresses, and asked what I wanted.

'We'll get back to you very shortly, and thank you,' James said.

Between us James, Spoony and I designed a lovely little lilac dress, cut away at the sides and with a fluffy bra top and short skirt, finished with thin straps across the hips. It was the skimpiest outfit anyone had ever worn on Strictly and the cut-away sections were something very new and daring, but I absolutely loved it.

'Wow!' James and Spoony both said when they saw it. 'It's amazing!

'Ola, you look so hot,' James said, his eyes popping out of his head.

I felt very confident in the dress, and it gave me a boost. The pressure of doing the show and all the changes I'd gone through in my life in recent months meant I'd lost weight not just from my ongoing dieting, but through stress. I hadn't been eating much at all and I was at the thinnest I'd ever been – less than seven and a half stone – and I felt really good. It was still a healthy weight for my height and I still had my curves in all the right places, but I was really trim and toned. I absolutely loved being that size.

In fact, the only issue I now had with my appearance was my skin problem. The spots I'd started to develop in Hong Kong had never gone away, and they seemed to flare up really badly whenever I was feeling stressed. Whatever I ate or didn't eat made no difference at all, by the way. Sometimes the healthier the food I was eating, the worse my skin was. I was starting to develop full-blown acne again in these early days at Strictly, and when I got an outbreak of spots they were raised and boil-like, as they had been many times in the past. They were also filled with blood, but you couldn't squeeze them or do anything to get rid of the blood and redness. It was horrific. I couldn't even go to training with Spoony without putting loads of make-up on my face, which was really inconvenient and demoralising.

'At least with my weight I know I can control it,' I cried to James. But this is out of my control. It's just not fair!'

When I met the Strictly make-up artists I explained the whole history of how the spots had appeared from nowhere when I was twenty-two, and how I'd treated them repeatedly with antibiotics over the previous couple of years but couldn't take the pills all the time. By now I'd also used loads of different medicated creams, been to countless dermatologists and resorted to some expensive facial peels. Nothing worked, and in fact the peels just left me with a pigmentation problem and meant I had to use factor 50 on my face in the sun at all times, and still do.

'Don't worry,' the make-up artists. 'We'll have you looking absolutely amazing!'

They were absolutely brilliant with me, never making me feel embarrassed and doing a fabulous job every time I sat in the chair. My foundation had to be incredibly thick, but the girls were very highly skilled at their job, and when I was on screen you would never have known how bad my skin was underneath. Even in the flesh I looked OK with the make-up on, though I was very conscious of how much I was wearing, and I was always concerned about what other people thought, and whether they could tell how thick the foundation was.

'You know the best thing is to take care to remove your make-up really well at the end of each day,' one of the other pro dancers said, giving me what seemed to be quite a patronising smile. 'Washing pillowcases and make-up brushes regularly is another good tip...' another dancer chipped in. This girl was practically wrinkling her nose at me. I felt uncomfortable under their glare and I wasn't sure if those dancers were genuinely trying to help me or were somehow attempting to undermine my confidence because we were competing against each other. They certainly didn't make me feel at ease like the lovely staff in the make-up department did. I smiled back sweetly, but what I really wanted to do was say, 'Do you think I haven't tried everything? This is a medical condition, not something that's happened because I don't know how to keep my face clean or because I am unhygienic!'

James wasn't getting on well with his partner Georgina at all. He came home fuming from training every night, complaining that she had turned up late even though he'd driven for more than two hours to start work promptly at the studio in Bristol.

'How late?'

'Like two hours late!'

'Why? Because of Casualty?'

'No! The other day she came in showing off her new nails. That's why she was late – she'd gone for a manicure! I've told her I can't help her learn the dance if she's not there, and if she's late again I'm calling the producer.'

'What did she say?'

James sighed. 'Ola, she basically said to me "let's not forget who the celebrity is here".'

After two weeks had gone by and James had been kept waiting time and time again he was at boiling point.

'It's like Georgina's put a brick wall up between us,' he complained, 'I just don't understand why she's behaving like this.'

Then something else happened, unrelated to Georgina, which really made him snap.

Before we signed up for Strictly, James and I already had a big competition booked in our diary, the International Championships at the Royal Albert Hall. One of the Strictly producers had agreed that we could still take part in it as it was pre-arranged, even though it would mean missing the Thursday of training before our very first live show. However, a few days beforehand the producer called James when he was in training, sounding annoyed.

'Are you OK?'

'No, not really, James. There's a bit of a problem. I hear you and Ola think you're taking a day off on Thursday.'

'That's right. We're competing at the Albert Hall. We agreed it.'

'No, you're not. You have to be in training. You both need to be rehearsing with your partners. It's only two days until the first live show and you have to be in training.'

'No! We agreed this before we signed the contracts, or we wouldn't have signed up. We're going to the competition. You put it in your diary, don't you remember?'

'No,' the producer told James flatly, 'and if you want to come back next year, I suggest you think very seriously about this. You have to be here. It's in your contract.'

James was already rattled by what was going on with Georgina, so this was like a red rag to a bull.

'No, I'm telling you that we're going to the competition, and if you don't like it you know what you can do with the contract!'

The producer put the phone down and then James kicked a chair across the room in a temper, ranting and swearing and calling her names. 'Who does she think she is!' he screamed.

An hour later the producer called James back.

'I'm SO sorry,' she said. 'I looked in my other diary and I see you have the time booked off. Can you forgive me?'

'Yes,' James said immediately, meaning it, as he is the sort of person who accepts apologies and moves on without holding a grudge. 'I understand that mistakes happen. Although I think I need to ask you if you will forgive me too…'

'What for James?'

He explained about how he'd kicked the chair and sworn and called her names. James had totally forgotten that the cameras were running all the time he was training in the studio, and his entire rant had been captured on film.

The producer listened and accepted his apology. 'I admire the way you stood up to me,' she said, 'not many would. And at least we got something out of it…'

James wasn't sure what she meant by this and nor was I. We did the competition at the Albert Hall, which turned out to be our last ever competition, incidentally. We were very glad we did it as we got a brilliant result, finishing in the top twelve professionals in the world.

Afterwards we found out what the producer had meant by her 'at least we got something out of it' comment. James's VT footage for the show was cut in such a way that it was made to look like he was ranting at Georgina for being late for rehearsals, rather than because he was cross with the producer. He and Georgina had genuinely rowed about her being late, but even so I was shocked at how the footage had been edited.

Then something else happened that stunned me even more: the story was leaked to the Sun newspaper. The Strictly press office tipped James off and unbelievably, it was splashed across the front page of the paper the next day, complete with an image of James looking as mad as hell and apparently seething with rage at Georgina.

'Dancer James's training walkout' read the headline, and James was quoted as saying: 'I'm cancelling practice with her. I'd do anything to make the show good but I've got the laziest cow ever.' The article claimed that Georgina fled to the toilet in tears, saying: 'He's very chauvinistic.'

'Ola, look at the picture!' James said. 'People are going to think I'm horrible and a troublemaker. I don't mind admitting I'm hot-headed when it comes to standing up for what I believe in, but this? This is going to stick. People don't forget things like this.'

We were both shocked. It was our first year and we couldn't believe something like this had happened. I hoped that it would blow over in time and be forgotten about but unfortunately James was right, and in hindsight his Strictly reputation was pretty much sealed that day.

After all this drama, and after working incredibly hard with Spoony for weeks, I was a bag of nerves when we finally got to the rehearsals at the BBC studio on the Friday before our first live show.

'Please welcome to the floor DJ Spoony and his dance partner Ola Jordan,' I heard the pre-recorded voiceover say.

I gasped, not just with nerves but because they had called me Ola. I had always used my full name of Aleksandra in competitions, and that was what I expected to hear.

'Are you OK with that?' James asked, as he was looking out for me and making sure I was coping.

'Yes, it's fine. Just leave it, I don't really mind.'

I had more important things to worry about, like the fact that I was going to be doing the Cha Cha Cha with Spoony on live TV in front of millions of people the following night.

To add to the build-up, my mum and dad were flying over to watch the show, and James's parents were going to be in the audience too. Each dancer gets two tickets per show, and James and I both wanted our parents to be there because without them we wouldn't have got this far. We had no idea how long we might last in the series, or whether we'd return the following year, so we wanted them to experience the excitement with us while they had the chance.

Friday rehearsals went well, even though I was incredibly nervous and I was feeling more stressed as every hour went by. On the Saturday night I'll never forget the moment my name was announced and the music started. My heart was beating out of my chest and I could feel the electricity bouncing off Spoony and me as we took to the floor.

We'd worked so hard and we desperately wanted to do well. My little lilac dress was perfect, we both loved the track we'd chosen and Spoony had turned out to be not half bad as a novice dancer. I'd had my spray tan, the hair and make-up girls had worked miracles, and now it was all down to us dancing the very best Cha Cha Cha we could.

I heard the first note of the music, and then I swear the next sound was that of applause. It was over, and I was standing next to a smiling Bruce Forsyth, who was making some very admiring comments about how I looked. I loved Sir Bruce from the moment I met him; he chatted to me and James in rehearsals as he knew Hong Kong and was interested in our lives there, and he just seemed to be such a genuine, lovely man.

I couldn't stop grinning as we stood before the judges. Our results weren't brilliant, but we survived, and I was incredibly relieved. It had been a baptism of fire, but I'd done it. James and Georgina got through to the next week too, which I was so pleased about.

Afterwards we all went to the bar with the other dancers and celebrities, and then some of us went out clubbing in London.

'I was more nervous for you than I was for myself,' James confided to me.

'I felt the same!' I giggled. 'Oh my God James, what have we got ourselves into? We must be mad!'

21

Spoony and I went out in the second week, which was disappointing, and Georgina and James survived until week three, which wasn't great either. The relationship between them remained tense although, many years later, Georgina phoned James out of the blue when he was on the golf course, to apologise for her behaviour on the show.

'Wow,' he said, taken aback, 'you didn't need to do that. Thank you.'

Very sweetly, Georgina told him she was older and wiser now and regretted what had happened between them. James was blown away that she took the trouble to make the call, especially after so many years. It was a lovely thing to do, and he really appreciated it.

Anyhow, neither James nor I were sure if the producers would ask us back for the next series after our early exits, and we figured that James's rant story in the press could go either way. The producers might think he was a bit of a liability, or maybe they would decide he was good for publicity? We had no idea at all; it was a whole new world to us and we didn't know the show or the TV industry well enough to predict which way it might go.

Even though Strictly had been nerve-racking and extremely hard work we were both in agreement that we wanted to give it another shot. We felt we had a lot more to give and, once I had time to reflect, I realised I'd coped better than I thought I would with the stress of being on TV, and talking on camera. My view was that it could only get easier, and I wanted the chance to stay in the competition for longer, if we were lucky enough to be invited back.

I'd enjoyed the excitement and drama of live TV much more than I'd bargained for. It was fun, and I loved the camaraderie back stage, particularly with the crew who were all lovely and very supportive. Meeting all the other pro dancers and celebs was interesting too, though we didn't get to know them well on that first series. I liked Flavia, Anton du Beke and Vincent Simone immediately as they were all friendly, genuine people. We'd met Brendan Cole before on the dance circuit, and he was very welcoming and easy to get on with.

James and I had shared the stage with characters like Mica Paris, Peter Schmeichel, Emma Bunton and the cricketer Mark Ramprakash, who won the series with Karen Hardy. I never got star-struck when I met any of the celebs, but it was good fun to have a drink in the bar with them and chat to all the different characters around the studio. As jobs went, you really couldn't complain; it was glamorous, exciting and really quite cool.

James and I stayed in the UK for Christmas that year, then headed back to Hong Kong so that James could carry on working while we waited for news about the next series. The pro dancers didn't get the call about whether or not they were being asked back for the following series until June – it's still the same now – so we had six months to wait.

I found it a struggle to go from working so intensely, in such a frenetic and exciting way, to returning to my normal routine in Hong Kong. I found it a bit boring going back to the gym and yoga classes on my own, I missed James when he was out for hours on end. In short, I had itchy feet and was ready to move on.

'I'm going out of my mind!' I started saying to James. 'I've had enough of Hong Kong! I'm lonely!'

I was dieting intensely again too which didn't help my mood, but I was adamant I wanted to keep my weight low. My skimpy dresses had been a hit on Strictly and I'd received a lot of publicity on the strength of how I looked. The papers spotted that I'd started a new trend for the tiny outfits and I needed to keep myself in really good shape if I wanted to keep up this reputation.

Thankfully, James completely understood how I felt and he was open to the idea of returning to the UK, even if we didn't get asked back to Strictly. We'd been asked to do all kinds of personal appearances, charity functions and performances at holiday resorts and on cruise ships on the strength of being on Strictly. We could both see how our careers could take off in a different direction, and that we could do all of those things, together, from a base back in England. If we did another series it would be ideal, as we'd be in a position to take on plenty of other work together during the months when we weren't filming the show.

All of this meant that when the call finally came from Strictly, inviting us back for series five, we said yes straight away, and we made plans to move back to the UK permanently in the August of 2007. This gave us time to get ourselves organised, say all of our goodbyes in Hong Kong and give Monica time to find another coach. Predictably, she was very supportive, even though she would really miss James.

'Thank you,' we told her, 'without you we might not have even taken the plunge in the first place.'

To this day I still feel grateful to her for telling us to 'take every opportunity that life throws at you'. It was exactly what we needed to hear.

It was sad leaving Hong Kong. It had been our home for a long time and we had a lot of very good friends there who we would miss, but as James said many times: 'As one door closes, another one opens.'

We moved back in with James's parents in Kent yet again while we looked for a house to buy.

'Last time!' we said, but they were very happy to have us and all our stuff. It was very good of them when I look back: we'd been charged £1,000 in excess luggage when we left Hong Kong, mostly because I'm a terrible hoarder and refused to throw out any of my clothes. Allan and Sharon must have wondered what on earth they'd agreed to.

James and I soon spotted a beautiful home that was being built on an upmarket development called Kings Hill, near the old English village of West Malling, not too far from where his parents lived. We snapped it up and loved it. Even though we'd had the little house in Iwade this felt like our first proper, grown-up house together. We'd made it, that's what I thought, but neither of us said those words. I remembered how James's dad had told his mum: 'We've made it!' when they moved into their dream home when James was a teenager, and then it all went wrong.

Of course, James remembered this very well indeed; the bankruptcy is something he talks about every so often, and every time I can see how deeply it affected him.

Because of our upbringings neither James nor I take anything for granted, ever. We shared the attitude that even though we had this great opportunity on Strictly, and this lovely new house, we had to keep working hard and doing our very best every day, as everything could slip away very quickly if we weren't careful.

'I've got Gabby Logan and I think you've got her husband!' James said when we started work on series five.

He was right. I'd been partnered with Gabby's rugby star husband Kenny Logan, and we were going to train together in a studio in Chiswick, next door to where James was teaching Gabby.

'Pardon?' I said the first time I met Kenny. It took me right back to the time when I couldn't understand the Scottish man who tried to make a booking at the hotel where I did the breakfasts. Kenny's accent was strong and I really struggled to get to grips with it.

Then, when he started doing a few dance steps I realised immediately that we had another problem. For a sportsman, Kenny's co-ordination was really bad, and he was probably the worst dancer in terms of natural ability I ever worked with on Strictly. He was the sweetest person, though. Every day Kenny paid for lunch for the whole crew as he said that was good luck, and he worked his socks off in the studio, really trying his best.

I left Kent at 6 a.m. every day and we started work at 9 a.m., when Kenny would always be waiting for me with a Starbucks in one hand and a skinny Red Bull in the other. He got the drinks for me as he knew I'd had a long journey and needed a boost. I really appreciated the thought. Then the work began, and I soon discovered that Kenny was a pleasure to teach. Even though dancing didn't come naturally to him at all he never gave up, even after we popped in to the studio next door one day and saw how well Gabby and James were doing.

'Oh my God, you two are going to win it,' Kenny cried, holding his head in his hands. 'We're miles behind you.' This actually really mattered to Kenny: he and Gabby were genuinely competitive with one another.

Kenny needed to train for long hours if he was to stand any chance at all in the competition, and he did so without complaint, day after day. I regularly got home at 8 p.m. after putting in an eight- or nine-hour day. Kenny's grit and determination, and the struggle he went through to perfect his technique, was all captured on the VT that was broadcast when the show first went on air. The film was honest and real, so the viewers got a true flavour of what we went through together in the studio. For this reason I think the public really warmed to Kenny, and when the competition started people at home fell in love with him.

Strangely, this wasn't the case with Gabby. The public warmed to her much less, maybe because she was just so impressive and high-achieving. She had twins, she was a former gymnast who could do the splits and she worked in the male-dominated world of sports presenting. Perhaps it was all a bit much for the public to take in? Who knows, but her performances didn't seem to go down as well as Kenny's even though she was a far better dancer. She and James were eliminated in week four, while Kenny and I lasted until week nine.

'Who's the better dancer?' Kenny would say, taunting Gabby cheekily when she came in to support us.

I was nervous every week, and my legs turned to jelly each time I heard the words: 'Will Kenny Logan and his dance partner Ola Jordan please take to the floor…'

When we did he Viennese Waltz in week six I was so nervous my mind went completely blank, but fortunately Kenny was on the ball and I just followed him. He was brilliant; I think the fact we were dancing to Flower of Scotland helped spur him on.

James came to help us train after he was eliminated, and when we did the Rumba I really needed some help. It was meant to be sexy and passionate, but Kenny was suddenly all coy and seemed to be afraid to get too close to me. One of the choreographed moves required him to run his hands up and down my thigh, as if he was caressing me and was madly in love with me.

'I can't do it!' he said, admitting that part of the problem was that he knew James was down the corridor, and it didn't seem right to be handling another man's wife in this way.

Then James appeared.

'Look mate, you have to act like you mean it,' he told Kenny. 'You have to look as if you want to make love to Ola. You have to really go for it. This is the Rumba!'

James then got a lot more than he bargained for, and so did I. Kenny suddenly switched into passionate lover mode, standing behind me and caressing me very sensually, with great enthusiasm. I felt his big hands run down my arms, brush past my boobs and land firmly on my hips.

'Is that good enough?' he said triumphantly, giving a roguish smirk.

James spluttered and said 'there was no need to go that far mate!' and I giggled.

'Too good,' I said.

Thankfully James saw the funny side and we all had a good laugh about it.

I can totally understand how male celebs can feel shy and worried about getting up close and personal with a scantily clad girl partner. Professional dancers don't give this a second thought, but of course celebs are not used to having such intimate contact and aren't sure how to deal with it. In Ballroom dancing the man has to press his right side into the woman, and all professional male dancers know that they have to 'dress to the left' when they are preparing to dance, as you connect right side to right side with your partner. The woman can feel absolutely everything – and I mean EVERYTHING! If the man hasn't 'dressed to the left' there is a danger he might get a bit excited, especially if he has to rub up against the woman during a routine. A lot of the male dancers on Strictly, James included, would do the decent thing and pass this information on to the male celebs when they started on the show.

'Listen mate, you need to point the old boy to the left,' was often how James put it.

'Why?' the celebs would say, often bemused by the advice.

They usually needed the whole thing explaining, which was always quite funny for the pro dancers and a bit of an eye-opener for the celebs.

Sometimes the male celebs forgot the advice and would be embarrassed when a female dancer had to say: 'Ooh, I think you need to move that to the other side.'

Occasionally, it was too late and some of the men inevitably got aroused. This happened to me with one or two of the celebs I danced with after Kenny. I'll never forget the first time.

'Oh dear,' I thought, 'that shouldn't be there!' I'd seen this particular celeb empty his pockets before we started rehearsing together so I knew that the bulge was what I feared it was. I didn't feel able to say anything and just tried to carry on as if nothing had happened, and the celeb did too. On another occasion, with a partner I felt more comfortable with, I decided to make a bit of a joke of it.

'Did you leave your mobile phone in your pocket?' I teased. We both laughed; I think that's the best way if you feel able to. 'Put your willy in the right place!' was something else I said, but only with the partners I got on really well with.

It wasn't uncommon to hear one of the other girl dancers backstage giggling and saying 'I think my partner got a little bit excited!' or 'I had to tell him to tuck it the other way! Oh my God I could feel absolutely everything!'

Farting was another problem for the male celebs. Without mentioning any names, over the years I've heard quite a few of my partners go 'pop' when they've lifted me up, because of the effort of the lift. Again I always tried to make a joke of it and say it was a common thing and not to worry, but there were one or two celebs along the way who were mortified and tried to pretend it hadn't happened. I'd keep a straight face so as not to embarrass them, but we both knew what had happened.

I was sad when Kenny and I were eliminated, but we'd had a great run and a really memorable experience.

Alesha Dixon went on to win with Matthew Cutler that series, beating contestants like Stephanie Beacham, Penny Lancaster, John Barnes and Letitia Dean to the glitterball trophy.

Alesha was lovely, lively and funny. James called her 'Muttley' because her laugh reminded him of Dick Dastardly's cartoon dog. We both really liked her and thought she deserved to win, although James wasn't pleased when it was later announced that she was returning as a judge, to replace Arlene Phillips. As lovely as she was, his view was that it didn't seem right that someone who had danced on the show for four months was going to be judging pro dancers with ten, twenty or thirty years' experience. I had to agree that James had a point, and his view was shared by a lot of the other dancers backstage.

The BBC was accused of ageism for letting Arlene go, but it claimed her departure had nothing to do with her age and was simply part of a refresh of the show. Who knows? If there was something else going on behind the scenes, we never got to hear of it.

The judges generally kept themselves to themselves and we only really saw them when they were actually judging us on air. I always liked Len Goodman because he was from the dancing world we'd grown up in. He generally gave James and me good marks, and he was fun and pleasant with it. Bruno made me laugh, of course, but neither James nor I could warm to Craig. Of course it was his job to be the Simon Cowell character on the panel, but more often than not we found him too rude and too irritating, not to mention predictable.

'It was a disaaarstar darling!' became a phrase that really got on our nerves, whoever it was aimed at.

James had a bit of a run-in with Stephanie Beacham during the series. She was partnered with Vincent, who is always very sweet and charming, whatever is going on around him. In James's opinion, Stephanie seemed a bit bossy and he teased Vincent about it.

'I wouldn't put up with that mate,' James would laugh, 'Does she think you are a lap dog?'

In typical style, Vincent would shrug his shoulders, throw his arms up and say: 'But what can I do, bella?' He'd then run after Stephanie while joking to James, 'I'm scared, bella!'

During a group dance Stephanie and Vincent were dancing beside Gabby and James, and Stephanie went up to James and said: 'I want you to move away from us. You make us look bad!'

James just brushed it off as a joke, but later I overheard Stephanie in the ladies, talking to Flavia.

'Honestly, that James Jordan is so RUDE!' Stephanie exclaimed.

Unbeknown to Stephanie I was behind her, washing my hands, and Flavia caught my eye as the pair of us tried not to crack up laughing.

Series five was also the year the 'dance off' was introduced, and James and Gabby's departure had come after a dance-off with Penny Lancaster and her partner Ian Waite.

There was a rumour going round that Penny won the dance-off because her husband Rod Stewart was performing on the show the following week, but I didn't get involved in the gossip and didn't believe it. I was very naive when it came to TV politics in those days, but even so it seemed unlikely and very ungenerous that anything untoward had gone on.

James was devastated to go out so early on as he'd had high hopes with Gabby, but nevertheless we agreed this series was far better than the last, for both of us. Best of all we made friends with Gabby and Kenny, and we're still good friends today.

At the wrap party all of the pro girl dancers and I decided to dress up in sexy Santa costumes from Ann Summers. Bruce was there and we all posed for a great photograph with him. He looked like he was in his element and he put a smile on all our faces. Everybody loved Brucie.

Every Saturday night before the live show Bruce would do the most fantastic warm-up. He'd get people up from the audience, do a bit of tap-dancing and come out with great banter, like pretending the costume girls had stolen the curtains from his dressing room to make the dresses for the dancers that night. It all seemed effortless because he was such a professional. He was awesome to watch and he'd have the audience in the palm of his hand every time.

Part of our rehearsals on the Saturday involved doing fake scores and chats. The dancers and celebs would run up the stairs to Tess's room as we did on the real show, and because it was a rehearsal we'd sometimes be a bit loud and rowdy on purpose, just for the fun of it. Brucie knew we were doing this to get a reaction, and he'd come charging up the stairs and slap us on the wrists like we were naughty children. It was all very funny.

If things went wrong Brucie always knew exactly what to do. For instance, when Mark Ramprakash was dancing the Salsa with Karen Hardy he got his microphone caught up in her dress on the live show. It could have been really awkward but Bruce made it very entertaining, very naturally. A woman ran on stage and Bruce asked her, 'Who are you?', which got a laugh, as it turned out she was one of the associate producers. Bruce then grabbed hold of the producer and started dancing with her to fill in a bit of time while the problem was sorted out in the background. It was brilliant.

Whenever you bumped into Bruce in the corridor at TV Centre he'd always make time to stop for a little chat and ask how things were going. He enjoyed asking James and me about Hong Kong as he knew it well, and this was often a topic of conversation. I loved the fact Brucie was so friendly and generous with his time, as he would stop and talk even when he was very busy. However, there was one time when I really wished he'd just hurried past without stopping.

James and I shared a dressing room at Wood Lane, and one time things got very passionate between us before a show. We'd been apart doing different rehearsals all week and had really missed each other.

'Ola you look amazing,' James said, pulling me towards him and looking at me longingly in my little sparkly dress.

I could tell immediately what was on his mind.

'What do you think? We'll be too tired when we get home later...'

'James! What do you mean? We can't have sex at the BBC!'

'Why not? Who'll know? We're a married couple. Come on Ola, I've missed you so much...'

James looked gorgeous and I couldn't say no. The sparks were flying between us.

'Well just don't mess up my hair and make-up!' I teased.

We were running late for rehearsals by the time we emerged from the studio, breathless and looking a little bit flustered, having hastily thrown our costumes back on.

'Ola! James!' a familiar voice boomed out.

To my dismay I knew immediately who this was: it was Brucie! His dressing room was close to ours and he had happened to be walking past our door at the exact moment we emerged.

'How lovely to see you. How are you both?'

'Fine!' we chirped.

'Ola, you're looking as lovely as ever. Radiant, in fact!'

I wanted the ground to swallow me up.

Bruce then proceeded to chat about the weather and goodness knows what else. When he finally walked away James and I collapsed into giggles.

'Aren't you meant to have a cigarette afterwards, not a chat with Bruce Forsyth?' James joked. We laughed about it for years afterwards, referring to it as the time we 'performed the Rumba' in our dressing room before rehearsals.

After this series ended, James and I were invited to take part in the Strictly Come Dancing Live! tour, which then meant travelling around the UK for about two months, putting on a choreographed show with other pro dancers and celebs who had appeared on Strictly, and performing in big arenas like the O2 and Wembley.

We jumped at the chance and it was great fun being on the road, especially as some of the people I got on best with, like Matthew and Nicole Cutler, Vincent and Flavia, were also on the tour.

The only downside was that I developed a stress fracture in my hip part way through, and I tried to cover it up as I really didn't want to drop out. Arlene Phillips was still involved in the tour at that time and, always the eagle-eyed pro, she spotted me limping on the floor one afternoon in rehearsals.

'I can't watch you do this,' she said, 'you have to have that looked at.'

Arlene convinced me to see a specialist and I went to one close by in Sheffield. I was in agony when I went for the appointment and it turned out the neck of my hip was thinning out. I knew this was serious; if you permanently damage that bone you won't ever dance again. To my dismay, after doing an MMR scan, the specialist put me on crutches and told me not to dance for a full six months.

'No,' I said, horrified, 'I can't do this!'

I saw my career flash before me and I started crying on the phone to James. I panicked about not being able to work, even in the short term. Oh my God this is going to be like Hong Kong all over again! James will be working and I'll be stuck on my own!

When I told Arlene the news she was extremely calm and helpful and sent me to a Harley Street physio called Ed, who is an expert in treating dancers and works with a lot of dancers on West End shows.

'Get off those crutches,' Ed said.

He then gave me some exercises to do and assured me I'd be fine in a few weeks' time. He was right, thank God. Within two weeks I was back on tour, and two weeks after the tour ended I was absolutely fine.

I was incredibly grateful to Arlene. This was such a relief, not least because after the tour James and I were flooded with more requests than ever to do shows, give private dance lessons and even deliver lectures on dance. We had taken on a lot of bookings for the summer and, thanks to Arlene, we were able fulfil them all. I surprised myself with what I could deliver in terms of the lectures and private talks and demonstrations. My English had improved a great deal, and even though I still had my recognisable 'Cockney Polish' accent I was fluent and understood everything. The people who hired us seemed to really appreciate our skills and it was a great confidence boost to be respected and treated like an expert, and to be in such demand.

'You bring me such fun!' one member of the audience said to me. I felt proud, and it reminded me why I'd got into dancing in the first place. I adored losing myself on the dance floor, and it was a privilege to share my passion for dance.

I even started getting fan mail. Little girls wrote to me and included sketches of dresses they had drawn that they thought I should wear on Strictly.

'My daughter wants to be a princess like you when she grows up,' mothers wrote.

Inevitably, there were negative comments online from the 'keyboard warriors', as James always called them, and some snide remarks made in the press too. I found those difficult to deal with in the beginning. I couldn't understand how members of the public and journalists who didn't know me could make horrible remarks about my dancing, my looks, my husband or anything else for that matter. It especially bothered me if people commented on my weight and skin. The first time I was called a 'fat, spotty bitch' by someone online really hurt. I wasn't a bad person and I wished I could tell the critics to their faces about the sacrifices I'd made to pursue my career, and how lucky I felt to have come this far, but of course I couldn't.

However, things were put in perspective for me one day when another mother wrote to me and said her daughter had cancer, and loved watching me on Strictly. Apparently, the little girl perked up whenever she saw me on TV. I felt humbled and very moved, and if I had to take a thousand criticisms to make a small difference like that to somebody's life, then I would take every one. Very sadly the little girl passed away some time afterwards. I won't ever forget her.

James and I really hoped to be asked back to Strictly, and once again we were delighted to get the call in the summer that the producers wanted us to return for series six, in 2008.

'I wonder who we'll get?' was the first thing we said to each other.

When we first joined Strictly, the public vote alone decided who stayed and who was eliminated. This meant that good dancers like

Spoony, for instance, could be voted off without the judges having a chance of saving them. Things had changed since then, and now the judges could save a good dancer if they felt it was worthwhile to do so, by giving them high scores and keeping them out of the danger zone at the bottom of the leaderboard. Of course the judges ultimately wanted a good dancer to go on and win. It was a dance competition after all, and they wanted the glitterball trophy to go to somebody who could actually dance, however charismatic and loved by the public they may or may not be.

All of this meant James and I hoped we'd get a naturally skilled dance partner this year, to boost our chances of progressing further in the competition or even winning, as we both hoped to do.

This time I was partnered with the former tennis player and GMTV presenter Andrew Castle, and James was paired with the actress Cherie Lunghi, who he knew best for her role in the long-running Kenco coffee adverts.

Neither James nor I had a clue how the dancing was going to go but we were both cautiously optimistic. Andrew had been the most amazing athlete in his day and Cherie had a reputation for being a charismatic actress with a string of impressive stage and screen roles under her belt. These were all good signs, but we'd just have to wait and see. In those days nobody knew how skilful the celebs might be until the day we hit the studio together and started training.

'I've got everything crossed,' James said.

'Exactly. Let's hope one of us has a winner!'

There was some healthy rivalry between me and James when we were competing against one another, but ultimately we knew we would both be equally pleased if the other won. It would mean the world to us, but would this be our year?

22

'She's a MILF!' one of the boys backstage giggled.

He was referring to Cherie Lunghi, who was in her fifties, a mother and extremely glamorous and attractive.

She didn't seem to mind the cheeky banter at all and one day, when they'd started to get to know one another in training, James asked: 'Cherie, do you actually know what a 'MILF' is?'

'Of course darling,' she replied with her usual panache. 'It stands for a 'mother I'd like to fondle.'

Everybody in the room fell about laughing.

Cherie proved to be a great partner for James. They scored the highest points of the first two weeks when they did the Foxtrot and then they went top of the leaderboard in week four with the Rumba, surviving until week nine when they lost in the dance-off against Lisa Snowdon.

James absolutely loved their Rumba routine and it's one of his all-time favourites from his whole Strictly career. It was very classy, very simple and was clean and beautiful.

'Pure Rumba!' James enthused, 'I loved it!'

James found he could really connect with Cherie, which of course helped their performances no end. He also loved her sense of humour, although one day she announced that she shouldn't be called a MILF any more. This worried James.

'Why not?' he asked, suddenly panicking that Cherie may have been offended by the word after all.

'Because I'm a grandmother now! You'll have to call me a GILF!'

James cracked up laughing as he congratulated Cherie on the good news.

Unfortunately, my relationship with Andrew Castle wasn't so great. Having been at the very top of his game as a tennis pro in the 1980s,

Andrew had a fine reputation to uphold. From the moment we started training together I could tell he was going to find his Strictly experience tough, as he was clearly worried about how he looked and found it difficult to throw himself into the steps, as you need to do. We had a height disadvantage too. Normally the producers tried to pair you with a celebrity of a suitable height, but Andrew was six foot three – a full foot taller than me. In hindsight I'd have been better matched with the rugby player Austin Healey, who was five foot ten.

'You have to not care if you look silly,' I told Andrew as we tried to train. 'On a show like this, at some point everyone will look silly.'

Andrew tried but he just couldn't seem to let himself go. I understood that a sportsman of his standing wouldn't want to look daft on national TV, but in my opinion he really needed to loosen up if we were going to make this work. I encouraged him and pushed him hard, but overall it was a difficult experience and the atmosphere was often tense in the studio.

'That's wrong,' I'd say. 'Do it again, like this.'

I wasn't rude, just forceful. We didn't have time for me to beat around the bush and I wanted our routines to be right so I told him what was what in a very straightforward way, which is how a lot of professional dancers are in the studio.

'No! I'm not doing it again,' he'd sometimes reply. 'Why do I need to do it again?'

I think one of the other problems was that Andrew was nearly twenty years older than me with two teenage daughters, so it wasn't easy for him to take orders from a twenty-six year old.

Our first dance was the Cha Cha Cha, and one day Andrew failed to catch me when I was demonstrating a move in training. My toes went crack and a shot of pain went through my foot: it turned out I'd fractured a small bone. My toes swelled up and looked misshapen, but we had to carry on. Then Andrew had his foot in the wrong position for another move, and I accidentally slammed the heel of my dance shoe onto his foot, fracturing two of his toes. Again, we had no choice but to keep practising. We needed every minute just to be able to hold our own, but it wasn't looking great.

Luckily, I did have a secret weapon this year. James and I had designed a catsuit for me to wear in round one, and I was delighted with it. It was James's idea, as he knew my body so well, and he knew how much it would suit me. We sketched out the design together and discussed it with the costume department, and they made a fabulous job of making it. The catsuit was made of a very stretchy, dark brown and black animal print material. The back was cut away to a point in the small of my back, and there was an elongated figure of eight section cut out of the front, from my neck to my navel. I absolutely loved it, and I felt fantastic it in.

Andrew and I danced our Cha Cha Cha to Mercy by Duffy, and the audience went wild. Not only that, people were tweeting about how 'hot' I looked in the catsuit and there was a lot of hype all over the internet about me. I found it all very flattering and also quite funny, and when I saw the papers the next day I was gobsmacked, because my picture was everywhere.

Andrew and I were eventually eliminated in week seven. I was disappointed, of course, but I can't say I was surprised. I hadn't had a very enjoyable couple of months and I'm sure the public must have picked up on the vibe. Andrew apologised to me some time afterwards, when he'd had chance to reflect.

'I wish I'd had a different experience,' he said. 'You were right, I was worried about looking stupid and I should have relaxed more and trusted what you were saying. It was my fault we didn't go further in the competition.'

I admired him for saying that, but I took some responsibility too. We were in it together and I was the teacher, so perhaps I should have found other ways to help him, who knows? The experience certainly didn't put me off Strictly: in fact, I think the opposite was true.

'I REALLY want to win next time,' I told James afterwards.

'So do I,' he replied. 'It would be incredible, wouldn't it, if either one of us got the trophy?'

We'd tease each other about who was going to win. Over the years, friends would joke that we should be happy if we got eliminated early on in the competition, because as a pro dancer you are paid the same money per series regardless of how long you survive. The suggestion always shocked us, even when it was said in jest.

'Once you're in it and competing, believe me you really do not want to go out,' I always said. 'You want to win and you want to win badly.'

Doing Strictly was absolutely exhausting, but even after three years James and I were both still loving it. We wanted more, and once again we wanted to be invited back again so we could have another chance of winning the glitterball trophy.

We would always stay in a hotel in London after the live Saturday show, because everyone would go for drinks in the bar and it was always a great night. Everyone would be high on adrenaline even before they'd had a drink, and the atmosphere was always buzzing, every week. Even if you'd been eliminated this was very often the routine, as you'd be taking part in the pro dances, or in specials like the annual Children in Need edition, and the friends and family you'd given your audience tickets to could join you at the bar as well.

I'd made good friends with Flavia by now, and I really liked her. She has a heart of gold and wouldn't hurt a fly, and of all the dancers she was the one I liked to socialise with. She'd had quite a tough time in the press after she had a relationship with one of her dance partners, the EastEnders actor Matt Di Angelo. The newspapers tried to make out the relationship with Matt was some kind of scandal as he was younger than her and she'd previously dated Vincent, but it wasn't scandalous at all. She stayed with Matt for a couple of years before they went their separate ways, and I'm happy to say she then went on to marry her lovely husband Jimi Mistry, who she partnered on Strictly in 2010. What nobody reported was that Flavia is the sweetest, most loyal person ever, and she had only ever had three serious relationships in her whole life.

Flavia and I giggled together sometimes about the perils of being in the spotlight, and the fact that the media was always searching for Strictly tales of backstage romance. It had all started in series one when there was obvious chemistry between the winners Brendan Cole and Natasha Kaplinsky and they both subsequently split from their partners, even though they didn't become a couple.

James and I kept well out of any gossip about who was doing what with whom. There were some tales the press never did get hold of, but I didn't really want to know. It's not unusual or illegal to have a relationship with someone you meet at work, is it? I couldn't see what all the fuss was about, and I certainly didn't like it when someone as sweet as Flavia got scrutinised unfairly.

'Ola, you won't run off with a dance partner, will you?' James would tease sometimes, coming up to me like a love-sick puppy.

'No,' I would say. 'I love you James, you know how much I love you. I would never do that. But if you want to run off for a little while, I really don't mind. I would like the break...'

We had a running joke like this, because James hates being alone and I am quite happy to be on my own every now and then. 'I'd enjoy the peace and quiet to be honest, James. It would give me a nice rest, but just make sure you come back eventually.'

Once you were eliminated from the competition, as well as doing specials like Children in Need, you also went to chat with Claudia Winkleman on Strictly's sister show, It Takes Two, and you returned for the Strictly Christmas Special.

It was busy, busy, busy every day, and you'd get to the end of December and be totally shattered and overdue a break.

Having said that, we always wanted to be invited to go on tour in the new year. Not every dancer was asked. Craig Revel Horwood was the creative director and he seemed to think he had the last say on which pro dancers and celebrities would take part and on all the choreography. In reality this was not the case, as the producers had the final say and were ultimately in control of the tour.

James and I did get invited on tour again after series six, and the 2009 tour was even better than the first one we did. Dancers from previous series often went on tour, and Kenny Logan came on this one. He was great fun and proved to be a huge party animal who was always at the hub of everything, wanting everybody to have a great time. We all loved him, and some of the girls in the crew would be swooning over him because he was so good-looking and charismatic.

'Drink this or I'll punch you in the gut,' became Kenny's catchphrase of the tour. We partied almost every night for two months. We had nothing to do during the day so typically the boys would go and play golf and the girls would go shopping, or we'd treat ourselves to a spa before we got ready for the show in the evening.

When we partied, Kenny would have a bottle of vodka in one hand and sambuca in the other. The bottles had pouring caps on top so he could easily dish out shots, and he would go around the room pouring shots straight into everyone's mouth. If you said no he literally grabbed your head, tilted it back and poured a drink down your throat. One night one of the production crew passed out and Vincent – whose natural reaction is to say 'OK bella!' to most things – was completely smashed. James had to carry him back to the hotel, where he was promptly sick in our bedroom. Through all of this, Kenny carried on drinking and being the life and soul of the party.

James and Kenny often fought like schoolboys in the changing rooms before we went on stage, but Kenny was massive compared with James and always came out on top. One time Kenny simply picked James up like a rag doll and threw him into a clothes rail, just for fun. His strength didn't surprise me at all. When we were training together Kenny used to pick me up with one arm and raise my whole body up and down in the air, like I was a tiny little dumbbell.

It was a brilliant tour, and James and I were both delighted when, a few months later, we were invited back for series seven.

This time I was to be partnered with BBC Breakfast's sport correspondent Chris Hollins, and James got the Footballers' Wives actress Zoe Lucker. Of course we didn't find out who our celeb partners were until a few months later, in the August, just before we started training with them.

'I'm gonna win this year!' James said, getting all competitive and trying to wind me up, like he does.

'No, I am going to win James. Watch this space. Now, where am I going to put that trophy?'

In truth, once again we had no idea how skilled our celebrity partners were going to be in the studio and so we didn't have a clue how this next series was going to pan out. It was exciting and daunting once more, but we wouldn't have wanted it any other way; Strictly had become a massive part of our lives.

23

'Oh my God,' I thought when I walked into the studio and saw Chris Hollins for the first time. He was short and didn't look particularly athletic. 'We'll never even make it halfway through the competition.'

Despite this initial reaction to my new dance partner I was determined I wanted to win this year, and I wasn't going to let anything put me off. I felt driven to succeed and I was really up for the challenge. I felt good in my skin, and this was because I was thin again, after doing a bit of yo-yoing over the previous few years. I was still on a constant diet, but I had good months and bad months and if I let myself slip even the tiniest but I'd put on weight very easily. I was bigger when I danced with Andrew Castle, and I'd then put on quite a bit more weight during the tour with Kenny because we were partying and drinking all the time. Immediately afterwards I had to slash my calories and work really hard in the gym to lose the extra pounds. It was hard, but I'd done well and was back to about seven and a half stone, which made me feel confident in myself.

Unfortunately, as soon as Chris and I took our first steps together I could tell he was no dancer, and I knew I had a lot of hard work of a different kind ahead of me. Chris did too.

'I'm going to have to be tough with you,' I told him.

'Bring it on,' he said. 'I'm in your hands, Ola. I'll do whatever you tell me to do, you're the expert here.'

As soon as Chris said that my spirits lifted, and very soon I started to feel really happy about dancing with him. Chris was a lovely, fun, genuine guy, and he didn't take himself too seriously. When I asked him to try a step he always put his heart and soul into it and he didn't care if he looked silly, despite being naturally self-conscious.

We called ourselves 'Team Cola' and Chris and I trained for twenty-five hours a week. I loved every minute. When I was in Hong Kong I was given the affectionate nickname Ola Chops by the boy dancers and it had stuck. James called me it all the time, and Chris soon picked up on the nickname and started calling me Ola Chops too. I bossed him around like we were an old married couple, and we snacked on cola bottle sweets because of our team name. It was a real blast from start to finish.

'Beat me,' he would joke, 'make me work harder Ola Chops!'

I did, always telling him it was 'tough love' when I got especially bossy.

'Do it again, that was terrible!' I'd shout.

He never argued and just got on with it. I said he was like an obedient workhorse, although his efforts didn't mean he always got it right.

'Chris, what are you doing with your hand?' I had to say all the time, as he had a limp wrist.

'I don't know. I have a naturally camp hand, I can't help it!'

We had such a laugh and got on really well together, and when we did the live shows I'm sure this came across and helped our performances. It was a rollercoaster nonetheless. We scored a good 30 in week one with our Rumba, despite the fact Len Goodman described us as 'dancing Hobbits', but then our scores dipped and never recovered until week nine, when we did the Paso Doble and scored 30 again.

'Yeah babe!' I cried.

Chris thought my accent was hilarious, and he always mimicked me. It became one of our catchphrases, and every week Chris would tell me he wanted to make me smile and come out with a 'yeah babe!' in my 'Polish Cockney' after the live show. We even got tee-shirts made up with the slogan on the front, to give us an extra boost.

Unbelievably, Chris got a 'yeah babe!' from me week after week as we stayed in the competition without once having to do a dance-off. Our next challenge was to do the Samba and Waltz in week twelve, in order to get through to the semi-final. I had drummed it into Chris from day one that if he made a mistake during a routine he just had to carry on, and that's exactly what he did when he made two small errors as we were rehearsing the Samba to the live band on the Saturday morning. I should have carried on too, but for some reason I stopped and looked, and then I shouted at Chris, pointing out where he'd gone wrong. To my dismay Chris then stormed off the floor. I burst into tears and James came over and gave me a hug before reassuring me everything would be fine, and going to Chris's dressing room.

'Mate, you've done nothing wrong,' James told Chris.

'Thanks James. I'm not upset. The reason I walked off was because I don't want to shout at Ola. I don't want to upset her.'

They both knew how stressed I was and how much it meant to me to get to the semi-final, and they were both doing all they could to get us there.

I'd got my head together in time for the live show, thank God, and Chris and I gained 39 points on the Samba and 41 on our Waltz. I couldn't believe it, because we really were in the semi-final, I was starting to see the finish line and to think it really was possible to lift the glitterball trophy. I could hardly believe it.

That same weekend James and I danced together on the results show, when Bette Midler sang The Rose. It was an unforgettable experience. Just before the performance, Bette turned to James and said: 'Make sure you don't go wrong.'

'Make sure you sing it right,' James quipped back, without pausing to think what he was saying. Bruce was within earshot and he snorted with laughter.

It was an honour to be chosen to be on stage with someone like Bette and the performance couldn't have gone better. The audience really loved it and so did we. I always felt at my best when dancing with James. I felt absolutely fantastic, in fact, and when I was back in the studio with Chris I was still on a massive high.

'Come on Chris, we can win this!'

He raised his eyes.

'Are you sure little Ola Chops?'

'Yeah babe!'

Winning definitely felt within reach, but we still had our work cut out. Chris had never danced before, but in those days it was possible for a non-dancer to get that far. While the judges could save good dancers by keeping them off the bottom of the leaderboard they didn't actively try to eliminate naturally poor dancers. Personality and the chemistry between the couple held a lot of sway back then, and that definitely went in our favour because Chris and I were genuinely fond of one another and sparked off each other. As time went on we could say anything to one another too, and sometimes this meant I really did hen-peck him, as if we were an old married couple.

'What are you doing?' I said one day.

'What do you mean, Ola?'

'You've had a drink! I can't believe you'd have a drink.'

Chris looked mortified. It was before a live show, and I'd smelt beer on his breath.

'I'm sorry, Ola. Joe Calzaghe insisted on getting me a beer. He dragged me to the bar. I'm really sorry. I won't do it again. I only had a couple of sips, I promise.'

It was hard to be cross with Chris for long, because he was just such a lovely guy, and he was looking at me like a guilty puppy.

Every time Chris was interviewed in the last few weeks of the competition journalists were trying to get him to say he wanted to win. He never exactly said that. Instead he always told them: 'I want to win for Ola.' He really meant this. He was stunned and delighted at how far he had come and anything else was a bonus as far as Chris was concerned, because we'd had such a great run. He wanted the win for me because dancing was my career and my life and he knew it would mean so much. For my part, I loved Chris to bits and wanted to win for him as much as for myself. I felt he really deserved it after all the enthusiasm and hard work he'd put in, and I thought it would be such a great victory for a non-dancer like Chris to lift the trophy.

In the semi-final we did the Rumba to Total Eclipse of the Heart and the Argentine Tango to Bust Your Windows. Both felt great and the audience loved them, but even so I was trembling with nerves as we waited for the judges' comments. When I found out we were safe I just went wild and screamed and jumped all over Chris. It was like a crazy dream – we were in the Strictly final, and we'd be competing against the Hollyoaks actor Ricky Whittle, who was a fantastic dancer and widely tipped to be the winner, and his partner Natalie Lowe, who is fabulous. Each couple had to prepare four dances, one of which was the Lindy Hop, which is like a swing jive. This dance was new to Strictly and even I didn't find it easy to learn, but when I tried to teach Chris he couldn't even get one step down. My emotions were running very high at this point and I burst into tears in training that week and called the producers.

'You can't make us do the Lindy Hop,' I said. 'Chris just can't do it.'

'You have to do it,' they said. 'The decision has been made.'

I was starting to think it was already over; the Lindy Hop would ruin us.

We also had to do a Foxtrot, the Charleston and our Showdance, which was to Do You Love Me? from Dirty Dancing. I was concerned about the Foxtrot as Chris had been criticised by the judges the last time we did it, for doing strange things with his hands and his mouth. Bruno had told him he looked like he was sucking a lemon, and he was also accused of having a 'trout pout'.

'We can't have that again,' I said to Chris.

'I know, but how do I stop? I don't even know I'm doing it!'

James and his partner Zoe Lucker had been eliminated in week seven, and so he came to the studio to give me and Chris some moral support. I really appreciated having James around. He'd bring cookies and coffees and cola bottle sweets and offer no end of encouragement. Of course he was disappointed that he hadn't gone further in the competition himself this time, but this didn't stop him rooting for me and Chris and giving us all the support he could. James wanted us to win just as much as we did, and he was also going through all the emotions I was feeling.

He had had a good run with Zoe. She and James got on really well and became quite close, so much so they really missed each other when it was all over. She was a really lovely girl, but James felt she was very fragile and incredibly nervous. He felt protective over her because she was so insecure about her dancing ability and he certainly couldn't bring himself to boss her in the way I did with Chris.

'I think she'd have just gone to pieces if I put her under pressure,' he said. 'It would have broken her if I shouted.'

James had no regrets about their run together and he saw it as a valuable experience. 'When you teach dance you never stop learning how to deal with different personalities,' he said.

James knew I was worried about Chris's hands and mouth in the Foxtrot, and he and the crew decided to try to help, in a way that might also lighten the increasingly tense atmosphere in the studio. They got some black gaffer tape and put it across Chris's mouth, and they also bound his fingers together, which was very funny.

'Now do as I tell you!' I ordered Chris. 'And don't even try to talk or move your hands. Do you hear me?'

Chris nodded his head up and down comically, joining in the joke. It was very funny, and having a laugh together did make us both calm down.

I had no qualms about performing the Charleston, because when we'd done it in week eleven to Fat Sam's Grand Slam it had gone down a storm. The audience went wild, we got fabulous feedback from the judges and it became one of my favourite routines ever, and is the one that people tend to remember from my time on Strictly. Looking back that was a defining moment in the competition for Chris and me, and our performance has since been described as one of the iconic moments on Strictly, and one the best routines ever performed, which makes me very proud indeed.

'You're gonna bloody win this thing!' James said when we came off stage afterwards. I can remember that my heart leaped because I felt he might be right, though I could scarcely take it in.

I was buzzing and so was Chris. Our routine was wacky and great fun and Bruno described it as 'a concoction of slapstick and dancing' which really summed it up. I wore a fabulous 1920s-style white feathered dress and headband and we threw everything in there: quirky smiles and waves at the camera and crazy moves like my 'swimming across the floor' segment, which saw me pretending to swim breaststroke on top of Chris, who was lying flat on his back on the floor.

We might have been confident about the Charleston for the final, but our Showdance to Do You Love Me? was a worry. For some reason every time we rehearsed we messed it up, and then on the Wednesday before the final Chris dropped me on my head not once but twice, when he was trying to spin me around with his arms. I was used to being manhandled and pulled in different directions. I could put up with feeling sick and dizzy, as I often did after being lifted in the air and spun around, but this was too much.

'Forget it,' I snapped. 'I'm not doing this dance!' With that I stormed off.

Lifts had been a bugbear throughout the competition and this was the final straw.

'Try this,' I'd said before he dropped me.

'I can't.'

'Then try this.'

'I can't!'

'What can you do?' I'd snapped.

We needed to put loads of lifts in or we didn't stand a chance in the Showdance. It was the one performance where you had free rein to be as creative and ambitious as you liked. I wanted it to be a real showstopper, but Chris was not helping. This was not through want of trying; he simply couldn't do what I was asking him to do. He tried his best but then he dropped me. It was just too much for me to take. I was very stressed and the pressure was really getting to me. This series was the longest ever, with sixteen celebs, and running over fourteen weeks rather than the usual twelve, so I was physically drained as well as nervously exhausted. I'd been working flat out for months, giving it my all seven days a week to make Chris into the best dancer I possibly could. The only time I'd relaxed just a little bit was for an hour or so on a Sunday morning when James and I went back home to Kings Hill from the hotel in London. It was never much of a break, though, because all the time I'd be thinking about the choreography for the next week, and what I was going to teach Chris the next morning, when I'd be back in London, meeting him straight after he came off air from his day job. He was shattered too, as he was getting up at the crack of dawn and presenting on BBC Breakfast before getting to training.

My parents were flying over for the final, to be in the audience with James's mum and dad. I wanted everything to be perfect and I wanted to win, for everybody's sake. James started stressing out too in the final week and he did everything he possibly could to help. He'd come to training to offer support and advice and Chris joked that he had the 'Jordans in stereo' as he had me in one ear and James in the other.

On the Friday, the day before the final, Chris and I messed up the Showdance three times on camera in rehearsals.

'Oh my God the show is tomorrow,' I said. 'We can't do it, but we have to! We have to pull it off!'

We had no opportunity to try again as the whole show needed to be rehearsed and there simply wasn't time.

By the time we got to the live show on the Saturday I was a complete bag of nerves. I couldn't eat, I could barely stand still, my legs felt like jelly and my head felt like it was about to explode. Strangely, my nerves seemed to get worse instead of better as I got older and I don't really understand why. Vincent and Flavia also suffered badly from nerves, and I could hear Vincent's strong Italian accent in my head. 'Bella, I feel not good! Why do we do it to ourselves?'

Vincent said that all the time backstage. Tonight, especially, I really didn't have an answer to the question.

Chris and I did the Foxtrot to Frank Sinatra's I Could Have Danced All Night and got four 9s and a 10, from Alesha. It wasn't good enough: Ricky and Natalie had five straight 10s.

Then all four of us had to do the Lindy Hop on the floor together, to Sing, Sing, Sing by Louis Prima. It was a lot of pressure to share the floor. My heart was thumping and I desperately didn't want Chris to look bad, as I knew how hard he had found it to learn. When the results came I couldn't believe it – we'd got four 9s and an 8, while Ricky and Natalie had one point less – three 9s and two 8s.

'We can do it,' I told myself. 'Keep going. Keep pushing.'

I could feel the heat and energy coming off Chris. The adrenaline was pumping around both our bodies like crazy and we were grinning at each other and doing all we could to keep each other going.

Darcey Bussell had joined the judging panel this year, as a guest judge for weeks twelve to fourteen. Next up was our Charleston, and my next memory is of Darcey giving us a dazzling smile telling us it was brilliant. 'You transported me to the golden era of the movies,' she said. I was thrilled. Darcey was always very gracious and absolutely lovely, and I really respected her and listened to what she had to say.

We were awarded five 10s from the judges. Now I felt like I was in a movie, but it could not have been more real: I was on live TV in front of more than eleven million viewers. The enormity of the occasion was difficult to take in. I'd read in the papers recently that Strictly had earned a place in the Guinness Book of World Records as the world's most successful reality TV format. Here I was, at the centre of this incredible TV tornado, and I really felt it. Sweat was pricking my brow, I had goose pimples and my blood was zapping around my body like crazy.

James was just as nervous and agitated as me as he watched from the green room, so much so the producer had a camera pointed on him to capture his reactions as the show unfolded. It must have been absolute agony for James. He was powerless to do anything but bite his nails and try to keep calm. He said he watched every second of the show like a hawk, his nerves frayed to pieces, willing us not to put a single foot wrong and praying like crazy that we'd pull it off.

I can't describe how badly I wanted to win. Being able to walk away with the glitterball trophy had become everything; taking second place would not be good enough. Chris and I had worked so hard. It felt like we'd had to work ten times harder because Chris was such a novice dancer. We'd pushed and pushed and I really wanted all the effort and Chris's dedication to pay off.

These and what seemed like a hundred other thoughts were chasing through my mind as I stood on the stage beside Chris, waiting for the final result. Ricky and Natalie were on the stage too and I really had no idea if Chris and I had done enough to beat them to the title. I was sweating under the heat of the lights and I can remember thinking that Ricky was the bookies' favourite. 'Oh my God, we might not win! Oh my God, I want to win so much, but have we done enough? Ricky is the favourite! Can we do it?'

It felt like Chris and I stood there for an absolute age before Brucie announced: 'The winners of Strictly Come Dancing 2009 are…'

I held my breath and expected him to say the names of the winners straight away, but then there was an agonising pause as Tess took over to make the final announcement.

'It's Chris and Ola!' she yelled a few moments later.

I felt like I could breathe again for the first time in ages. Suddenly, Bruce was beside me and I was crying and trying to take the news in. We had won! Chris and I had actually won the glitterball trophy. Oh my God! Is this for real?

I was so happy and I couldn't stop the tears from streaming down my cheeks. I found out later that James had fallen to his knees in the wings and Joe Calzaghe had to pick him off the floor because he was completely bowled over with the emotion of it all. Afterwards, James told me that, without a shadow of a doubt, this was the highlight of his Strictly experience too. He'd seen how much effort Chris and I had put in and he totally shared my hopes and dreams.

Chris and I hugged and looked at each other in utter amazement as we stood on the stage. Suddenly, it was like being in the middle of a carnival. Flashbulbs were popping all around us, glitter was falling from the ceiling and pyrotechnics were exploding behind us and lighting up the stage.

'Little Ola chops,' Chris said when the noise died down and we were presented with our prize – the coveted glitterball trophy. 'Thank you so much for believing in me all the way along, I did test you a little bit, the Jive and the Quickstep come to mind! Thank you so much you lovely little girl.'

I felt overcome and I told Chris he'd been the best partner. 'You've been a dream to work with – thank you so much because that experience was fantastic for me.'

This was the greatest moment of my life. It wasn't just a reward for all the hard work I'd put in with Chris, it felt like a reward for all the work I'd put into my dancing throughout my life. If anyone had told me when I moved to the UK that I would be standing on this stage, holding this trophy and speaking fluent English I would not have believed it. The past decade had been unbelievable, and I really felt the decisions I'd made had been exactly the right ones. This was the best feeling in the world and I was deliriously happy.

Mum and Dad and Allan and Sharon were all in the audience to see me lift the trophy. I was so glad they shared the night with us, because James and I owed all four of them a huge debt: I would not have been holding that trophy without them, that is for sure.

The wrap party is a bit of a blur. I was emotionally spent and it was very surreal, listening to what felt like a million cries of 'congratulations!' The next day was even odder. It was snowing when we got back to Kent and the house seemed so quiet and empty. We'd lived on Kings Hill for three years by now but we'd been so busy with Strictly we hadn't had chance to do much to it. When we had time off we went on holiday to some lovely places like Mauritius and Jamaica and the rest of the time we were very busy with our corporate work, teaching lessons and attending events. We also went to Poland as often as we could to see my parents, so even when we weren't tied up with Strictly from August to December we were often away from home.

It felt odd to be in the house, in such peaceful and uncluttered surroundings, and I collapsed on the sofa and watched the snow falling outside the window.

The glitterball trophy was on the table in front of me, and when I looked at it I felt a surge of pride and satisfaction for a job well done. I also felt a crushing sense of anticlimax. I think one of the things that kept Chris and me going, week-in and week-out, was that we genuinely didn't want to stop dancing together. He had become like a brother and a best friend to me and we had developed a special bond that ran deep because of our shared experience. The past few months had been so intense and now it was all over. I felt uneasy as I took this in, and I wondered about the future. I'd won, so now what was my goal? Could I really do this all again and if not, then what would I do?

'Are you OK?' James asked.

James understood what I'd experienced for so many weeks and months and I told him exactly how I felt.

'I didn't want it to end,' I found myself saying. 'I feel a bit lost, I think. A bit uncertain about what happens next.'

'Ola,' James said, 'you have just ensured that the world is your oyster. You don't have to worry about a thing. Enjoy the moment, and let the future take care of itself. I'm so proud of you.'

24

'I'm going to New York!' James announced.

'Wow, lucky you,' I said. 'I'm going up north!'

It was 2010 and for this series of Strictly James had been partnered with Pamela Stephenson who lived in New York with her husband Billy Connolly. James was delighted that he was going to get to train in the Big Apple, not least because he'd also get to meet the Big Yin himself, who James had been a massive fan of for years.

This time I'd been partnered with the magician Paul Daniels. After my win the previous year I had a good idea that I wouldn't be given someone who had a chance of winning, as it was common knowledge backstage that the producers ideally wouldn't want the same pro dancer to walk off with the trophy two years running.

Paul was in his early seventies by then, and he wasn't a dancer by any stretch. I reckoned we'd be very lucky to survive even for a few weeks. Having said that, the experience of journalist John Sergeant was still fresh in my mind. John had competed in series six in 2008 and he repeatedly ended up in last place after the judges' votes. However, the public loved his performances and their phone votes kept him in week after week. John eventually chose to leave the competition in week ten after saying that he felt there was a danger he might actually win, which would have been 'a joke too far'. The rumour behind the scenes was that John was booked for a public appearance on a cruise ship and left because he wanted to fulfil that commitment, having wrongly anticipated he'd be well clear of Strictly by the time the ship sailed. Whether that was true or not, John's experience had shown me that you could never be sure how the British public would react.

I tried to be positive about how things might go with Paul; maybe we'd go further than I thought? I knew how popular his magic shows had been on TV over the years, and I knew he was loved by the public and had been for a very long time, so who knew how things could pan out? Paul was on tour in the north of England and I had to travel around up there with him so we could rehearse.

'I'll teach you a card trick,' Paul said, almost as soon as we'd met.

He was polite and we got on fine, but it's safe to say he was a lot more interested in magic than learning to dance, even when we were in the studio, ready to go.

'Right, one trick and then we'll get started…'

'You'll like it, not a lot, but you'll like it, Ola! Watch this, very carefully…'

I concentrated as Paul showed me a really clever trick. I had a go but couldn't get it right, so he patiently said he'd show me again the next day.

'Oh God,' I thought. 'I won't remember a single thing by tomorrow.'

I was right, and I think Paul was thinking the same about the dancing. He wasn't a natural and, given his age, we were limited with what we could do.

We started with the Cha Cha Cha, and when I began explaining what Cha Cha Cha stood for he joked that it meant 'three cups of tea'. I didn't know what he meant. 'No,' I said. 'It stands for 'four and one'. It was like we were speaking completely different languages, but nevertheless I really wanted to do my best by Paul and make him feel confident and look as good as possible on the dance floor.

Paul's wife Debbie McGee came to training to see us a few times and she was absolutely lovely. As a couple they were very nice and sweet together, like teenagers in love. We all laughed when one of the Sunday papers published a photo of Paul standing with his arm around me, while Debbie supposedly looked at us 'green-eyed' and 'ready to tell Paul Daniels to Foxtrot Oscar'.

'So Debbie, do you like seeing Paul with his arm around sexy Ola? NOT A LOT!' ran the headline. Honestly, that tells you all you need to know about how naughty the tabloid press can be!

I'd decided to get hair extensions after the previous series, because my own hair had been destroyed by what it had gone through over the years on Strictly. When I first joined the show I had long, healthy hair, but it became progressively weaker from all the backcombing and styling. When you do the dress run on a Saturday you of course have full hair and make-up, and then after the rehearsal everything is totally re-done, so it is perfect for the live show in the evening. All curls and plaits and hairspray are completely brushed out – often in a very necessary hurry – and then more rollers are put in and more grips and spray applied as the whole process is repeated. It's so bad for your hair, and mine had become thin and weak, and had ended up looking terrible.

Lots of other dancers had extensions and a friend recommended them, so I gave them a go. The process was time-consuming and expensive as I had natural hair woven into my own. It would have to be re-done every four months too, but I loved the results. It didn't help my confidence when my hair was wrecked, so it felt great to have strong hair tumbling down my back again.

I don't blame the hairdressers at Strictly at all for how my hair became damaged, by the way. They were all brilliant at what they did and I was constantly amazed at what they could achieve in a short space of time, often under intense pressure. Hardly surprisingly, they did have the occasional mishap because of the volume of work they had to cope with and the stress of meeting TV deadlines. It's well known backstage that one of the hairdressers left the show several years ago after mixing up the dyes for two of the professional dancers. The girl who was meant to go red ended up brown and vice versa – and to make matters worse the two dancers in question didn't like each other. It was such a shame, but these things happen when you are working in such a high-pressure environment.

There was a different drama in more recent times, when one of the professional dancers refused to dye her hair the colour the producers wanted her to. Image is so important on Strictly, so I guess it's no surprise that something like this can blow up into a row. This was a big one, and the dancer in question threatened to take legal action as she felt so strongly that the producers couldn't force her to dye her hair.

I was coping a little bit better with my skin by this time. After years of trial and error, and seeing different skin specialists, I'd started to build up a really good collection of natural products. I was still prone to acne and had to cover myself in make-up just for training, but I was now using some really good skincare products by the likes of La Roche-Posay and Jan Marini that agreed with me and were recommended by dermatologists. They didn't cure the spots entirely but they soothed them and reduced the flare-ups that gave me the red boils. This was a huge relief, although I was always on the look-out for a cure or the next expert who might be able to come up with an even better plan.

As far as my diet went, I was now about half a stone heavier than when I first joined Strictly four years earlier. It hadn't been a steady rise, of course; I'd yo-yoed, and I'd come to accept that I was always going to gain and lose weight according to how strict I was with my diet and that I had an ongoing struggle on my hands. The advantage of carrying more weight was that I'd become noticeably more curvy, which people seemed to like. I'd worn a very daring red lacy catsuit with cut-out sides when I was dancing the Cha Cha Cha with Chris Hollins one week. It had caused another big stir and got a lot of coverage in the press and all over the internet, with a lot of fans saying how much they loved it. Again I found this a bit embarrassing: I never got used to this kind of attention, particularly as I was conscious about my weight and appearance in general. However, I did appreciate that it was good to have fans and viewers on my side, saying nice things.

Bruce always loved my catsuits and never made a secret of the fact he liked all of my skimpy costumes. Whenever he remarked on my outfits I'd giggle, and I'm sure Bruce's banter could only have added to the way my reputation was growing: the papers had started to routinely call me 'sexy Ola'.

I was being asked to model lingerie and advertisers were approaching me to promote various products. It was all very flattering and I understood that I had a body a lot of people would have loved to have themselves, but I still wasn't confident about my appearance and I still wanted to be thinner. When you're wearing next to nothing and dancing in front of millions of people you have to feel right, but I didn't, because I knew I was a little on the heavy side. I also had some cellulite and there were areas of my body I wished were more toned, like my bum and my tummy. I'd go to the gym when I wasn't training and I was still eating very cleanly, partly because dermatologists told me this would help my skin too. My diet was made up of a lot of whole fruits and vegetables, and plenty of lean protein like chicken and salmon. I had stopped drinking Coke, which I used to love, and was drinking green tea and lots of water instead. Despite this, the weight just seemed to stick to me.

'Do you really want that?' James would say to me if I had a moment of weakness and treated myself to something naughty, like sweets or pizza.

I'd scowl at him, as I always did in those situations, but I knew he was only trying to help me stay on track and to stop me gaining any more weight. He'd call me a 'chunky monkey' too, saying things like 'are you sure you should be eating that, chunky monkey?' As had happened in the past, if other people heard James speak to me like this they were shocked and gave him disapproving looks. I'd have to reassure them he was on my side, and that he only did it because he knew I would get miserable and feel self-conscious on TV if I put on more weight, but even so I could tell that some people were not impressed with him!

Disappointingly, Paul Daniels and I were eliminated in week three. I cried when I had to leave the competition so early on; it was still only the middle of October.

Our time together had been short but sweet.

I was very sad when I heard the news that Paul had passed away, in March 2016. I had just started writing this book and all my memories of him came back to me. I sent my condolences to Debbie. Paul was a legend, and it was a privilege to meet him.

James had a fine old time with Pamela Stephenson. As planned they did two weeks of their training in New York, and James had the pleasure of going out to lunch with Pamela and Billy Connolly.

'Why are ya troosers so tight laddie?' Billy asked James memorably.

'I didn't think they were that tight!' James laughed.

'They are laddie. How'd ya dance in those?'

Pamela was driven and passionate, and could characterise the dances really well; being a comedienne and a sex psychologist clearly stood her in good stead, and she had a fabulous attitude. Despite being a grandma, she was incredibly energetic too and threw herself into the competition with everything she had, losing about three stone in weight along the way.

'Well done granny!' James would tease. The two of them got some great feedback, especially for their Viennese Waltz and Quickstep, which they got top marks in.

They also had lots of laughs along the way.

'Feel free to tell me about your sex life, I might be able to offer advice,' Pamela said to a gobsmacked James one day – and, believe me, it takes a lot for James to be gobsmacked.

When they did the Salsa on the live show, James spun Pamela around very dramatically on the floor in her bright scarlet dress. Unfortunately, when she stood up, she lost control and almost fell over before spinning off towards the judges, grinning and shimmying as she tried to stay upright. Claudia Winkleman played the clip several times when she interviewed James and Pamela on It Takes Two afterwards. She cracked up laughing, branding it Pamela's 'firecracker moment'. When James tells the story I can't stop laughing either, as he says Pamela's arms were whirling like windmill sails and she danced off looking like the Leaning Tower of Pisa, which is a very funny and accurate description.

Despite the mistake, Pamela and James ended up top of the leaderboard and they came third overall in the competition. It was a really fantastic result for them, and James's best-ever position.

It had been an interesting series. Unbelievably, we'd done five years on Strictly by now. It had gone in the blink of an eye, and any doubts I'd had about the future after winning with Chris had faded. I knew the day would come when the show would be over, but I wasn't ready for that day yet, no way.

25

'Come on James!' I shouted excitedly.

He was on a running track in Nottingham, preparing to race against none other than Olympic hurdler Colin Jackson.

Colin was runner-up on the third series of Strictly, before we joined the show, and he had been invited onto the 2011 live tour along with James and me, Pamela Stephenson and several other celebrities and pro dancers. It was a two-month tour, covering venues all over the country throughout January and February.

As usual, we were all looking for things to do during the daytime, when we generally had plenty of free time. I'd shop and have a spa treatment occasionally, although one time this went badly wrong when I decided to go for a full bikini wax. I'd never had an extreme waxing like that before, and it was horrific. When I got back to the hotel I was on fire and I had to sit with my legs in the air, fanning myself with a magazine. James, of course, thought it was very funny.

Anyhow, Colin Jackson was a really fun guy, and one day he fixed up a running contest for the crew and dancers. The winners of the heats would compete against Colin himself in the final, which got everyone going. James really wanted to win his heat, and he was buzzing when he did really well and easily made the grand final.

'Wow,' James thought, finding himself in the blocks right next to Colin. Fired up on adrenaline, he then told himself: 'Come on James, you can do this! You've smashed your heat. You can beat Colin Jackson!'

James even thought about how he was ten years younger than Colin and started to imagine he might have an advantage on him because of the age difference.

'I'll do it. I'll beat him. I can do it!'

When the starting pistol went off, James left the blocks at full pelt.

He felt like a whippet, but when he looked up he saw that Colin was already four metres ahead. James pushed on with all his might and then, to his surprise and delight, he starting catching Colin up. James could hardly believe it, and this fired him up to run faster still.

'Run harder,' he told himself as he closed the gap on Colin inch by inch. Unbelievably, James actually caught Colin up. James was on fire, and I was clapping and cheering and jumping up and down on the side of the track. Maybe he really could beat Colin Jackson?

A split second later, Colin looked across at James and laughed in his face. At that point Colin stepped up his pace and left James for dead, which of course had been his cheeky plan all along.

'How could I ever have even contemplated trying to beat Colin Jackson?' James laughed afterwards, 'what an arrogant idiot I am!'

'No you're not,' I said, '… well, not really!'

'Cheers Ola!'

Colin had really played the joke well, which was typical of him; he loved a laugh and had a great sense of humour.

Colin was my dance partner on the tour and we got on really well together and started off enjoying all the rehearsals and shows. However, we encountered a problem with the set at one particular venue. We were doing the Quickstep, and at the start of the performance Colin and I were asked to run through a very narrow gap around the edge of the stage. It was dimly lit and didn't seem safe. I looked at it and wasn't happy, but didn't want to make a fuss.

James, typically, had no such qualms.

'You're gonna trip and snap a leg, Ola!' he said. 'There isn't enough room and with the lights in your face you could have a nasty accident.'

Clearly, Colin didn't want to risk any kind of injury either, so James approached Craig Revel Horwood, who was once again the director of the tour.

'Can we move this section?' James asked Craig, politely.

'No, we can't,' came the curt reply.

James stuck to his guns, explaining the reason for the request, but then

Craig suddenly lost his temper and shouted at him.

'You do as you're told! You're just a dancer,' he bellowed, in front of the crew and several other colleagues.

The red mist descended in front of James's eyes and he totally lost it, threatening Craig and shouting at him.

'I've never been spoken to like that in my life before,' James complained to the producer later. 'It's just not on. It's bullying behaviour and totally unacceptable.' James conceded that he should not have lost his temper so badly, or threatened Craig as he did, even though in the circumstances he really didn't feel inclined to apologise.

The producer heard him out but ultimately nothing was done about James's complaint against Craig, or the steps that concerned us in the routine. We just had to get on with it and hope for the best.

'I don't understand why the BBC lets him carry on like that,' James complained to me privately. 'Has he got some kind of hold over them? It's almost like they are trying to protect him.'

I had no answer.

Apart from that incident, the rest of the tour turned out to be very enjoyable, and we had a lot of laughs.

In one of the group dances we performed the men had to spin the girls around just once and then put them down and step back. James was partnering Pamela Stephenson, and I was once again dancing with Colin. The two boys were particularly naughty when they were together, and they hatched a plot to liven things up a bit. Unbeknown to the girls, all the boys had decided to spin us around five times instead of the once. The first I knew of it was when my head span, as well as my body. Colin was spinning me so fast I practically had dribble coming out of my mouth but somehow I coped and managed to find my feet when he put me down. Poor Pamela, who was dancing with James, wasn't so lucky. In true style she kept smiling as she tried to regain her composure, then all of sudden she crashed to the ground with a loud thump. She was the only one to fall and most of the other girls danced over her with a 'show must go on' determination, while the rest of us burst out laughing.

The next day James was taken into a meeting room by the producers. They had some film footage from the night before, and they had the recording frozen on James's laughing face.

'What on earth do you think you were playing at?'

'It wasn't just me who was laughing! Why have you only called me in?'

Apparently, James was the worst offender. It was true that his partner was the only one to fall, but even so he still felt it was unfair to single him out. All the boys had been in on it and he could not understand why he was the only one in trouble.

James thought it was wrong to be so stuffy on tour. 'I think we should have fun on the tour,' he protested. This sort of caper is what a tour should be all about. The audience love it. It's entertainment! Nobody got hurt, it's just clean, safe fun.'

I had to agree with him, because the audiences always loved it when something went wrong, or when they spotted we were mucking about. The producers were having none of it, though. James didn't care, and he carried on regardless, often behaving like a naughty schoolboy.

As a result some of our funniest memories of Strictly happened when we were on the road. We also did a Gothic number on this tour that started off with two pro girl dancers standing back to back wearing long cloaks. James had to wait at the back before he came on stage, and he always complained about how boring it was to be crouched in the dark, waiting for his cue. One night, a little devil popped up on his shoulder and told him to have some fun. The first the rest of us knew about it was when the two girls began to walk away from each other towards opposite sides of the stage. All of a sudden both their necks jerked backwards and then there was an almighty scramble to untie the strings of their cloaks, which some joker had knotted together: James, of course. The girls gave him evil looks and eventually managed to carry on, while James was told off once more by a producer.

'It's entertainment!' he protested. 'The audience loved it!'

The tour management didn't see the funny side and they didn't agree with James's view. It seemed he'd never shaken off the 'bad boy' image he was painted with on our very first series and they saw him not as a harmless joker, but as a troublemaker who needed to be kept firmly in line. He wasn't prepared to play ball, though, so I guess he was partly to blame for the fact his bad boy image persisted.

One time, James was wearing a kilt, and for a laugh he put on a nude thong and did a cartwheel on stage. He also took off his shirt and went topless. We were performing in Glasgow and the audience loved and it started stamping their feet and cheering. Nevertheless, James was told not to repeat the performance, as it didn't fit in with the way the BBC wanted to present itself.

'But it went down a storm!' James protested. Once again the producers were not amused and wouldn't budge.

The previous year we'd taken part in The Professionals Tour along with Vincent and Flavia and several other pro dancers. In one number we were all dressed up in smart London suits and the boys had bowler hats, which they passed to the girls part way through the routine. All the girls then did a routine lifting the hat on and off their head. The choreography was arranged so that Flavia would be handed Vincent's bowler hat before going to the front of the stage and leading the girls in a fairly long segment of the performance.

However, what actually happened was that when the boys were still at the back of the stage, James grabbed Vincent's hat and threw it into the band. James did this on the spur of the moment and hadn't really thought it through. He only intended to cause Flavia a momentary panic when she got no hat from Vincent but of course she was then exposed at the front of the stage, trying to do something very weird and wonderful with her hands with no prop to work with. It was very funny, and at one point she just shrugged and grinned while members of the audience could be heard saying: 'Look! She's got no hat!' as she waved her empty hands around.

The clip ended up on YouTube where it was viewed about eight thousand times, though I don't think this did anything to pacify the producers.

We'd sometimes go out to a club after the show to let our hair down. One time, all the dancers bought a different fancy dress outfit then we each pulled our name out of a hat to see which costume we had to wear out that night.

Flavia was a duck, Matthew Cutler was a baby, James was the guy in the tight black leathers and cap from Village People, Ian Waite was Ronald McDonald and I was in a wacky red wig with a red top and England flag trousers. We went to a gay club – we never got any trouble from anybody in the gay clubs, even when we were dressed up like that – and it was a brilliant night.

Back on stage, it wasn't just the boys who mucked about. On one of our earlier tours there was a routine in which all the dance partners wore matching colours. Kenny Logan and I were in vibrant pink while other couples complemented each other in bright green, red, yellow and so on. One night, feeling mischievous, all the girls decided to swap dresses to confuse the boys. I swapped with Jodie Kidd, and it was worth it to see all the boys do a double take when we came onto the dance floor. That was as far as we wanted the joke to go, but what we didn't realise was the cameramen who filmed the show ever night to project it onto the large screens in the arenas followed the colours of the dresses, not the individual girls. It was a shambles, and to make matters worse the lighting was rigged differently for different coloured dresses so that was all wrong too, and the whole routine descended into chaos.

The boys were not averse to swapping clothes either. The most memorable occasion was when Kenny and Vincent swapped tops, and Kenny was bursting out of Vincent's shirt looking like the Incredible Hulk.

One of my all-time favourite stories from tour happened when Arlene Phillips was still a judge. She had told Len Goodman off for mentioning Tesco on air on a live show, because of the BBC's strict rules on advertising. This presented a golden opportunity for a joke, and James and some of the other boys came up with a plan.

'Wouldn't it be funny if we all name brands when Kate Thornton interviews us on stage?' James said.

Nearly all the dancers agreed, and when Kate came on to do the interviews in front of the arena audience everybody was ready.

'How did you enjoy the show tonight?' Kate asked Vincent.

'I loved it! It was like driving a Ferrari!'

'Your hair looks lovely,' she told another dancer.

'Thanks! I went to Toni & Guy to have it done today!'

Arlene was the Creative Director on this tour and she was watching and listening to every word, cottoning on to what we were doing and getting very cross. Somebody else said doing the show was 'more fun than changing Pampers'. Arlene was really annoyed now, but she couldn't say anything or attempt to control us because we were in front of a packed audience. Afterwards, she went mad backstage, and she told James off especially, as she guessed he was behind it.

'How come you didn't get told off Ola?' he said afterwards. 'Why always me? Why nobody else?'

I raised my eyebrows.

'James, you have a reputation and you keep fuelling it. You are your own worst enemy!'

He giggled and his eyes twinkled. He knew it, but he wasn't going to change any time soon. In fact, my guess was he was only going to get worse.

26

'W hen are we going to have a baby?' I said one day when James and I were snuggled up together.

This was a question we had started asking each other, because we both wanted to start a family at some point. I was going to turn thirty the following year, while James was already thirty-three. Neither of us wanted to leave it too late, but we both agreed that it was difficult to know when the time is right.

'When is the right time, James? What do you think?'

He'd asked me the same question in the past, and now he gave me the same answer I had given him: 'I just don't know. I wish I did.'

I never wanted to combine being a mum with being on Strictly. James's mum had suggested that I could plan to have a baby in the summer when Strictly was off the air and then go back to work in the autumn. This never appealed to me at all. I wanted to be a hands-on mum, and that would just not be possible with the demands of Strictly. James agreed with me wholeheartedly on this and even though we had these conversations from time to time, when one or other of us felt a bit broody, we both knew that we'd just have to wait until the time was right, and hope that we'd know when this was. We weren't quite there yet, even though I was starting to think more and more about having kids. For now it felt right to keep doing Strictly. Our run wouldn't last forever, so why not do another year or so while we were still enjoying ourselves on the show?

We were very happy to return to Strictly for the 2011 series, but in hindsight that was the year when we started to experience a few problems with the show.

I was partnered with Robbie Savage and I was very pleased I'd been put with him. Not only was Robbie a genuinely friendly guy and good fun, but as an ex-footballer he was competitive and had a positive attitude that I could see would really help his dancing. Even in the very beginning when we had a long way to go, he was saying: 'Come on, I can do this!', and he was working really hard in training every day, giving it his all.

I took the train up to Manchester on Mondays straight after pro rehearsals for the group dances that we had to do, and I stayed in a hotel near where Robbie and I practised. Every day I absolutely loved dancing with Robbie. We always had some good banter going on, often about Robbie's looks. He'd tease me that his blonde highlights were better than mine, his teeth whiter and his eyes prettier.

'You're such a girl!' I'd say, and it came as no surprise when Robbie would be first in the queue for the spray tan before the live shows. He'd also take longer having his hair done than me, and he'd pout in the mirror, which I really took the mickey out of.

After one long day in the studio we went out for something to eat in Manchester.

'Where are you?' James asked when he phoned for a chat, as he did every evening.

'Oh, just having an Italian with Robbie.'

'Right.'

I could almost hear the thump of his heart. James and I always missed each other when we were apart during the week, and I knew it didn't help that I was out with Robbie. I guess no husband wants their wife to go out to dinner with a good-looking sportsman, whatever the circumstances, and James knew better than anyone how close the relationship can become with your dancing partner.

On this occasion, Robbie and I were photographed coming out of the restaurant together, and even though James knew there was nothing going on, he'd still get in a bit of a mood about it.

'I'm sorry,' he said afterwards. 'I'm jealous, I admit it. It's not your fault Ola, but I'm just telling you how I feel.'

Robbie and I would get the train down to London together on the

Thursday night, ready for the studio rehearsals on Friday. When we arrived at Euston, Robbie would have a taxi waiting for him and his luggage, as would the camera crew, which was understandable given the amount of kit they carried. All of this was provided by Strictly, but dancers had to make their own travel arrangements, whatever time of day it was. This meant I'd have to lug my big suitcase on the underground before catching the train back to Kent, and I'd be lucky to get home before 11 p.m. Then I'd have to be back in London to start work very early the next morning. I'd be exhausted, and I also found the set-up demoralising and embarrassing as it was so obvious to everyone that we dancers were not treated as well as the celebrities. It wasn't that I wanted any star treatment of any kind; that was absolutely not the case. It just seemed unnecessarily penny-pinching of the BBC to put me in this situation.

There had been a few other occasions in recent times when both James and I had felt uncomfortable with the way we were treated. For instance, one time a member of the production team came into the studio where all the dancers and celebrities were gathered.

'Right! Celebrities, you all go to that room, where you have lunch waiting for you.'

'What about us?' one of the dancers asked.

'Sorry, lunch is only provided for celebrities today.'

All the dancers were left to rush outside and grab themselves something to eat. We'd been training for four hours and were hungry, and it seemed churlish that the bosses couldn't lay on a few extra sandwiches for us. It's not as if dancers are big eaters, after all. It would have been a small gesture, but it would have meant a lot.

Another time, James and I arrived in our dressing room to find fruit and champagne set out.

'How nice!' we thought.

It wasn't that we particularly wanted fruit or champagne; we didn't. The gesture meant a great deal, though. It made us feel appreciated... that is, until a runner turned up in a fluster.

'Sorry! My mistake,' she said, hurriedly gathering up the goodies. 'This is just for celebs!'

When James got to hear about what happened at Euston with the taxis he went mad. He rang the producer and said he didn't think it was on that I didn't have a car provided, particularly when the others did and when it was after 9 p.m. It didn't seem fair. I didn't want any special treatment, I just wanted to be looked after in the same way as my dance partner and the camera crew.

The response was less than favourable. 'We only provide taxis for celebrities,' James was told bluntly.

That was the end of it; there was no negotiation.

James was dancing with The One Show presenter Alex Jones this time, and they survived for eleven weeks, until the semi-final. James got on well with all his partners and was chatty and cuddly and flirty with all of them. I know it's just the way James is, and of course I understand it's par for the course when you are dancing closely with someone for weeks on end. You have to get close, and you inevitably become attached to your partner to a certain extent.

This had never bothered me in the past as James and me were in the same boat, but if I'm honest I did find it a bit difficult to see how close his bond was with Alex, and how much fun they had together.

'We had such a laugh in the studio,' James said one night, when he phoned me in Manchester as usual.

'What happened today?'

I was on my own in a hotel in Manchester, exhausted after having danced with Robbie all day.

James explained that Alex had worn leggings that went see-through and exposed her thong when she bent over. She didn't realise this, and so James and the camera guys had some fun with it.

'Just bend over and touch your toes,' James told Alex, 'I want to see how flexible you are…'

Alex was facing James, but her bottom was pointing at the camera crew, who giggled and gave James the thumbs up. Alex cottoned on and laughed, saying 'very funny, James!' She didn't mind at all, as she totally got James's sense of humour and realised he was a prankster.

'It was hysterical!' James hooted.

I laughed because he told the story well and made it sound very funny, but really I was thinking: 'Great! And I'm two hundred miles away!'

I wasn't jealous, but I don't think I'd have been human if I hadn't felt a pang at the thought of an attractive woman like Alex larking around and having such great rapport with my husband.

There was controversy on the show when Alex and James did the Rumba in week four. Alex knew she wasn't a natural dancer but she still tried really hard to do her best, and most importantly she was enjoying her Strictly experience. She and James performed what I thought was an acceptable Rumba, but Craig completely burst Alex's bubble when he came out with his comments. 'Sexless, cold and stiff' was his shocking verdict. Alex's face fell, James argued back, and I gasped from Tess's area, as I thought this was very rude and unfair of Craig.

'The public seemed to like it,' James said, which brought cheers from the audience.

Afterwards, when James and Alex joined us in Tess's room, James started shouting down from the balcony, heckling the judges and letting them know what he thought of Craig's comments.

At one point Len Goodman shouted up to James: 'All you have to do is turn up, keep up and shut up.'

'You used that line last year,' James shouted back, enjoying the spat.

As the temperature rose, Brucie was practically running on the spot, not knowing what to do. James's mum was in the audience and she started shaking her head at James to show her disapproval and warn him he'd gone too far and that he should shut up now.

Later, in the bar, Sharon told James she thought he was really out of order giving cheek to Len Goodman like that.

'You're no son of mine, behaving like that,' she said, shaking her head and looking disappointed in him.

Moments later, Ant and Dec appeared, as they happened to be in the bar that night.

'James, that was awesome,' they said before turning to Sharon and saying, 'You must be so proud of your son!'

'Er, yes, I am,' Sharon stuttered, suddenly changing her tune as she didn't want to disagree with Ant and Dec. It was a very funny exchange, but afterwards I had mixed feelings about the events of that evening. Part of me felt proud of James for standing up for himself. I also liked the fact I knew I could rely on him to watch both of our backs as I knew he always would, but I felt uneasy too. Was it wise to rock the boat like that? It wasn't my style at all, and I really wasn't sure.

Robbie and I survived until week ten, and we'd had a real blast. During our time together I'd discovered that Robbie had an unexpected soft side. Even though he was prepared to work really hard in training he'd have some vulnerable moments too, when he'd say: 'please don't expect too much Ola!'

He also had a very silly streak, and he had a habit of pulling down people's jogging bottoms when they least expected it. One day he did this to Brendan Cole. We all knew that Brendan didn't wear any underwear but, very funnily, it came as quite a shock to Robbie. Another time Robbie very unexpectedly asked Audley Harrison: 'Why didn't you throw a punch against David Haye?'

'Oh my God Robbie,' I was thinking, 'Why?' I wished the ground would swallow us both up.

Every week, as we walked down the stairs for the live show and the VT was played to the audience and viewers, Robbie would panic and say to me: 'Which leg do I start with?'

I was always nervous too, but I knew that deep down he was thinking what he'd thought from day one: 'Come on, I can do this!' He was brilliant every week in the live shows and never put a foot wrong. He loved the attention and the drama and the whole experience of doing Strictly, and I think people watching could really see that. The time we performed the Salsa to Robbie Williams's Let Me Entertain You at Wembley was perhaps the best example of this. We opened the whole show and Robbie said he felt like a rock star. The audience went wild, even though it wasn't our best technical performance and we didn't get the best marks: Alex and James topped the leaderboard that night, and Robbie and me were second from bottom.

Unfortunately, at the wrap party, there was another problem to contend with. Everybody was celebrating after having worked so hard for months on end and James and I were in really good spirits and enjoying a drink together. Then someone from the press team called James's mobile.

'Just to let you know, there's going to be a story coming out in the papers tomorrow, saying you are sacked.'

'What? SACKED? Well can't you stop it?'

'No, sorry, that's why we just wanted to warn you in advance.'

'Why can't you stop it? Why can't you put out a statement saying it is untrue? It's nonsense.'

'It's too late, sorry James.'

We couldn't understand why the press office couldn't issue a denial, however late in the day it was. The story was a load of rubbish and it was upsetting and unsettling to have lies like that circulating. Why let people assume it was true? It didn't make any sense for the press office to tip us off but do nothing.

'It's obviously good publicity for Strictly,' James concluded, shaking his head. 'But what about my feelings? It's not exactly good for morale, is it?'

When we looked back over the various glitches and issues we'd had this series we both had to admit there had been a sea change this year, in the way we were viewed and treated by the powers that be. It seemed to us that we were not as popular with the bosses as we had been in the past. Then, for the first time since we joined Strictly, we were not invited on the tour. We were told in an email at short notice that we were 'not needed'. We'd had a great run on the tours and it was understood that not all the dancers were invited every year, but even so this was a bit of a blow. The way the news was delivered didn't help, and then stories appeared in the press suggesting the decision was made because of James's 'strops' behind the scenes. Reports also suggested that bosses thought James had got too big for his boots and needed a 'reality check.'

I was asked by various people if I was angry with James for the way he had behaved, and I would tell them truthfully: 'Not at all. I agree with everything he says. We are a team and I support him all the way because he only sticks up for what he believes is right.'

The truth was that as time went on I wished I could have been more like him, and I wished I could have the confidence to stand up for myself on Strictly as much as he did, and in life in general.

What most people didn't know was that I actually had started to become stronger and more outspoken myself, although I was still nowhere near as bold as James. The two of us had a joke that he was like one of those clockwork monkeys that you had to wind up before setting them off. Whenever I was stressed about something I'd load James up with the ammunition, wind him up and set him off. He was fighting the battles for both of us, so I really couldn't blame him for any of the consequences.

We looked on the bright side. We'd have a break in the new year, take a holiday and start afresh for series ten. We were moving from Kings Hill to a beautiful country house in nearby Wateringbury, so we had plenty to keep ourselves busy with.

We ended up having the most fantastic holiday to the Bahamas in the spring of 2012, where we swam with wild pigs in the clear blue waters around Pig Beach. It was a surreal experience, and we learned that the feral pigs, they look like wild boars, just pitch up to the shores of the uninhabited island whenever they fancy a swim, and when they are hoping to be fed by the holidaymakers. It was amazing. James and I loved every minute of that trip and had a really relaxing time. His parents came too, which was lovely. I felt very happy and content, and I really recharged my batteries and had a good rest.

Little did I know how good the timing of this holiday was, because 2012 turned out to be an incredibly busy and testing year, for all kinds of reasons I could not have foreseen.

27

'**O**la, your mum was taken to hospital last night.'

It was Dad calling from Poland and I was in a hotel in London as I was in the middle of training with my latest dance partner, the EastEnders actor Sid Owen.

'Last night? What happened? What time?'

I stayed outwardly calm but I could feel the blood coursing through my veins. It was surreal, like my world was collapsing around me and I was getting ready to fight. Dad explained that Mum had been taken to hospital at 11 p.m. the night before, after throwing up at home and then suffering a heart attack.

'She is stable now, Ola. She's fine. They are putting stents in.'

'I'll fly home straight away. I want to see her.'

'Ola, there is no need to rush here. She is being well looked after. I am with her, and I can tell you everything that is happening.'

It was a Thursday in October, and Sid and I were rehearsing the Tango for Saturday's live show. I desperately didn't want to let Sid down, but my instinct was to go and see Mum.

'Ola, you are working,' Dad insisted. 'Mum is fine, honestly. I will let you know if anything changes.'

'But Dad, I want to see her.'

'Ola, really, there is no need. Don't do anything hasty. She is going to be fine, honestly, wait for more news…'

Sid had worked really hard and was a great guy who had potential. I thought he could go quite far in the competition and I didn't want to wreck his chances, but of course my loyalties lay with my family. I stayed in London that night and went into the studio the next day for rehearsals, with Dad's words ringing in my ears. I was trying to be strong and heed his advice, but I couldn't. I suddenly lost it in the middle of the studio and just burst into tears, sobbing uncontrollably. Glen, the lovely producer at the time, came to talk to me.

'I don't want to let people down,' I cried, 'but I want to see my mum.'

'Ola, whatever your decision we'll support you. You have to do what is right for you.'

As it was Saturday the next day, I took the decision to stay for the live show then fly to Poland first thing on the Sunday morning. In hindsight, I don't think it was a good idea. My mind was on Mum every minute and I was struggling to focus. Sid and I only got seventeen points, though we did enough to stay in the competition. It was arranged that while I was away, one of the other pro dancers who had already been eliminated, Iveta, would teach Sid the choreography for our next dance, the Cha Cha Cha to Ghostbusters for Halloween week. All being well I would then return on the Thursday to rehearse with Sid ahead of the next live show. Sid was gutted I had to go, though of course he also understood completely and wished me and my family all the very best.

The flight was horrible. I was counting off the minutes, just wanting to get to Mum and wishing we could fly faster and faster. Dad picked me up at the airport and took me straight to the hospital. It was awful because Dad looked lost, and then it was a terrible shock to see Mum lying in a hospital bed. I had never seen her like that. She had no colour in her skin but even so she smiled when she saw me. Softly and slowly she described to me how she'd had a pain in her arm before she had the heart attack.

I'd last seen my parents just a few weeks beforehand, as it had been my thirtieth birthday at the end of September and James flew them over as a surprise. The first I knew of this was when I came in tired from practice with Sid one night and heard the doorbell ring. We were in our new house in Wateringbury, and you can see the driveway from the open-plan lounge area beyond the kitchen at the front.

I was sitting on the sofa, and I looked out of the front window and saw that James's mum and dad's car was outside.

'James, your mum and dad are here!' I said, puzzled, as they never normally turned up unannounced.

'Are they? Can you answer the door?'

I hauled myself off the sofa and went to let them in. When I opened the front door I couldn't believe my eyes. Sharon and Allan had picked my parents up from the airport and driven them to our house from Gatwick.

'This is amazing!' I said. 'I'm so happy to see you!'

I was completely taken aback, and James really could not have planned a better surprise. We went for a lovely family meal together and had a great weekend to celebrate my birthday, but when I thought about it now I could tell that my mum wasn't in the best of health. She'd told me she'd been feeling a bit sickly and had had a few tests, but of course none of us anticipated what would happen next. 'Let me know your results,' I'd said. 'Maybe you are a bit tired and run down.'

Thankfully, we discovered the heart attack had been minor, but even so Mum had had a terrible shock and I felt very sorry for her. She was only in her sixties but in that moment, lying on the ward, she looked older than her years. One blessing was that, despite the physical blow she'd suffered, she remained as strong-minded and uncomplaining as ever.

'I've told all the ladies about you,' she said. 'They're all very interested in you and your dancing!'

Mum always carried around a bunch of photographs of me in her handbag, and she'd shown the nurses and other patients pictures of me on Strictly, proudly telling them all about my career.

I smiled, and then we reminisced about the old days, when Dad made my costumes and drove me to practice, and the two of then cheered me on in competitions. Mum brightened up a bit as we chatted and it was very comforting to see; I knew she was going to be OK.

I stayed in the apartment with Dad and I could see he was totally lost without Mum. He didn't know where anything was, and I hated to think of him alone there. In many ways he was in a worse state than she was.

I looked around and remembered being a child, lying on the floor watching TV, and gazing in awe at the ballroom dancing shows. Mum and Dad were both heavy smokers, and my eyes used to sting when I watched TV, because for years they smoked inside the tiny flat. When I was older and they knew the health risks they started smoking on the balcony. Now, inevitably, the doctors were telling Mum she had to stop smoking completely, and I'm happy to say that after the heart attack she never smoked again.

Mum was going to be discharged from hospital within the week and she and Dad insisted I took my flight back on the Thursday, so I could be in the Halloween show. I did as they wanted, and it seemed the right thing all round, not least for Sid.

'We will worry if you miss any more work,' they both said. 'You must go, Ola.'

I flew back to London, and during my flight I thought about what was important in life. My family and loved ones came first, without a doubt.

There had been a drama backstage early on during this series of Strictly, when we started the pro dance rehearsals. I thought about this too. A producer had arrived in the training studio and said to all the pro dancers 'here's your water bottle for the series.' We were normally given a plentiful supply of disposable water bottles when we practised the pro group dances, but we were told these were being taken away. Now we were going to have to use plastic refillable gym bottles – the type I used for a gym session at home. This was fine for a workout in the local gym, but not on Strictly.

It meant all the pro dancers would have to keep running out of the studio to fill up these plastic bottles when we were rehearsing for eight hours at a time, and sweating our heads off. We needed water to hand all the time, but the nearest fountain was down a corridor. It really wasn't on.

There was a big row about this and the scandal became known as 'watergate' behind the scenes. In hindsight it's quite amusing, but it wasn't at the time. We won our argument in the end, thank God, eventually getting our disposable bottles of water back, but not before Brendan had thrown his refillable bottle across the studio in a strop.

'If they can argue about giving us water they are capable of arguing about anything!' one of the other dancers commented.

This all seemed so silly and unimportant now, as I sat on the plane back to London. It had been so important to me in the heat of the moment, but it wasn't really. My job and what happened on Strictly was important to me, but nothing was more important than my mum and dad, James and both our families. My trip home had given me a timely reality check.

When I got back to work I discovered that, despite Iveta being a fantastic dancer and teacher, Sid had really struggled with the change of partner. He'd cancelled a few rehearsals with Iveta, so when we met up to practise on the Friday Sid and I really had our work cut out.

'I really don't want us to go out tomorrow,' I told Sid. 'Come on, we can do it!'

I was trying to be enthusiastic but the truth is I was mentally and physically exhausted, and our performance in the live show was shocking. Craig quite rightly described it as a 'Halloween nightmare'. We got just seventeen points again, and this time Sid and I were eliminated from the competition. We'd survived just four weeks, and I still feel guilty about how Sid's Strictly experience turned out.

James fared much better. He was dancing with Denise van Outen and she was driven and competitive and responded really well to being pushed by James. They lasted until week twelve and were runners up in the final, missing out to Flavia and the gymnast Louis Smith. This was a great result for James, not least because he'd had a few injuries to put up with.

Injuries are par for the course for dancers. Many years previously I'd accidentally split James's eyebrow open with my elbow during one energetic routine. We were performing in a club in Lewisham, and James's mum and dad were in the audience. When we clashed blood started pumping out of James's eyebrow all over the beige trousers and shirt he was wearing. James wiped the blood away and tried to carry on, not wanting to cause any more fuss, but then his mum ran on the dance floor shouting 'my baby!'

'Mum, sit down!' James hissed while I started telling him we had to stop. It was a shambles.

Now I was having déjà vu, because during a group dance I split James's skin just above his right eye once again. He was wearing a white tee-shirt this time, and in the next moment it turned red as it was completely covered in blood.

It was the first year Darcey had joined the show as a permanent judge, and I can remember looking up and seeing a totally horrified, startled expression on her face, and she was holding her hands over her mouth in shock.

'I'll continue,' James said, because it was a recording of a group number in front of a live studio audience and he knew that if he left the floor it would hold up the whole show.

A floor manager scuttled on.

'I'm sorry James, you have to leave the floor. People in the audience are feeling faint.'

Two weeks later, during a group dance practice again, James was spinning me around on his shoulders whilst I was wearing a dress that had big coin sequins on it. The skirt of the dress was really slippery, and as James spun me I flew off to one side. My head was going down and so James grabbed one of my legs, at which point I caught him square on the nose with my shoe. He fell to the floor like he'd been hit by a truck yelping: 'Ola! You've broken my nose!'

I was mortified and it was clear he was in a lot of pain. James had broken his nose on several occasions in the past, not just through dancing but once in a fight with a boy at school, when he was fifteen and was headbutted. He had to go to hospital and have a huge cast on his nose, and since then he had learned that he could click his nose back into place if he broke it. It was excruciating and horrific to watch, but James said it was far preferable to going to hospital and having surgery again.

'Don't worry, I know what to do,' he told the producer who had rushed to help him, 'I'll just click it back...'

'No, James, please don't do that...'

It was too late. There was a stomach-turning crack and James's nose was straight on his face again. He was as white as a sheet, though, because of the shock and the pain.

Unbelievably, James suffered yet another injury on that same series. He and Brendan Cole had a habit of mucking around backstage and they would wind each other up no end and pull silly stunts on one another. Usually these were harmless and funny. For example, Brendan had a reputation for being clumsy and James would often deliberately trip him up on the pro dances. Then one time James tied Brendan to a chair in the studio, just for a laugh and to stop him 'getting in the way'. On another occasion, as James ran up the stairs on the set to be interviewed after his performance, Brendan lifted up James's shirt and slapped his bare chest really hard. Poor James had to go through a live interview with Tess Daly trying not to wince, as the slap really stung him.

This time Brendan gave James a bit of a shove on the stairs, just in a jokey way, messing around like they often did. He didn't mean to hurt him, but unfortunately James stumbled down the stairs and landed awkwardly. One of his feet swelled up like a balloon and it was so bad that he had to ask Ian Waite to go through the dance routine he was working on with Denise van Outen that week. James sat in the studio while Denise and Ian rehearsed the Paso Doble, and for entertainment value Denise proceeded to wind James up, pretending she preferred dancing with Ian and making out he was taller and more handsome and a better mover than James. It was all good fun on camera, but behind the scenes there was actually quite a serious argument unfolding. The producers told James he would have to pay for his treatment himself, as the injury to his foot was self-inflicted. He argued that it was an unlucky accident, and that nobody could have anticipated that such an injury would result from such a minor shove. James felt the show should pay as it happened on Strictly stairs, during working hours.

James continued to argue and Strictly did pay in the end, but when he went for treatment the physio said he couldn't dance for two weeks. Frustrated, James got his GP to sign him off after three days, and he and

Denise did a fantastic Paso Doble together the following Saturday, even though James was in agony and his foot was red and swollen.

I was proud of him, and what's more he and Denise got to final. It was a real triumph for them. I was thrilled to bits, and for the first time I really understood what James had been through when Chris and I were in the final. I was as nervous as hell, and on the night I felt as if I was competing myself, because I wanted James and Denise to win so much. My nerves were snapping and my heart was literally aching for them to lift the trophy.

When I watched from the green room as James and Denise took to the floor all I could think was I hope they don't go wrong, I hope they don't go wrong. I'd seen them in training and I knew all the choreography so I was watching every move very carefully and I knew exactly what should come next, and what shouldn't.

They performed brilliantly and their Showdance to the Flashdance song What a Feeling was absolutely incredible. It was a true showstopper, earning then a perfect score of forty from the judges. It was mesmerising to watch and, honestly, it was one of the best Showdances I'd ever seen in the history of Strictly. Unfortunately it wasn't enough, as Flavia and her partner, the gymnast Louis Smith, were absolutely awesome. Louis was incredibly popular too, having made history with his performances at the London Olympics earlier that year. By contrast, Denise had come in for a lot of stick because she had had some previous dance training, which I my opinion was very unfair as there were many other celebs over the years who'd also had training but didn't get a bad press because of it – the talented Lisa Riley perhaps being the best example of this.

Nevertheless, I was delighted for Flavia that she'd won and I was incredibly proud of James for getting so far against the odds.

It had been a tough series for me, but James's success made everything better and worthwhile. We were a strong and loyal team, and we shared each other's pain and triumphs. I could not have been happier for James for doing so well, and I was very proud of him too.

28

In April 2013, it was announced that a new executive producer, Louise Rainbow, was taking over at Strictly. James and I didn't know her but we hoped for great things. Strictly had become extremely important to the BBC, pulling in an average of more than ten million viewers each week. It had won a clutch of awards by now too, including Best TV Reality Programme at the TRIC awards and Best Reality Competition Show at the National Reality TV Awards. It was also named the highest rating entertainment series of the year in 2012. Clearly, a show of Strictly's calibre could attract the best production talent in the industry and we were excited to see what Louise Rainbow would bring to the table.

Just before the 2013 series started, with Louise installed at the helm, James and I took part in a P&O cruise organised by BBC Worldwide. This meant putting on a show at sea and doing meet and greets and Q&A sessions for guests on the cruise, which was going around the Med and the Canaries.

The cruise was fun and I was enjoying myself, and after the show in the evenings it was always nice to wind down in the bar with some of the other dancers and members of the production team. Craig Revel Horwood and Darcey Bussell were there, and one night I found myself in the bar with both of them, plus two representatives from BBC Worldwide and some other dancers and producers. James had decided to go to the ship's casino, and he'd told me he'd meet me in the bar later.

'Have a good time!' I smiled.

Things were fine with Craig by now; the run-ins James and I had had with him were in the past as far as I was concerned, and this trip was going really well.

However, by the time James arrived at the bar later on that evening

Craig had had a lot to drink, and things turned nasty. It was not unusual to see Craig in this state. He would often drink after the Saturday night Strictly show, and there would be bottles of wine waiting for him on a reserved table.

First of all he started slagging off one of the long-serving pro girls. What he had to say was so vile I would never repeat it, and then he turned his attention to Arlene Phillips.

'She was shit at her job and that's why she went,' he said. 'It had nothing to do with ageism.'

Darcey tried to shut him up diplomatically.

'I do hope that when I leave the show you won't speak about me like this,' she said, but Craig carried on regardless.

Len Goodman was next in his firing line.

'So he's written another book? Who wants to hear about him? He's a boring old man.'

He still hadn't finished, and next he got started on Brendan Cole. By that point James had had enough and was ready to blow.

'Craig,' he said. 'I don't appreciate you talking about my friends like this. It's not right, and there are other people here.'

It was an intimate bar and besides our party there were various members of the P&O entertainments team enjoying a quiet drink. They could all hear what was being said and it was very embarrassing.

'Who are you, James?' Craig retorted loudly. 'You were nothing before Strictly. You're a no-one!'

'I'm a no-one? You were just a backing dancer for Arlene Phillips before Strictly,' James snapped back. 'But you know what you are now Craig?'

James then used a very rude word to describe Craig before saying to me 'Ola, I think it's time to leave. He's drunk.' We both left the bar, leaving Darcey and the rest of the party open-mouthed. I was pleased James had stuck up for our friends but I was also very upset this had happened, and that the night had been ruined in such an awful way, in front of other people too.

Thankfully, we finished the trip without incident but back in London James was called to a meeting with Louise Rainbow and two other senior BBC executives.

'We understand there was an altercation on the P&O cruise and you behaved in an unacceptable manner, James,' Louise said.

'Has Craig been called in too?' James asked.

'No.'

'Well I think you need to talk to him because I was only responding to what he was saying.'

James was asked if he'd used a rude term to describe Craig.

'Yes I did,' James said.

There was a momentary pause before James made it clear he had no regrets because of Craig's 'vile' behaviour.

'He was slagging off my friends in front of strangers. He's meant to be a Strictly representative but he was drunk and he was a total disgrace and what he was saying was nasty and vicious.'

James was asked if he felt he could move forward and work with Craig again.

'Yes. All he does is judge me on the live shows. I don't have anything to do with him the rest of the time.'

James made it clear that he thought it was very unfair they were not calling Craig in, but it seemed that was the end of the meeting.

I felt uneasy when James reported all this to me. I was concerned about how it would affect both of us on the show, though I really admired him for sticking to his principles. James would not be James if he hid his feelings and didn't speak the truth, so I took a deep breath and hoped for the best.

When we got started on the 2013 series in the August, Louise Rainbow introduced a lot of changes, very quickly. I really wasn't optimistic about how this was all going to pan out, especially for James.

I was partnered with the Hollyoaks actor Ashley Taylor Dawson this time. I was over the moon about this and I'd been secretly hoping I'd be partnered with him. In my opinion Ashley was the best boy out of the bunch in terms of his dancing potential, and he was young and good-looking too.

James was with Vanessa Feltz. She was not a prime contender to lift the glitterball trophy, and James wondered if this was a deliberate slap down from the bosses, as the likelihood was he wouldn't last too long in the competition.

That was not the only thing on both our minds.

Traditionally, we had a lot of say in our outfit and song choices, but suddenly it was very different. I was told I was not allowed to wear a catsuit, which had become my trademark, even though other dancers were allowed to. Instead of working with the costume department to come up with ideas together, as all the dancers normally did, now we were just being told what to wear by the producers, without discussion. All the dancers would be given their clothes on the Friday after rehearsals and if you hated the costume there was virtually nothing you could do about it, as it was too late to change. James and I both thought about the problem we'd had on our very first series, when I was initially given the yellow and green dress I didn't like. The producers had ended up being very helpful and let me design my own dress back then, but this was different.

'It looks like we're going to have no input at all this year in what we wear,' James said.

It was an order from above that we had to comply with, so that was the end of it; there would be no chance for negotiation this time.

'I don't understand it,' James complained. 'All the pro dancers know what suits them and what is going to work well in a routine. Why are they doing this?'

'I have no idea,' I said, bemused. 'It doesn't make sense to me.'

James did have a theory about my catsuits. He suspected the bosses thought they were too sexy and this gave me an unfair advantage, as I always made a big impact whenever I wore one. There would be headlines in the press and I'd receive a lot of comments, and people would be tweeting me, asking when I was going to wear one again.

I didn't see the problem. Surely if people liked to see me in the catsuits and they suited me I should be allowed to wear them? They made me feel special and I loved wearing them, so I really didn't see what the issue was.

I wasn't only confused, I felt like my creativity was being suppressed. To my mind the finished performance would be so much better if the dancers had an input into all the different elements, including their outfits.

When it came to the music, we started to find that putting up good ideas for songs to accompany particular dances was counterproductive. The same went for ideas about concepts for our routines, such as whether to have certain props on stage. We found the producers would knock back our ideas, sometimes blaming the budget, but often simply saying they didn't like the idea. This was usually a personal opinion, from one person, and we couldn't understand how this was dictating our whole performance.

We tried to accept this at first, but then we started to find that our suggestions were being given to other dancers who we suspected the producers favoured. It clearly wasn't a budget issue at all.

It was very frustrating and annoying because all James and I were trying to do was put on the best performances we could, and we couldn't see how having this control taken off us would improve the enjoyment of the show for the people who mattered most – the audience and viewers.

'What is going on?' James said, 'It has to be all about control, doesn't it? All the control is being taken away from us, but why? Why try to fix something when it isn't broken? We know what we're doing; we've been doing it successfully for years.'

Though I was confused and very irritated too, I was less outspoken than James, and I was more prepared than he was to comply and see how things panned out. There had been changes through the years on Strictly that I had taken in my stride. For instance the way the VTs were made had changed completely since we joined the show. I was filmed for eight hours a day in training with the partners I had in the early days, like Spoony, Kenny Logan, Andrew Castle and Chris Hollins. The resulting VT was a natural, edited version of what had happened in training, showing the progress made, and how we'd got to know each other and perfected the steps. Now the film crew was only with us for a couple of hours. They told us what they wanted us to say and edited the footage heavily, often in a gimmicky way, using props and graphics to spice things up. I'd accepted that without argument, but the changes that were taking place now were far more drastic and I was very worried about where this was going.

Luckily, one big plus for me this year was that Ashley was a great guy, really open and friendly, and he had a great sense of humour. He didn't take himself too seriously and was a mickey-taker, like James.

'My girlfriend was glad I was partnered with you because you're married,' he laughed the first time we met.

'Oh God, I can't believe that is even an issue!'

Unfortunately, after various dancers had been rumoured to have flings with their celebrity partners, it seemed the pro dancers had all been tarred with the same brush. Partners and spouses of celebs were becoming more and more anxious about what might happen between dancing partners on Strictly, and I'd heard on the grapevine that it was becoming more difficult to find male celebs for the show, as their wives didn't want them to go on.

James and I were about to celebrate our tenth wedding anniversary, and I told Ashley this, joking that this should put his girlfriend's mind at rest. She was pregnant, and I didn't want her to have a single second of worry.

'Your girlfriend does not have to worry about a thing,' I laughed. 'James might have a reputation as a Strictly 'bad boy', but I love him to bits and I'm very happy to be Mrs Jordan!'

'Wow – congratulations on ten years!' Ashley smiled. 'That's an achievement!' This was one of many positive responses I got when people heard about our wedding anniversary, although Zoe Ball did cheekily say to me on air: 'Ten years with James Jordan? How on earth have you managed that Ola?!' James and Zoe got on really well; she knew what James was like and they always had great banter.

By coincidence, it turned out that our actual wedding anniversary, 12th October, fell on 'love week' on Strictly. To this day I have no idea if the bosses realised this, but I suspect they may have, because they made the night very special and used our anniversary to great effect. James and I played a bride and groom in one of the group numbers. It was amazing, and we even got to splatter custard pies in Craig's face, as he played the priest. Afterwards, in Tess's room, James and I were presented with a fantastic cake. It was a lovely gesture and came as a complete surprise, and we both really appreciated it. We were very proud to have been married for ten years but we didn't for one minute expect to share our special anniversary with millions of TV viewers! It's a moment we won't forget.

For my training with Ashley I had to travel to Liverpool, where he was in the middle of filming a big storyline for Hollyoaks. His schedule was really demanding and he was on set until 8 p.m. every night, which meant we had to train from 8.30 p.m. until midnight or sometimes 1 a.m. to fit the hours in.

It was exhausting for Ashley, and it wasn't ideal for me either. I was on my own all day in a city where I knew nobody, plus the studio was in a red light district. When Ashley and I came out at midnight there were often prostitutes on the pavement, which I really didn't like to see. The BBC provided taxis for me this time, as I was outside of the M25 area, but they often didn't turn up. Ashley always had his own car as he drove straight from Hollyoaks and on many occasions he ended up taking me back to my hotel, which was out of his way. He was a real gentleman and would never have left me on my own, and he never complained about driving me. Even so, I felt bad about this. I wasn't Ashley's responsibility and the last thing he needed was to be worrying about me at the end of such a long day. I complained to the producers and asked them to provide me with some more reliable transport, but nothing came of it.

Another problem that came up during this series was that the producers changed the way the pro dances were done. Up until 2009, the pros just used to work out the routines together. It took a few hours and was fun, but the system was changed and now we had to do a whole month of rehearsals before we met our celebs. It seemed a bit over the top to have so much rehearsal time when we'd managed with much less in the past, but it did work and it was fun. There was always a strong sense of camaraderie amongst dancers like James and me, Vincent, Flavia, Brendan, Ian Waite, Camilla Dallerup and Matthew and Nicole Cutler. We'd all take it in turns to work out the choreography together and there'd often be shouting and screaming as dancers argued over steps. But it was done in a high-energy, passionate way and above all it was fun, and the studio would often be filled with laughter.

'Learn your steps!' you'd hear regularly as we crashed into each other. 'I told you you're heavy!' was another frequent comment if anyone struggled with a lift or got dropped. Brendan was one of the most notorious for dropping partners, but even if it was the girl's fault and she let go by accident, as Katya did in one particular lift, we all still teased Brendan, just for the fun of it. It was hard work but at the end of the day we always had a great laugh.

Now the BBC brought in choreographers to do the pro dances, and it wasn't so much fun.

'Dance full out! More energy!' they'd scold.

'It's like being at school,' James would whisper to Brendan, and they'd snigger like naughty boys at the back of the class. It was impossible to dance 'full out' for eight hours in rehearsals and we'd have to explain to the choreographers that we'd do that when we were actually on the show, but we couldn't work flat out at that level for so many hours.

A lot of the dancers were feeling riled and unappreciated, and it didn't make for the best environment in which to practise. It was such a shame to have bad feelings like this in the air, and it felt like a step backwards for the show. Looking back, it seems like I had one complaint after another during this series, but unfortunately this was the way it was. I hadn't changed but the show had, and it was tough trying to cope with so many issues I hadn't had to deal with before.

Towards the end of October we were told we were going to be doing a hip-hop number for a group dance on the Halloween show. All the pros gathered in the studio at Elstree early on a Monday to learn the dance, after which we'd all go off and train with our celebs. As soon as the rehearsal started I felt uncomfortable with the choreography. As well as doing this complicated hip-hop routine we had to hold ourselves like puppets. I really didn't like it. I tried my best but I felt stupid and I was struggling with the steps as I wasn't used to doing hip-hop. James wasn't finding it easy either and questioned the choreography, and some of the professional dancers were unhappy too. Arguments started breaking out.

'I'm struggling here!' James said. 'Can't we change the step?'

'No,' some of the other dancers said. 'We think you should leave it.'

It was mostly the newer dancers who wanted to leave it and carry on; I guess they either had more experience of hip-hop or were just more eager than we were to please the producers, as they were newer to the show.

Karen Hauer was one of the dancers who disagreed with James, as was her boyfriend, now husband, Kevin Clifton.

'Why don't you just do it?' Karen snapped at James aggressively. Kevin got stuck in and shouted and screamed at James, telling him to stop complaining and do the dance.

The heat was clearly rising in the studio and so James sensibly took himself outside for a break to calm down. I stayed in position and tried to carry on but there were still a lot of arguments going on. I admitted I was finding the routine a real struggle and that I agreed with James and thought we should change the step so we would all be happy.

'Why don't you just get on with it?' Karen then shouted directly at me. Kevin shouted at me too, and they both just started going mental. I was taken aback, and all of a sudden Karen was right in my face, shouting at me and waving her arms. The way she was carrying on reminded me of some kind of gangster having an argument in a New York ghetto. It was completely over the top and I could feel my pulse racing with nerves.

'Let's talk about it,' I stuttered, but Karen was not listening and just kept going on about how I should just shut up and do the routine.

'Karen, let's talk.'

'No!'

'Then what? What are you going to do?'

'I'll fuck you up,' she screamed in my face.

Karen was inches from me and I thought she was going to hit me. Pasha Kovalev and Artem Chigvintsev rushed forward and pulled Karen away. I tried to compose myself but it was no good. Two minutes later I ran out of the studio and burst into tears, and then Pasha and Artem ran out to find James.

'Who was in the wrong?' was one of the first questions James asked, after making sure I was OK.

'Ola did nothing wrong,' they replied.

James saw red and charged back to the studio. Karen had gone but he saw Kevin and gave him a piece of his mind. Meanwhile I ran to find a producer, but Karen had beaten me to it and was already talking to a junior producer in the corridor.

'Why is she allowed to do this?' I asked. 'How can she behave like this?'

'Fuck off, you're a shit dancer,' Karen spat at me. 'That's why they put you at the back. You're shit!'

The producer consoled me and tried to diffuse the situation, but I was shaking and feeling very upset. I couldn't believe what had just happened and I wanted to get as far away from Karen as possible. The pro rehearsals all stopped that morning and so I quickly left the studio and headed to Liverpool to train with Ashley. I was glad to get away.

Louise Rainbow called me and said 'I'm so sorry'. Nearly all of the other dancers had described how it had been an unprovoked attack.

'It's unacceptable,' I said.

Karen was told to ring me and apologise but I wasn't ready to speak to her, though I agreed to go to a meeting with Karen and the producers when I was back in London on the Friday. I was dreading it all week but I knew I had to be there. This had been a really bad experience and was very upsetting, and I needed to draw a line under it.

Karen was calm and she did apologise. That was supposedly the end of the matter and I wished it was, but deep down I couldn't forget how she made me feel. Also, I wasn't sure the BBC bosses understood how awful it had been for me, as I felt Karen was let off very lightly, simply having to say she was sorry for her behaviour. Unbelievably, James was also called to a meeting and was told off for shouting at Kevin; it was almost like he got into as much trouble as Karen, which really did not seem fair at all. In hindsight, this was another nail in the coffin for James's career on Strictly. He was really fed up about that and felt not just unsupported, but picked on.

I wanted to put this behind me, but unfortunately the story was leaked to the press and there were headlines written about the fact Karen had 'bullied' me. I was angry and upset on so many levels. The facts of the story weren't all there, I didn't like the word 'bullying' as this had been a one-off attack, and I was also annoyed the press office hadn't managed to keep this out of the public domain. The only reason I'm talking about it now is because I want to explain the truthful version of events. It's not fair that people are selling stories about Strictly dancers, and it adds insult to injury when only half the story is told.

As a result of the media coverage Karen got a lot of abuse online, with people calling her a bully. They were effectively bullying her, and I didn't like it. In the end I stuck up for her on Twitter, telling people to stop sending her nasty tweets and accusing her of bullying. I made it clear that Karen had apologised and we had moved on. This was true. It took a bit of time, but Karen and I did patch things up and we are fine now. This wasn't quite the end of the story, though, because when I eventually left Strictly I had to speak out again about Karen. People suggested I was leaving because of Karen's bullying, and I had to point out this was utter nonsense. She had not bullied me, and the way she behaved towards me that day had nothing to do with my decision to quit.

James and Vanessa Feltz were the second couple to be eliminated on this series. James had a theory that he'd been partnered with Vanessa as the producers thought they'd create drama, tantrums and fireworks together, as Vanessa was as strong-minded and self-assured as James. This didn't happen, but Vanessa was very straight-talking.

'You don't need to kiss my arse darling,' she told one of he producers at the start. 'I've had all that for years!'

James admired the fact that Vanessa was outspoken, and they got on very well and seemed to understand each other. Vanessa was a savvy, clever woman, and James discovered she was also very sweet when you got to know her.

At one point during rehearsals a producer came on to the dance floor on set and asked Vanessa to take hold of her dress and swish it about as she danced. This irritated James and Vanessa.

'Get off the dance floor!' James said, 'and please don't interrupt and tell Vanessa what to do with her dancing.'

Vanessa supported James wholeheartedly.

'I only listen to James when it comes to dancing,' she said firmly. That told the producer, who was forced to leave the floor.

'Vanessa's a lovely woman but I wouldn't like to be on the bad side of her!' James told me afterwards.

Once he was out of the competition James decided to come up to Liverpool. I had nothing to do all day and so James could keep me company, and in the evening he could come to the studio with me. Not only could he help out as I trained Ashley, but having him there would solve the problem of me being on my own in a rough part of the city late at night when training ended.

It was common practice for dancers to help one another out once they had been eliminated and had free time. On many occasions Vincent helped Flavia, Anton would help Erin, Matthew and Nicole frequently helped each other out and so did Robin and Kristina. Similarly, Karen

Hauer sometimes had help from her now husband Kevin Clifton, even before he was on the show.

None of this was a secret; we all mucked in when we could, because why wouldn't we? As professional dancers we all wanted to strive for the best performances we could, to make the show better for the viewers.

Unfortunately, Louise Rainbow found out that James was in Liverpool with Ashley and me and she was very unhappy about it.

'I understand you're in Ola's training room,' she said sharply, calling James on his mobile.

'Yes I am. Is there an issue with that?'

Louise said there was an issue, and James had to leave.

'No, I'm not leaving. Ola is on her own in Liverpool and I'm going to help her.' James pointed out the long history of Strictly pro dancers helping each other out. He also reminded Louise that I was alone in a red light area of the city and that he wanted to look after me, particularly as I'd had problems with my taxis not turning up when I finished work at midnight and 1 a.m. Louise was having none of it, and she was getting more and more annoyed.

'I'm the executive producer and I'm telling you that you can't help Ola,' she said.

'I don't care who you are,' he retorted. 'I'm not leaving the studio. I'm staying here to help my wife in training and to protect her when she comes out of work, and you can't stop me.'

He switched his phone off.

'Oh my God!' I said as I heard the conversation unfold. 'James, you've got some balls!'

'I don't care, Ola. I've had enough, I really have. It's like working under a dictatorship. I want out!'

James had been talking about leaving the show for weeks and weeks now as more changes came in.

'It's not the same,' he'd said many times during this series. 'I'm not happy. I feel like the bosses just want us to be puppets and that's not my style. I'm stifled.'

Until now I hadn't been convinced that James was serious about leaving Strictly, or whether he was just letting off steam. Now, though, I could tell he really had reached breaking point. To make matters worse, we were also told that from now on all the dancers were going to have someone come into the studio to check out the choreography we put together.

'It is to help you and your celeb partner,' is how the bosses explained this to us.

I was really confused. Why couldn't I have James in my training room? He was an amazing teacher. Why was someone else coming in?

James shared my concerns. 'It doesn't make sense and it's undermining!' he said. 'We've been doing this for years. We don't need people to tell us what to do! We're professional dancers.'

'If I was going to choose who to help me I'd pick you James,' I said. 'What on earth is going on? Don't they trust us?'

In the event a choreographer did travel from London to work with me for an hour every now and then. I'd just listen and go along with what he said then do my own thing anyway. If James was there he'd say to Ashley afterwards: 'Forget everything he said, just listen to Ola.'

'I've told you, Ola, the show isn't the same,' James said to me privately. 'We're being dictated to. First the costumes, then the music and now all this interference. I just can't work like this, it's a joke! I've done eight years and the first seven were brilliant. Now it's just not the same at all and I can't see it getting better. I'd rather quit while I'm at the top of my game.'

'Quit, really?'

'Yes, really. I want to quit.'

James was adamant.

I listened and I told James that I would support him whatever his decision, even though I didn't feel exactly the same way as him. Yes, I was unhappy with the way the outfits and music were being chosen for us, and no, I didn't like the whole 'one rule for the celebs, another for the dancers' mentality, because I found it unnecessary and demoralising. As for having my choreography checked up on, that was an insult in my eyes.

My personality is so different to James's, though. My natural instinct was, and still is, to comply and try to avoid conflict. Even though I didn't agree with the new way of working, I hoped I could learn to deal with it, because ultimately I still loved being on the show and didn't want to leave. Strictly was glamorous and exciting, but most of all I loved dancing every day. Even after all these years, dancing was still my great passion in life. I always enjoyed meeting a new partner and going through their dancing 'journey' with them. The live shows were the icing on the cake. Even though they were nerve-racking I loved them and I couldn't imagine life without Strictly, not yet. It was a dream job for me, and so I was prepared to take the rough with the smooth and see how it went.

I wasn't worried at all about James if he quit. Strictly was only one part of our working lives, taking up less than half the year. We would still do our corporate events and private lessons together when we weren't doing Strictly, and he could take up offers of other TV work that regularly came in, which he had been wanting to do more of for a long time.

All of these thoughts were in our heads when, two days after the row with Louise Rainbow, James received an email from one of the Strictly bosses. She wanted to see James in her office, and Louise would also be there.

Just prior to this James had tweeted 'Vote for Ola' on Twitter, to show his support for me and Ashley. In the email James was told that he was not allowed to ask for votes and he was also told he was in breach of contract, for refusing to do the Christmas special. It was true that he'd turned down the forthcoming Christmas special, but he had good reason for this as he'd injured himself recently, dancing with Torvill and Dean on Children in Need. Unfortunately, James popped a facet joint in his spine as he practised lifts with Jane Torvill, so it would have been impossible for him to do the Christmas special.

'I'm still in agony,' he told the bosses when they met. 'I'm not physically fit enough to do it, so how can I be in breach of contract?'

They said they didn't know that and apologised.

'I have mentioned it before and I've got pictures of myself in a neck brace. I'm surprised you didn't realise I wasn't fit.'

James was very annoyed. He also argued the rule about asking for votes only applied to asking for votes for yourself.

'I tweeted for people to vote for Ola!' he said indignantly when this point was raised. 'My contract only says I can't ask for votes for myself so why are you bringing this up?'

There didn't seem to be an answer and they moved on to the issue of James helping me and Ashley in training.

'You know pros always help each other out so why are you picking on me? I know for a fact that several of the other pros have been helping each other out this year.'

There wasn't really an answer to this either and James left the meeting with a sour taste in his mouth after telling Louise Rainbow pointedly: 'Something is different this year. Something isn't working.'

James wanted to add: 'I think you want to get rid of me, Louise, and I don't think you want Ola to win this year,' but for once he held his tongue and saved this conversation for when just the two of us were together later.

Despite all of this going on behind the scenes, I was absolutely loving dancing with Ashley and we were doing well every week. He completely threw himself into rehearsals; in fact, the only thing he held back on was the spray tan, as he couldn't be too tanned when he was filming Hollyoaks. We reached the quarter-finals, but then James was given some unsettling news. He was told by another pro dancer that she had been asked to help choreograph for the final week, and the music had already been chosen. The chosen song was Here Come The Girls.

James passed this on to me and told me not to get my hopes up of getting any further in the competition.

'What do you mean?'

'Ola, this means that the celebs who make the final are going to be girls. You can't make the final with Ashley.'

There had been speculation from all the professional dancers for years about how it was possible for the judges to manipulate the positions on the leaderboard by over- and under-marking, but I didn't want to believe the final was being stitched up this far in advance in the way people were suggesting.

James was past caring by now. The gloves were off as far as he was concerned and he cheekily tweeted: 'Wouldn't it be good if we had Here Come The Girls in the final?'

Ashley and I did a really good Salsa in the quarter-final and were in a great position, near the top of the leaderboard but then there was a silly little 'swingathon' in which all the couples had to do a swing jive on the dance floor at the same time. This was billed as something that was a bit of fun, but in fact it had a massive impact on the positions on the leaderboard. Only the judges had a vote, there was no input from the public, and after the swingathon, Ashley and I were dropped down to a vulnerable position and were eliminated. This would have been highly unlikely without the swingathon.

'Told you,' James said.

I frowned. I still didn't want to believe the show I'd loved and been a part of for all these years had suddenly changed and was now being run the way James thought it was, but he was absolutely convinced the scoreboard was being massaged to suit the results the bosses wanted.

'It's not a swingathon, it's a fixathon,' James said to me. This was something a lot of people were talking about backstage and on Twitter, and on a popular Strictly forum on the internet.

James had a theory about the way judges tied the scores. If, for example, three dancers were tied at the top of the leaderboard and two dancers tied in the middle, this effectively meant that either couple in the middle could leap up the leaderboard after the public vote, avoiding the risk of elimination. James said it was a way of keeping a couple the bosses didn't want to lose off the bottom position, where they were in much more danger, and vice versa.

'You have no proof,' I said, although I had to admit his theory did sound feasible, especially after what happened to me and Ashley in the swingathon.

If Here Come The Girls really had been the original song choice for the 2013 final, it was changed, possibly due to James's tweet. However, as James predicted, it really was an all-girl final that year. Abbey Clancey won with Aljaz Skorjanec, who I have to say were absolutely amazing and thoroughly deserved to win.

I think the so-called fixathon had been the final straw for James and by the end of the series he'd made up his mind once and for all that he was going to leave. It was a big deal for me to take this on board, and even though I supported James one hundred per cent, part of me was worried. What would it be like doing Strictly without James? I couldn't imagine it at all and I wasn't sure if I wanted to stay without him. I had a big decision to make.

29

'If it's going to be the same as last year, please don't ask me back, as I'm not interested.'

James had gone in for another meeting with Louise Rainbow, in March 2014. This was a few months before it was announced which dancers would be returning for the next series. It was a meeting we had every year around this time, when we'd typically be asked what we thought of the last series and whether we'd like to return, if we were asked back when the final decisions were made on the pro dancers in June.

James was well aware of the consequences of his bold statement because he had a very good idea that the show would be run the same way as it was the year before, and that Louise would not be changing the way she ran Strictly.

'The last series simply wasn't the same,' James explained. 'I felt like you wanted me to be a puppet, and I can't work like that. I didn't enjoy it.'

He'd basically given Louise Rainbow an ultimatum: if you don't change the way things are done, please count me out.

When it was my turn to have this meeting with the bosses I said I'd like to come back, although I made it clear I shared some of James's reservations and I hadn't completely made my mind up yet.

We both went away, did some corporate events and lessons, had a relaxing holiday in the sun and enjoyed spending time with our families and friends like we normally did at this time of year. By now James's sister Kelly had three children – Lewis, Sophie and Rose – and my sister Monika had two daughters – Dominika, who I used to babysit for back in Poland, and Antosia. James and I got on well with our sisters' husbands and we all enjoyed getting together and chilling out whenever we could.

The phone calls from Strictly came in the June.

Louise told James that she could potentially offer him the chance to do a weekly slot on It Takes Two, the Children In Need special plus the Strictly Christmas Special, rather than giving him a role as a full-time pro dancer.

James asked what he would be paid for this, if he wasn't hired as a pro dancer for the full series, but Louise didn't give him an answer. It seemed the offer was informal, and there was no actual money on the table at this stage.

'Effectively, you're offering me nothing,' James concluded. 'If there is no offer in writing and no firm offer of money then you are not offering me a job at all. Really, you are sacking me.'

Louise said this would not be a sacking, it would merely be a reduction of his role on Strictly. The conversation more or less ended there, with James making it clear he was not happy with this flaky situation.

'Oh well, we both saw that coming,' I said when he put the phone down.

We had seen this coming after his meeting in March, but nevertheless it still came as a bit of a shock and I didn't find it easy to just accept this. It was a massive deal, and I was concerned for James.

'Ola, I forced their hand,' he said. 'Don't worry. It's what I wanted and it's time for me to go. I'm not at all surprised this has happened, and it's what I wanted if the show is staying the same, which it obviously is.'

Ten minutes later my phone rang.

'Ola, we would love you to come back,' Louise said.

'No thank you,' I found myself blurting out. This was my gut reaction. I felt emotional and my loyalties were with my husband. 'I'm not coming back without James. We started the show together and we'll finish the show together.'

Louise sounded disappointed and a little surprised.

'If you change your mind give us a call,' she said.

I put the phone down and looked at James.

'Ola, why did you say no?' he said. 'You should do it.'

We'd already had conversations about this scenario and James had told me several times that he thought I should carry on without him. I thought he was right, but when it came to the crunch I'd followed my heart not my head, and I'd instinctively said no.

'I want to be loyal to you,' I replied. 'How can I do Strictly without you?'

James was touched by my support, but he didn't think I'd made the right decision.

'Babe,' he said, 'I think you should do it. Call Louise back and tell her you'll do it.'

'No.'

'Why not?'

'Because of you.'

'Forget about me. I wanted to go but you don't want to go, do you Ola?'

'Well, not really.'

'Exactly! You wouldn't have considered saying no if I was going back, would you?'

'No, but you're not going back James. Things are different, and I'm really not sure if I want to go back without you.'

'Ola, do you want to do another series or not?'

'Well, yes, I'd like to carry on for a bit longer, at least another year or maybe two…'

'Then do it! Call Louise right back and tell her you'd love to do it.'

I did, there and then, and as soon as I made the call it felt like the right decision. Louise was pleased and I was too, though I felt nervous, imagining how it would be going to work without James. We had always known that Strictly wasn't forever. Every year I'd thought this could be the last year. I had always told myself that if I wasn't invited back I wouldn't be upset; instead I'd be very grateful and appreciative for the great years Strictly had given me, because it really had been a blast. I wasn't prepared for just one of us leaving, though. This was strange and I felt like I was about to enter the unknown. I really wasn't sure if I was going to enjoy it in the same way without James there supporting me, as he always had done.

The BBC asked us if we would keep quiet about James's departure as a full-time pro dancer until after they had made the official announcement, and we agreed to this. However, when the news came out James was not happy at all, as the statement simply said James was offered a reduced role on the show but declined it.

'I was sacked!' he shouted, 'they didn't offer me anything!' In time he went public with this, as he wanted to set the record straight. The papers were already speculating that he'd been 'axed', as they described it, and James wanted people to know the full truth.

'I forced the BBC's hand,' he admitted, 'but the truth is I was sacked. I was not invited back to do the job I had been doing for eight years, and in my book that means I was sacked. This 'reduced role' business is a smokescreen. I believe the BBC didn't want to be seen to be sacking me, but that is effectively what they did.'

I felt uncomfortable about the negative publicity and the fact James's departure had caused all this fuss and bad feeling, and I really agonised over whether I'd done the right thing in agreeing to go back. It was too late now, though. I'd signed up for the next series, and James was supporting me all the way. He had other irons in the fire, and he urged me to go ahead and make the most of the next series.

'You can only regret what you don't do, Ola,' he said. 'Give it a go. If it doesn't work out then you don't have to sign for the next series.'

James was invited to appear on Celebrity Big Brother, in August 2014, and he had no hesitation in saying yes.

'Are you mad?' I joked, as it would be my idea of hell.

'Ola, you know me, and I know what my traits are. I know I can't hold my tongue and I know if anyone annoys me I won't hold back. People will either love or hate me, but I think once people get to see the real me they'll like my honesty.'

I raised my eyebrows, but I did have to admit that Big Brother was right up James's street. He had a thick skin on top of all this, and he was prepared to laugh at himself. He'd proved this a few months earlier, when a photographer snatched a picture of him outside our house, shirtless and putting a pizza box in the bin outside on a Sunday morning.

'PAUNCHING above his weight,' the headline mocked. 'Dancer

James Jordan reveals a rounder physique after easing off his Strictly exercise regime.'

James's reaction was to make the unflattering picture his profile picture on Twitter.

'You'll be good on Big Brother,' I conceded, 'and I'll get a break from you too, so it's a win-win situation...'

James knew I was joking. I didn't relish the prospect of us spending up to thirty days apart with him locked away in the Big Brother house, but I fully supported him. Over the years we'd done a few TV shows together besides Strictly, including a celebrity version of Total Wipeout, a one-off show called Dancing on Wheels and All Star Mr & Mrs, which we won, raising £30,000 for a children's charity. We always had fun taking part on different shows like that, and James especially loved trying his hand at new stuff on TV. He presented a behind-the-scenes segment for Strictly from the Tower Ballroom in Blackpool the year I won with Chris Hollins and was in his element, and now he was exploring all sorts of other options on TV.

James went into the Big Brother house a few weeks before I started working again on Strictly. This year I was to be partnered with Steve Backshall, the wildlife presenter, which I was happy about. The only thing was that James and I had always shared the excitement of finding out which celeb we'd been partnered with. This year there was none of that and it wasn't the same at all. In fact, it was so odd that it felt like half of me had left Strictly, not having James with me every step of the way.

It didn't help that James was not only missing the usual build-up of excitement, but he was away from me completely, locked in the Big Brother house. Our lives had changed so much, and it all seemed to happen very quickly. I missed James a lot and I'd sit on my own feeling lonely, watching him on TV and wondering what would happen in the house night after night. I found it quite fascinating to see how the show unfolded. How James had relished the chance of taking part was beyond me; I was out of my comfort zone just watching him.

I can remember cringing on the sofa one night, hiding behind a cushion and drinking a glass of wine, when James suddenly came out with the line: 'I'm the Brad Pitt of the dance world.'

'Oh my God, why would he say that?' I spluttered.

Afterwards I panicked to James's parents on the phone about how he was coming across, because I was worried he might be making a big mistake.

'What are you worried about? We think it's brilliant!' they replied. 'He's doing really well and we think he's very funny!'

I went on Twitter to say that James was joking about being the Brad Pitt of the dance world, because I knew not everyone watching would get his sense of humour. The line was already out there now, though, and of course James was subsequently mocked something rotten. When word spread I was inevitably teased about it too, so I started to take the mickey out of myself first, saying to people 'Just call me Angelina.'

I feared what else James was going to do or say and each night I'd watch with my heart in my mouth. I gasped when he commented that all the dancers on Strictly were a bit 'beige' except him and Anton Du Beke, not least because I knew James didn't believe this for one minute and was very good friends with Brendan, Artem, Vincent, Pasha and several others. On top of this, I'd have to go and face them all at work the next morning – I couldn't believe it!

There was a drama very early on when James was accused of bullying the Lethal Weapon actor Gary Busey, who had speculated about James being gay because he wasn't afraid to camp it up. It got very heated on air and there was a backlash in the press. Ashley Taylor Dawson was glued to the show and called me to see if I was alright, along with many of James's friends, which I really appreciated.

'I'm fine,' I told them. 'You know James. I don't know why he does it to himself, but I know he can handle it.'

One night James commented that when Sir Bruce – as he now was, after being knighted in 2011 – stepped down as the main host of Strictly he should have been replaced by a man instead of Claudia Winkleman.

'But you love Claudia!' I was shouting at the TV. 'Oh my God James, why?' I was cringing all over again.

James is a huge fan of Claudia, and I think she had a bit of a soft spot for him. 'It's James Jordan!' she'd shout when she saw him, and he loved her kooky ways.

'I'm absolutely shitting myself,' she always said before we went live on air.

'Not as much as me,' James would quip, and they'd both laugh together.

Claudia would often ease everybody's nerves by doing something silly, like pretending to adjust her boobs in the split second before the camera was on her.

We all loved her and were delighted she'd taken over as the main host earlier that year. I knew James's comments must have been taken out of context and could come across all wrong, but what would viewers make of it? I dreaded to think.

Some of the other dancers talked to me about James being on Big Brother, but others didn't. In fact, some never mentioned his name again after he left Strictly. I think James had hit the nail on the head. People either loved him or hated him, and I'd seen over the years how a lot of people he encountered really did not like the way he spoke his mind and was so brutally honest.

Ultimately, I wasn't sure James had done himself any favours going on Big Brother but it was too late now, and I knew there was no telling him in any case. He wears his heart on his sleeve and this can be difficult to accept when you don't know the man inside, but thankfully I did.

'I love you James!' I'd shout at the TV some nights when he was being given a hard time, and when I missed him a lot.

When I was at Strictly I was in the building right next door and I'd shout across really loudly to the Big Brother house 'I love you James!' The crew thought it was very funny and would laugh at me, but it wasn't a joke because I really hoped he would hear me.

James eventually came third in the series and was happy to get to the final, even though he said he also missed me massively after staying in the house for the best part of a month. I went to the wrap party and expected to have a fantastic time, meeting some of the housemates, but it was actually quite an eye-opening ordeal.

It was fantastic being out with James again but then the evening went rapidly downhill. James tried to introduce me to Kellie Maloney, who he had clashed with massively on the show, and unbelievably she swore at us. She'd obviously taken the whole ordeal to heart.

'It was just a game in there!' James said, but Kellie clearly didn't think so. The next minute we were surrounded by bouncers, and the producers told James and Kellie to leave it and stay apart, as it looked like things could get nasty.

I was also alarmed to learn that before going into the house James had been so nervous the producers gave him Imodium because his stomach was churning and his bowels were in a terrible state. He'd found it a very testing experience and had struggled with the extremes of temperatures they had in house, which made all his skin crack and brought him out in a rash.

He was still glad he'd taken part. 'It was a life experience,' he said. 'And, in my opinion, if you stop taking risks and opportunities like this, you might as well pack it in.'

I couldn't disagree with that. This was one of the reasons I had carried on with Strictly. Even after all these years I still got incredibly nervous and every time I prepared for a live show I asked myself 'why am I doing this?', but I knew the answer. Life is for living, and you have to push yourself to reap rewards. I still wasn't quite done with Strictly. I loved it, and even though it wasn't the same without James I was prepared to put up with the stress and nerves and the physical work to keep doing something I enjoyed very much indeed: not just dancing, but dancing for a living.

30

'I'd love to do this!' I said. 'It's a great opportunity to learn how to ski. What do you think, James?'

'It's your decision. What's the worst that could happen? You break your leg.'

'Well that wouldn't be great…'

'No, but seriously, what are the chances Ola? And even if you did break your leg it wouldn't be the end of the world. Broken legs heal pretty fast.'

I agreed with James. We were discussing the fact I'd been invited to take part in The Jump, the Channel 4 show that challenges celebs in ski jumps and other winter sports. It appealed to me and seemed like an opportunity not to be missed, and I reckoned I would be being overly cautious and pessimistic to turn it down on the grounds I might injure myself.

The initial training would start mid-December but the show wasn't filmed in Austria until the start of 2015. The timing fitted my schedule as I wasn't invited on the Strictly tour this season, and I wouldn't have done it without James in any case.

James was a good skier and had been trying to get me to learn for years but I'd never got round to it. This was another reason to take this chance. I imagined I'd love skiing and that James and I would be able to have some good ski holidays together once I got up to his level.

'I'm going to do it, I don't think I'll regret it.'

I wanted to be open and honest with Strictly about what I was planning and so I called a meeting and told my bosses that I was considering taking part in The Jump. They didn't want me to and even said they would give me a five-year contract on Strictly if I didn't sign up. I knew I didn't want to stay for another five years and I told them this. My bosses conceded it was my decision as I was not under any exclusive agreement with them, and so I went ahead and signed up for The Jump. As soon as I'd done so I told the Strictly bosses exactly what I was doing. I was looking forward to it; it would make a change to do something so different to dancing and I thought it would be great fun.

Steve Backshall and I had a good run on the dance floor and survived until week nine. He was a lovely partner and I enjoyed dancing with him, but it hadn't been the best series for me. The main reason for this was because it was reported in the national press and all over the internet that I'd bullied Steve in training, and that he'd lodged a complaint against me to the BBC. This was completely untrue and very hurtful. I was told by the press office the day before that the story was coming out, and I made it clear to them that it was not true and asked if they could do anything to stop it. The press office said they couldn't and I argued with them, because I was very disappointed about it. As had happened in the past, it seemed like they were just not protecting me as I felt they could.

When I saw Steve in the training room he told me that he had had nothing to do with the story, and that it had certainly not come from him. He could see how upset I was, and the next day he turned up with a bunch of flowers.

It was just so wrong and unnecessary that we both had to deal with this and I cried on and off for days after I read the story. One of the biggest headlines read: 'Strictly Ola is bullying me, moans Steve Backshall (who's dived with Great White sharks and poisonous snakes)'.

The newspaper article went on to claim that bosses had to give us a chaperone, and that I'd dented Steve's confidence with my 'rude and impatient' manner. I couldn't understand why such lies were being published. I knew that once a story was in the public domain people would believe it, no matter that it was untrue and even if we could prove it was lies. Other reports suggested the BBC was fed up with my popularity and was trying to turn the public against me. James was furious and ranted on Twitter about how he had heard in the past the BBC leaked stories deliberately to increase publicity for the show, even when they knew they were not true and were generally to the detriment of the pro dancers.

We didn't know for sure if this is what had happened this time, but how else had the story come out like this? Steve kept reassuring me that none of this had come from him. He didn't need to say that; I knew that he would never do such a thing.

The stress of dealing with the lies undoubtedly took its toll and spoilt our experience as we were forced to spend time addressing the false stories rather than putting all our energies into our dancing. Everything went to pot really after those allegations were printed, and two weeks later we were out of the competition, which was such a shame. Steve wasn't a brilliant dancer and he had a lot of old injuries that meant he had trouble with his feet and back, but he did a good job and worked hard. We could have gone further, I'm sure, if we hadn't received such a battering in the press. It broke us, it really did.

Unfortunately, there was another tabloid story going around too, this one focused on James. The gossip was that he was banned from coming in to the Strictly studio with me. It was true that he never did come in with me, as he chose not to once he'd left, but this got me wondering if there really was a ban in place. I started to become more vocal after James left, for the simple reason that he wasn't there to do the talking for both of us anymore and I asked Louise Rainbow directly: 'Is it true? Is James banned from coming in?'

She said he wasn't banned at all and the reports were untrue. This was a relief to know, although James still chose not to come in with me. He said he was happier watching the show on TV and didn't fancy tagging along with me after his very public departure.

I worried about James every time I went out to training and to the live shows without him, but he reassured me that he was fine. He was busy. He was writing several columns for magazines and newspapers which came on the back of his success on Big Brother, plus he was still teaching and doing personal appearances. When he had free time he had all his good friends from home around him and they'd play golf and keep him occupied. This was great as he was rarely alone, even when I was flat out on the show.

We talked from time to time about how he felt now he was no longer a part of Strictly.

'Ola, the truth is I'd have ended up really blowing up and resenting Strictly if I'd stayed any longer. I didn't want that to happen. I wanted to go out on a high. I have no regrets.'

James was proud he had stuck to his principles and not clung on when he sensed his Strictly heyday was over.

'I've had a fantastic time, but they were starting to kill my passion for the show,' I heard him say several times when friends asked him how he felt. 'I didn't want to have all of my enthusiasm crushed out of me, that would have been terrible.'

One time James did come in, to meet some of the other dancers and me at a hotel in Elstree, after a live show. We had a lovely meal and it was a good evening, though it wasn't the same as the old days, how could it be? He'd moved on.

James particularly missed the crew and I know he would have liked to have gone into the studio to see all the production staff who he'd worked with for years, but it didn't feel the right thing to do. He always got on really well with everyone in the crew: the runners, the guys on costume and props and the camera operators, plus all the great girls and guys in hair and make-up.

'It's not the same without James here!' several of the staff in make-up had said to me, and I had to agree. James had been loud and had brought a lot of fun and energy backstage. He and the crew would always have a laugh and James has great memories of the make-up room. The make-up artists were so skilled that one time, when they did James's Halloween make-up the year he was dancing with Pamela Stephenson, the producers had to tell them to tone it down.

'Why?' James asked, fake blood dripping alarmingly down his face.

'Look in the mirror! It's too scary. The viewers will be terrified!'

James had a reputation for being one of the best at getting the audience going before a show, which he didn't have to do but always enjoyed. Anton and Brendan did this too, and did it well.

After Steve and I were eliminated I still had to take part in the group pro dances and the final show of the series, when all the dancer and their celebrities were reunited. I was lucky enough to be partnered with Pasha for the pro group numbers, which was one thing I'd asked the producers for when I agreed to come back without James.

Very politely, and unbeknown to me until later, Pasha called James before the show had even started to make sure he was happy about us dancing together.

'Of course mate!' James said. 'It's so good of you to even ask, that's the sweetest thing ever!'

We both loved Pasha. Not only is he a brilliant dancer and choreographer, he is a very straightforward guy. You always knew where you stood with him on Strictly, despite the fact that he liked to keep himself to himself, and more often than not he'd be on his own when we had downtime backstage, playing video games on his phone or iPad.

On December 12th, I was due to be at the BBC's Elstree studios at 9 a.m. for rehearsals for Strictly's semi-final show. Coincidentally, I had the chance of doing a ski training session for The Jump at the nearby Snow Centre in Hemel Hempstead early that same morning. I'd only had two ski lessons so far and needed all the practice I could get, and so I decided to squeeze in a couple of hours on the artificial slope before going to Strictly. I would never have done this if I was still in the competition, but after Steve and I had been eliminated I was only taking part in group dances now, and besides I didn't think I was taking a risk.

I arranged with The Jump that I'd be at the Snow Centre between 6 a.m. and 8 a.m. This would give me plenty of time to get myself to Elstree for the dance rehearsal. I didn't tell Strictly what I was doing, because I didn't think they needed to know.

Everything started off well on the ski slope. Right from the start I enjoyed being on skis and I felt very comfortable that morning, dressed in my pink salopettes. I was even thinking I might become quite good at skiing because I had the balance as a dancer, and I was also used to wakeboarding and water skiing. I was fit too, after months of dancing with Steve, and I figured all of these things went in my favour despite the fact I was a novice.

I had to be taught all the basics and I took things slowly and listened very carefully to everything my instructor said. It was all going fine. I mastered getting on and off the little button lift that took me up the slope so I could practise a snow plough, and after about an hour I was starting to get the hang of the plough and was coming down the slope tentatively on my own. I was followed by a camera, and at 7.30 a.m, when I had made a slow descent with no problem at all and was right near the bottom of the artificial slope, something totally unexpected happened. To this day I'm not even sure what, but for some reason I lost my balance and I fell to the right side. My left ski stayed in place and my knee popped. I felt the pop and I heard the pop. I didn't immediately feel any pain, but when I tried to move my legs to get myself up I couldn't. That's when I realised something was very wrong.

'Oh my God,' I gasped.

Suddenly loads of people surrounded me. My boots were still attached to my skis. I wanted to get my feet out of my ski boots and I tried again to stand up or just move my legs, but I couldn't put weight on my left leg.

'There's something not right,' I said, feeling sick with fear. 'Why can't I feel my knee?'

A stretcher was brought over and there were TV producers, members of the crew and medics and physios milling all around. Nobody was saying anything.

'I think my kneecap has popped off,' I said at one point, as that was exactly how it felt.

'No,' one of the physios said after assessing the damage, 'I think your kneecap is fine.'

'Then what is it?'

The physio couldn't look me in the eye, and I knew in that moment this was something very serious, but he just couldn't bring himself to say it.

One of the girls on the production crew for The Jump also worked on Strictly. I'd been stretchered to a room away from the slope, and I heard her outside the window.

'What's happened?' she asked, knowing someone had taken a fall. 'Who's fallen? I hope it's not Ola.'

Then she looked through the window. 'Oh no! It can't be Ola, it just can't be Ola!'

The physio put me in a wheelchair and I called James.

'Something's happened to my leg,' I cried.

James says I sounded absolutely distraught and that he felt like he was going to have a panic attack when he heard me, though he managed to hold himself together. I explained I was being taken to hospital for an MRI scan, and I told him not to rush to the hospital. There was no point yet – I would call him as soon as there was any more news. I ended the call by asking him to call Strictly and tell them I was not going to come in that day.

'I don't know what's wrong yet, so please just tell them I'm sick.'

When we arrived at the hospital I was in a lot of pain but I managed to get out of the wheelchair and hobble into the room for my MRI scan. Afterwards the guy who did the scan said: 'I don't know how you managed to walk at all. Sit down right now. You have snapped your ACL.'

I burst into tears. From years of working in the dance world I knew exactly what an ACL was. It stands for anterior cruciate ligament and it is the tough band of tissue joining the thigh bone to the shin bone at the knee joint. It runs diagonally through the inside of the knee, to make the knee stable. Snapping it is very serious. Frighteningly, I knew you needed surgery and a long time off work, and there is no guarantee you'll make a perfect recovery. In other words, for me it was career-threatening and I may never dance again. When all this began to sink in I felt like my whole world was collapsing around me.

James's words came back to me.

'What's the worst that could happen? You break your leg,' he'd said.

I'd agreed with him and refused to be pessimistic about The Jump.

How wrong we'd been. Snapping your ACL is far worse than breaking your leg, or even breaking both legs. Bones heal much faster than a damaged ACL. This was the very worst thing that could have happened, and I couldn't stop crying and felt sick with worry. I was absolutely distraught.

My career flashed before my eyes. Oh my God, imagine if I really couldn't dance again? Imagine if my career was over, just like that, because of one stupid fall on an artificial ski slope? I thought about how I had been skiing really slowly and was almost on the flat when I fell over. It seemed unbelievable I could have done so much damage in those conditions. I had expert teachers and all the best equipment too, so how could it have gone so wrong? I had been incredibly unlucky, and now what was I going to do? What about Strictly? Oh my God, what about Strictly?

While I waited to see a doctor I Googled 'snapped ACL' and to my horror I read the recovery is generally twelve to eighteen months.

'Even if the treatment works I might not be able to dance again until 2018,' I thought, panicking even more.

After I saw the doctor I was put in a brace from my calf up to my thigh and told I'd need reconstructive surgery followed by intense physiotherapy.

'Will I be able to dance on Strictly next autumn?' was my first question. The Jump was already a busted deal – filming in Austria was due to start the following month.

The doctor paused.

'I can't guarantee that,' he said. 'It generally takes longer than eight or nine months to recover from a snapped ACL.'

I had a hard lump in my throat and a sickening knot in my stomach. There was nothing else that could be done that day and I was given painkillers and sent home in a taxi, having told James not to come and collect me as it would have taken him a good couple of hours from Kent.

I desperately wanted to call James and chat to him when I was on my way home, but the taxi driver was being really nosy and I was afraid of what might get out.

'You're Ola off Strictly, aren't you? You snapped your leg then?'

I really didn't want to speak to him and I was annoyed and fed up that I couldn't talk to James either. I had no idea who the taxi driver might talk to, and risking having this story in the press was the last thing I needed right now. I just told him I didn't feel like chatting and stayed quiet.

James threw the front door open as the car pulled up our drive. His face was a picture of shock and pity when he saw the brace and crutches I'd been given, and he dashed out to help me into the house.

'I'm sorry,' I said.

'Ola, it's not your fault. It was an accident.'

'I know but I'm so sorry.'

As well as worrying about returning to Strictly next year I'd started to think about the impact on James and all the corporate events and shows we did together. This was not only going to affect my career but his too, in a massive way.

James settled me on the sofa and fussed around me. His focus was on making me comfortable and just looking after me, which was very sweet.

'What can I do to help?' he asked as soon as he'd got me everything I needed. 'What else can I get you? Is there anything you need?'

The truth was there was really nothing he could do, except bring me food and drinks and support me when I needed to get up to hobble from one room to the next. It was frustrating for James; he said it was the very first time in our relationship when something had happened that he didn't feel he could fix it, or at least make it a lot better.

There was one important thing I needed him to do for me, and that was to let the Strictly bosses know I was not returning for the rest of the series. I was feeling really guilty about letting everyone down, especially Steve as he would have no partner for the final group dance, when all the pro dancers and their celebrities performed for the last time.

'What did they say?' I asked when James came off the phone My heart was in my mouth as I was really nervous about their reaction. The reason I'd asked James to call was because I would have been too upset and cried if I'd made the call myself.

'They said how sorry they are and they wish you a speedy recovery.'

I was relieved this call had been made and that Strictly had been so understanding; at least that was one thing off my mind for now.

I was not the best patient. I cried my eyes out for hours, and by the first evening I was a real mess. 'Just get me wine, James!' I wailed. He poured me a glass and went to put the bottle back in the fridge.

'You can leave the bottle there, where I can reach it!' I said.

I sat there watching TV with my leg propped up, drinking the wine while James made beans on toast for our dinner. He has never been a cook and this was the best meal he could come up with. I never usually ate a lot of bread as it made me bloated, and normally I'd be careful about what time I ate in the evening, and what I drank, but I just thought: 'you know what, stuff it.'

The latest dermatologist I was seeing had encouraged me to give up milk, which I didn't find difficult. It did help my skin a lot, and for the time being I decided that was the only rule I was going to stick to. What was the point in stressing about my diet at this point in time? I certainly wasn't going to be putting on a catsuit or skimpy outfit any time soon, if ever again.

Knowing that a snapped ACL is an injury that affects footballers and rugby players I canvassed opinion about where to go for my surgery from some of the sportsmen I knew, including Robbie Savage, Kenny Logan and Austin Healey. I was insured by The Jump and so I didn't have to worry about the cost, thank God. James and I would have to cancel all the bookings we had for personal appearances and so on over the coming months, so at least this was one less worry.

My sportsmen friends unanimously recommended a consultant knee surgeon called Andy Williams.

'He's the best in the business,' I was told. 'Don't go anywhere else, Ola.'

We called Andy straightaway but unfortunately he had no appointments until February. However, to my relief, I got a call the very next day saying he could see me after all. We later found out that his mum was a huge Strictly fan – perhaps that was why the slot came up? I don't know, but I was very grateful that Andy could fit me in, as I didn't know who else to ask. I cried with relief, and in fact, I cried on and off every single day for weeks. Every morning when I work up I wondered if it had all been a bad dream. Then I tried to move my leg and remembered all over again what had happened on the ski slope. It was like a recurring nightmare, and I went through this shock and upset every single morning, crying every time.

After my initial consultation with Andy he booked me in for the operation on January 6th. This was the earliest date the operation could be done, as I had to wait four weeks for the swelling in my knee to go down. The plan was that after the surgery I would have on-going physiotherapy on a daily basis.

I began to feel more optimistic now I knew what was going to happen, and I even started to get it into my head that if everything went well I could return to Strictly in August for the next series, if I was asked back of course. As usual I had no idea if I would be asked back at this stage, and before the accident I hadn't even thought about the 2015 series, but now it became very important to me. Psychologically, I needed a goal. I wanted to be asked back so I had something to aim for, something that would keep me going through the intensive physio. When I spoke about this the medical staff kept quiet. Nobody could guarantee I'd be back on my feet by August, and to be honest I think they thought I was crazy to even consider it with such a serious injury.

The operation and physio I was facing did sound absolutely terrible, and I'm not surprised at all that the medics were being careful not to get my hopes up. I learned the snapped ligament would be replaced with a graft of tissue taken from my hamstring, via three small incisions made diagonally above and below the knee. Once the new ligament was in place it would be tightened, a bit like stretching a piece of elastic, to hold my knee joint in position. After that I'd have to go up to Harley Street every single day for at least six or seven months for the intensive physio sessions. This would mean getting up at 5 a.m. to get to London, and having five hours of physio before returning to Kent.

'Let's just try and enjoy Christmas first,' I said to James, once all these plans were in place.

'You're right, but we're not very organised, are we Ola?' he replied, frowning and looking around the room.

This was an understatement. We'd done nothing at all to prepare for Christmas. Now it was just days to go and we had my mum and dad coming over. The original plan was that James and I would go to Poland for Christmas, but now everything had changed. Mum and Dad were coming to us to help me out, and my sister and her family were going to join us for Christmas dinner. Monika had actually moved to England the year before and was now living and working close to us, on Kings Hill, so at least we could all be together.

'Everyone understands why we're not organised,' I said to James. 'It'll just be good to get the family together.'

I wouldn't normally be this laid back, but when you've had a health scare I think it makes you put things in perspective. I had James, we were going to be surrounded by lots of people we loved, and I was going to get better, eventually. I didn't have the energy or the headspace to start stressing out any more than I already had. Besides, what else could possibly go wrong?

As it happened, James swung into action and did absolutely everything, from decorating the house and putting up the Christmas tree to doing all the shopping, buying gifts and wrapping everything up. I love shopping and normally took charge of the presents but I have to hand it to James, he did a brilliant job.

On top of this he was doing a really good job of looking after me. I had to sit on the sofa with my leg elevated and iced, and he was forever running out to buy more ice for my ice machine. He never once complained. He also had to help me in and out of the shower, as

I couldn't even do that for myself. The only time he pulled a face was when I accidentally overstepped the mark one day.

'James, this tea is too strong,' I said, not thinking.

I'm not surprised he took exception to that!

'Why don't you go to the gym or something?' I suggested afterwards. 'You don't have to wait on me all day long.'

He never did; he wanted to be there for me every minute, and he could not have done more for me.

31

'James? Are you alright?'

I was sitting on the sofa as usual, watching TV with my leg propped up to reduce the pain of the blood rushing through it, when James appeared in the doorway. He was clutching his stomach and looked at me as if he was about to speak, but no words came out. I could see in his eyes that he was in pain, and he very obviously needed help.

'James! What is it?' I said, pushing myself up as quickly as I could and reaching for my crutches.

It was Christmas Eve. My parents had arrived, the tree was twinkling and I was feeling Christmassy at last, thinking about the next day when we would all sit around the table together. James had organised the turkey with all the trimmings and my mum was going to help with the cooking. I was really looking forward to it, and I hoped the day would be a real tonic for James. He'd spent the best part of two weeks fetching and carrying for me, and trying to cook dinner every night.

'What's wrong with you, you've only made beans on toast!' I'd tease at the end of each day, trying to cheer him up when I could see he was tired and a bit fraught.

'Excuse me, I did beans *and* cheese on toast,' he would retort, tongue in cheek.

It wasn't a great situation, but we'd kept our sense of humour and we'd been managing, or at least I thought we had.

Seeing James in the doorway clutching his stomach like this gave me a sharp reality check. Something was badly wrong with him, and when I look back now the truth was he hadn't been completely himself ever since my injury. He'd mentioned he'd had stomach pains and that he hadn't been sleeping particularly well. I'd put it all down to the upheaval of my situation, but then again he'd stopped playing golf too.

This should have been a red flag, because it took a lot to keep James off the golf course on a day off, even in winter. When my parents arrived I told James to let them help him, so he could rest. He did, but he'd clearly been in more trouble than I realised.

'James!' I called, hauling myself up and heading towards him on my crutches.

By now James had managed to stagger across the kitchen into the open-plan lounge area at the back of the house, where I'd been sitting on the sofa. All of a sudden, without warning, he threw up on the floor.

'James! James!'

He didn't respond and looked like he was losing consciousness. I started panicking, dashing around on my crutches, grabbing my phone and calling an ambulance. James had panic in his eyes. The whites of his eyes had gone red and he seemed to be staring straight through me. My sister and brother-in-law and their two children were all in the house at this moment, as well as my parents, and they all appeared, looking on in panic.

'It hurts like hell,' James moaned, gasping and clutching his stomach. 'Oh my God, this is killing me, Ola. What the hell is wrong with me…'

It was very, very frightening and I was talking to James, trying to keep him awake while trying to stay as calm as possible. I thought about Hong Kong, and when he was ill over there. It seemed like a repeat episode, but what was it? We'd never got to the bottom of it last time. Was this the same thing?

'Ola,' he gasped once more, this time more dramatically than before. James told me at this moment he knew he was going to collapse, and suddenly he keeled over. Thankfully, my brother-in-law managed to break his fall.

I grabbed the phone and dialled 999. An ambulance came very quickly and James was rushed to Pembury Hospital, near Tunbridge Wells. I travelled in the ambulance with him, leaving my family at him. The journey was an awful experience for us both. James threw up about ten times on the way to hospital.

'Why is it green?' he stammered after he gagged and vomited.

The paramedic said he'd been sick so many times he was most probably throwing up bile.

I started to panic that maybe James really did have some serious condition that should have been diagnosed when he was ill in Hong Kong. Had the doctors missed something after all?

I looked at James clutching his stomach, his eyes glazed and rolling around his head because he was in so much pain, and I looked down at my injured leg and crutches.

'What an absolute mess,' I thought. 'How have we come to this, and on Christmas Eve too?'

'You're James and Ola from Strictly, aren't you?' someone said as we limped and hobbled into the hospital, aided by the paramedics.

The person looked quite stunned to see us like that and I'm not surprised. You really couldn't have made it up; in that moment we could not have looked less like a pair of professional dancers.

A nurse asked James to describe the level of pain he was experiencing.

'My pain threshold is high,' he panted. 'But this is not just painful – this is absolutely excruciating.'

Doctors thought James might have gallstones, as had been suspected when he had his episode in Hong Kong, and a similar barrage of testing began.

'We're going to put a camera down your throat,' a doctor told James, turning to a nurse and asking her to give him a half dose of sedation.

I knew what a horrible experience this had been for James last time, and I could see that he was terrified of having an endoscopy tube put down his throat again.

'Ah ont it awl,' James stuttered as the plastic restraint was strapped over his mouth, to hold it open ready to receive the tube.

'He wants it all,' I translated. 'Please just give him as much sedation as you can.'

James ended up staying in hospital for three days and I spent as much time as possible with him.

On Christmas Day, James's sister Kelly texted us a picture of their family Christmas dinner, sending love and best wishes and asking if there was anything she could do. Both our families were brilliant. Everybody rallied round, all taking turns to visit James over those three days and helping me out with lifts, as, of course, I couldn't drive.

As it was Christmas there was only a skeleton staff working at the hospital, which was frustrating as not much seemed to be happening.

'Where is everyone?' James moaned. 'I'm in pain. I need drugs, now!'

I can't remember if we exchanged presents in hospital; it is a blur, and in my memory it wasn't really Christmas at all. The holiday had been hijacked, and all I can remember clearly is seeing James in a hospital bed with his name written in marker pen on the white board above his pillow, and the smell of hospital food and disinfectant. He was attached to a painkilling drip while he waited for all the various blood and urine tests and scan results to come back.

Every single test came back negative, and so James was discharged with a course of strong painkillers and told to take it as easy as he could for a while.

'I don't believe it,' James said, sounding utterly dejected. 'It's exactly like last time. It's so frustrating…'

'I know,' I lamented. 'It has to be stress related, doesn't it? It's probably because of what's happened to me. What do you think? Has all the stress caught up with you?'

James conceded this was the only explanation. When he looked back he had to admit he'd been experiencing pain in his stomach for weeks before he collapsed but he played it down, because of my knee. He hoped he'd just get better, as I was getting better, but his body clearly couldn't take any more.

Despite still being on crutches and in the leg brace, now it was my turn to fetch and carry for James. Even with the painkillers he was struggling to cope and spent a lot of time in bed, writhing in agony as his stomach cramped.

'Are you trying to steal my thunder?' I teased as I hobbled around after him, 'or did you just get bored of beans and cheese on toast and thought it was my turn to cook...'

We had to laugh or we would have both cried.

On the day I was due to have my operation James woke up in total agony, but he insisted he wanted to be with me at the Cromwell Hospital in London and he drove me there. Then, as I was wheeled down to theatre, he walked alongside the trolley even though he was doubled up in pain yet again.

'You have to say goodbye now,' a member of the nursing staff said as we approached the theatre.

I started bawling my eyes out. I'd never been in for an operation before and I was really worried, but it was the look on James's face that really set me off. He looked absolutely awful; terrified and distraught.

'Go home,' I told him, 'and get yourself to hospital.'

The operation went well. I can remember waking up feeling groggy. When I pushed back into my room James was still sitting there, waiting for me.

'Are you OK?' I asked him. I could see in his eyes that he was really unwell and after a couple of hours I encouraged him to leave.

I could feel pain in my leg and I was pumping the button next to my bed that delivered morphine. I took as much as I was allowed, and reached for more the moment I was allowed to take another dose. I felt great. The bed was so comfortable and I thought morphine was the best thing ever; I'd never felt so good!

The next day a physio came to see me and asked if I could stand up and walk. She wanted me to go along the corridor and see if I could walk up and down the stairs. I couldn't, however much I tried.

'I need to lay down,' I said, exhausted by the small effort.

The physio took one look at the amount of morphine I'd be on, and later on somebody came and took it away from me. I felt wiped out, and I ended up staying in for two nights instead of one as originally planned. I think I'd possibly overdone it on the morphine, but in any case an extra day in hospital did me no harm.

Once I was home James told me that he had gone back to Pembury Hospital, as I'd told him to. He hadn't wanted to tell me this until afterwards, in case I worried, but after doing a bit of research and talking to a few people he'd got it into his head that it must be his pancreas that was causing him the trouble.

'Just take it out!' he'd said when he arrived at the hospital, once again doubled up in pain.

This time he was given a coloured liquid to drink and then given a scan of his internal organs. It didn't show up any problem, but despite this James carried on insisting: 'Please, take my pancreas. Take something, you have to take something!' He was in so much pain he had started to get very desperate.

Once again he was eventually sent home with painkillers, and so we began a horrible time of us both being at home, taking 'his and hers' painkillers and just trying to get through the days.

It was boring and very frustrating, then after about five days I started going up to Harley Street every day for my physio. As planned a car would pick me up at home at 5 a.m. each morning and take me for my treatment. It was worse than watching paint dry. I had to do the most monotonous exercises over and over again, like lifting my leg up and down very slightly and slowly, or doing exercise in a pool of water. I had to rotate my leg as if I was on a bike. I'd be doing this at 7 a.m. thinking 'Oh my God'. I was normally so active, on the go all the time, and it was incredibly hard for me to be stuck in physio like that. I'd do five hours and then had a two-hour journey home, and that was my life for the foreseeable future.

'This is a nightmare!' I complained to James.

It was draining just to do all the travelling every day, and I was struggling mentally, trying to stay positive when I just felt like screaming.

'You have to do it, Ola,' I told myself. 'This is your career. You need to get better. It'll be worth it.' I thought about Strictly, and I hoped I'd be asked back, as I really needed that goal.

James did his best to support me but he was having a difficult time too. He was still in pain, though it was subsiding little by little as I started to make slow progress too.

By February we badly needed a break and James surprised me by booking a holiday to Dubai for seven days. It was the first time we'd ever been there and we loved it; I also really appreciated the thought James put into it when he wasn't well. His pain was under control by now, but I was still on crutches.

We really relaxed and enjoyed ourselves, just sunbathing and chilling out and having the chance to chat and take stock away from hospitals and doctors and physios for a while. It felt like paradise. It was Valentine's Day while we were away, which James had deliberately planned around, and he took me for a lovely meal in a beautiful restaurant.

'Things could be so much worse,' we said to each other as we reflected on what had happened over the last few months. 'In the big scheme of things we're really very lucky.' We felt this strongly. Compared with so many other people in the world we still had incredibly charmed lives, and we kept telling ourselves that.

The only downside of going on holiday was that I put on weight. I was already more than nine stone before we went away because I'd been so immobile and my diet had gone to pot after the injury, and now I piled on several more pounds. I've had people saying to me over the years: 'Ola, I don't know why you worry about what you eat or how much you weigh – you look fantastic.'

I'd always say: 'I have to watch my weight. You'd be shocked at how big I'd be if I wasn't permanently counting calories.'

Unfortunately, now I was proving this point and my weight was creeping up and up. A couple of months after the Dubai holiday James and I attended an award ceremony in London. I wore a clinging blue maxi dress, and to my horror one of the celebrity guests came over and said she had just heard James saying he had some good news. Whatever he was talking about was certainly not what she imagined.

'Congratulations!' she said to me. 'I didn't like to say anything before…'

I had to stop her, because I suddenly realised what she was about to say.

'I'm not pregnant, I'm just fat!' I laughed.

Needless to say she was absolutely mortified.

All told I had put on a stone since my leg injury. I decided to explain myself on Twitter the next day, when people all over the internet started speculating that James and I were expecting our first child.

'BREAKING NEWS… I'm not pregnant I'm just fat,' I tweeted.

If this had happened at the start of my Strictly career I'd have been devastated. To this day I can still vividly remember the pain I felt whenever I was criticised online or in the press in those early days. People had a go at me for everything: smiling in the wrong way, picking the wrong choreography, my figure, my hair, my fake tan. It was cruel and it hurt, but by now all this 'keyboard warrior' nonsense went over my head, thank goodness.

James of course loves a bit of banter on Twitter and he got in on the act later, tweeting: 'Good to see you're not in denial babe… Don't worry about what others think & at least u can say u r with Brad Pitt!'

We laughed about it a lot, but afterwards I knew I had my work cut out. I really wanted to be able to go back to Strictly for the 2015 series if I was asked and I was determined to get fit. However, there was no way I was going to dance in skimpy dresses when I was this size.

'Pass the salad,' I said to James with a heavy heart.

'I'd better start now. This may take some time…'

I was invited in to chat to the producers in April. As usual this was an opportunity to talk about the last series and let the producers know how I felt about returning to the show once again.

I had just come off my crutches, and I decided that I was going to go to the meeting looking my best, and as if nothing had happened. It was very important to me the bosses would still consider me for the next series, and I didn't want them to have any doubts about my fitness.

I dressed in a short skirt and high heels and when I looked in the mirror at home I was pleased with what I saw. I'd spent months wearing sweat pants and flat shoes and hobbling around on crutches, but now

I finally looked like my old self again. I took time doing my hair and make-up, and when I got to Elstree I put my shoulders back and walked into Strictly looking happy, carefree and confident.

I apologised to the producers for missing the end of the last series and they were very kind about it, and was asked if I wanted to return.

'Absolutely,' I said. 'There's nothing I'd like more.'

I walked out of the meeting on my stilettos, smiling and telling the producers I looked forward to hearing from them in June, when they would have made their decisions on all the pro dancers and I would get the call about whether or not they wanted me back.

In my head I was thinking I could end the physio at the end of June, spend July in the gym, getting back to dancing, and then I'd be ready to start work on Strictly at the beginning of August. The reality was I had no guarantees this was going to be possible. As soon as I got out of the meeting that day I immediately took off the high heels and went back to my flat shoes. I was still learning to walk without crutches, let alone in heels, and my feet and legs were killing me. I'd hidden it well, though; James said I looked amazing.

I persevered with my physio, and in mid-June I got the call inviting me back to Strictly. I was delighted, and it made me more determined than ever to get back to full fitness. I didn't want to let anybody down, and I asked the physio to sign me off so I could spend the month in the gym, strengthening my legs and practising my dancing. He agreed, signing me off on 1st July, though I don't think he was optimistic about me dancing again so soon. In fact, when I looked in his eyes I reckoned he was thinking I had absolutely no chance.

I spent the whole of July going to the gym and doing exercises on my legs like squats, then tentatively dancing by myself and eventually training with James. He came with me to the gym and we danced together every day, to see what I could cope with. It wasn't great. I wanted to prove myself, but at the same time I was very scared of damaging my leg again. If it hurt, which it did with certain steps, I listened to my body and didn't push it. I was especially afraid of doing turns, and again it was a case of persevering and being patient, working on my fitness every single day.

If I had a bad day James would say to me, 'Ola, the worst case scenario is you have to pull out.'

'Don't say that! The last thing I want to do is pull out and let anybody down. I've got the be ready.'

By the start of August, thank God, I actually did feel ready to go to the pro dance rehearsals. I was not perfectly fit, but I knew I'd be able to manage if I was careful. The BBC sent me for a medical, which is a routine procedure to protect themselves, and I passed it. This was a huge relief and I felt a great sense of achievement for having got that far.

It was quite a moment walking back into the studio. There had been many times over the past eight months when I thought I may never step foot in a dance studio again, let alone the Strictly studio, so it was a day to remember.

Once again Pasha was my pro dance partner. It was really good to see him and I knew he would support me and look after me.

'You need to be careful with me,' I said quietly.

'No problem at all.'

Pasha was brilliant. I occasionally said I'd miss out a jump, just to be on the safe side, and he took this in his stride, never making a fuss and helping me as much as he could. Occasionally I felt a twinge in my knee and I'd just take a ten-minute break without anyone but Pasha knowing. I had my heart in my mouth, but the last thing I wanted to do was have my knee swelling up. I didn't want to have to put ice on it at Strictly, and Pasha completely understood this and made it as easy as possible for me.

James phoned me about four times a day, worrying and checking I was OK.

'I'm doing fine,' I said. 'I can't believe it, but I really am back on my feet. I'm getting better every day.'

It would be wrong to suggest the injury was behind me and I had completely moved on. I had moments when I reflected on what a horrible, long-winded and painful experience it had been, and despite the fact I'd physically healed I knew the injury would affect me for the rest of my life.

Even outside the dance studio I found myself being much more cautious than I was before my accident, and I have stayed that way to this day. I don't water ski or wakeboard on holiday like I used to as it just isn't worth it; I'd be too distraught if I had a set-back after all the work I put into getting fit and mobile again. In time I started to do heavier weights in the gym and use the cross-trainer, treadmill and bikes to build up the strength in my leg. I can now work really hard again, like I used to before the accident. I love doing explosive leg work, like box jumps, but nevertheless I'm always acutely aware of my injury.

One time, after doing squats, I walked out of the gym and felt something go.

'Oh my God, James!' I shrieked, grabbing his arm in the car park.

James went white.

'What is it?'

'I don't know. Oh God, I can't walk!'

He helped me to the car and thankfully the pain subsided, but it had given us both a very nasty shock. I took it as a reminder of just how careful I had to be, every single day. My legs are my career. I should have taken more care of them in the first place.

32

'James, I've got boils!' I sobbed down the phone. 'I look so bad!'

I was absolutely distraught. It was the day of the launch show for the 2015 series and I was alone in a hotel near the Strictly studio. I'd just woken up and looked in the mirror, and I couldn't believe what I was seeing. I had the worst outbreak of spots and blood-filled boiled that I'd ever had. They covered my face and were red and angry and just absolutely horrific. I'd been excited about the show the night before, even though I was nervous too, but now I was just devastated. I had no idea how I was going to get through this and I was crying so hard when I phoned James that he could hardly understand what I was saying at first.

'Ola, are you OK? Just take a deep breath and calm down. I'm sure it'll be alright.'

He was trying to soothe me but it was no good. I was in floods of tears, crying my heart out like he had never heard me before.

James desperately wished he could hold me in his arms and make everything better, but of course he couldn't. He was two hours away, and I was due at Strictly within the hour, to meet my celeb for the first time on the launch show of the new series.

It took me a while to calm down. James was very patient and kind and said all the right things about how the make-up girls and boys would work their magic and how nobody would ever know when I was in front of the camera. I took some convincing, because these spots really were far worse than anything I'd ever had to deal with before. Eventually I stopped sobbing, but it took a great deal of effort and I was biting my lip and trying not to burst into tears all over again.

'Ola, as soon as we can we'll do whatever it takes to sort this out,' James said. 'I'll start researching the best dermatologists now. This is a turning point. Trust me, this will get sorted now.'

James encouraged me to get myself to make-up as soon as I could, which I did. On the way to the studio I tried to make sense of why this had happened. I'd been eating really healthily and had lost weight steadily over the summer in preparation for the show. Despite the injury and everything I'd gone through with my recovery I actually felt really good now. I was positive about the show, and I was starting to feel more and more confident about how my leg would hold out in the series.

The make-up crew were brilliant. They didn't bat an eyelid and as James had predicted they really did work a miracle. I was so grateful to them and I knew I would look fine on camera, but my confidence had still taking a battering and I was giving myself a good talking to as I started work on the launch show that day.

'Smile. Be yourself. Don't let anybody think about your injury or your skin or anything else. Be positive! Show them you are back and better than ever!'

I was trying really hard to keep the smile on my face, but somehow I did manage to go out and do my job like I always had.

This year I was paired with the Olympic sprinter-turned-sports commentator Iwan Thomas and, for the launch show, I was wearing a little red bra top and a red skirt. There was nothing wrong with the outfit, but when I was introduced to Iwan on the show I had a bit of a wardrobe malfunction. As soon as I was announced as Iwan's partner he picked me up, threw me around his back and started doing squats with me. Being a big strapping athlete he did this effortlessly and energetically. Unfortunately, the skirt ripped, I broke a nail and, worst of all, my boobs popped out of my dress. I had to scrabble around, trying to cover myself up with my little hands, just as I had done all those years earlier when I'd fallen out of that lilac dress when I was doing the Paso Doble with James as a teenager.

I couldn't believe it. There was me worrying about my skin and now I was flashing my boobs. You really couldn't make it up.

I laughed it off on Twitter. 'This is going to be a great series,' I tweeted.

I really hoped it would be; surely things could only get better?

After the launch show I trained with Iwan for five days instead of the normal three weeks, because he had other work commitments, in Japan. I think we did very well in the circumstances. Iwan was a good guy to work with and I was optimistic we could still do well despite this limited practise. However, when he was away in Japan something awful happened which really upset me and threw us off course.

Yet another false story was leaked to the press, claiming I'd had a 'massive meltdown' and was 'ranting and raving' because I'd wanted to be paired with Peter Andre instead of with Iwan.

I was devastated when I heard about it, and I immediately texted Iwan and told him that I had no idea where the story had come from, and that he was not to believe a word of it. I was gutted by the thought he might be hurt by the story, but thankfully Iwan was very understanding and kind and tried to console me.

The damage had already been done, though, and I felt so angry and upset this had made it into print, to be read by thousands of people all over the country.

The story claimed that I'd wanted Peter Andre as my partner because I thought we could win the competition together, and it also said that I was unhappy that Iwan was based miles away and claimed that I didn't even like him. All of this was lies; in fact we got on so well in the short time we had together that we have stayed in contact to this day.

To make matters worse, Peter was dancing with Janette Manrara, who I'd become friends with on the show the year before. She's a lovely girl and a fabulous dancer, and there is no way in the world I would suggest that I had a better chance with Peter than she did. It was all utterly ridiculous. I always liked being paired with sportsmen, because of their drive and work ethic. I was hopeful Iwan could go far in the competition and in any case, whoever I was paired with, I always started off feeling optimistic and hoping for the best.

Once again I was disappointed the press office hadn't done something to stop this, and I called Louise Rainbow.

'Why is there so much negative press about me?'

'I'm so sorry, we don't know where this story has come from, although we suspect it's someone in the Strictly family.'

I felt very let down, all over again, and I couldn't understand how the bosses could do nothing to help.

'The press team knows the stories before they come out, so why can't they stop them? Can't you find out who is giving untrue stories to the press and stop it?'

There was no answer to that and so I was no better off having spoken to Louise.

The furore in the press took its toll on Iwan and I. When we got back to training together he found it hard to pick up the steps. I loved his company and it was my job to teach him so I coped with that, but we also had all the usual problems behind the scenes, dealing with costumes and song choices, and having choreographers interfering. I wasn't in the best place, which was hardly surprising

'I feel like the bosses are trying to stop me being myself,' I said to James one night. We were talking specifically about the problems with costumes, and the fact that I wasn't allowed to wear catsuits anymore, which was something that still annoyed and confused me.

'I'm not surprised you feel that way. I think that is exactly what's happening. They're trying to marginalise you, Ola.'

There had been talk in the press in the past, before James left, about the BBC trying to 'put a stop to the James and Ola show'. Sadly it did seem that, even though James had gone, the bosses were now trying to keep me down. As the show became more and more successful year on year, the regular pro dancers like me naturally got more exposure in the media. I had no desire to be a celebrity; that isn't what I set out do at all. However, I had become very well known to Strictly fans and I was in the press a lot, more often than not through no choice of my own. My theory is that I don't think the bosses were comfortable with this. The real celebrities were the ones they wanted in the spotlight and I understood that, but I hadn't asked to be in this position, and so the way I was being treated didn't seem fair.

In the first week, Iwan and I danced the Tango to Keep On Running. I wasn't happy. It wasn't my song choice and I'd been told we had to use a superimposed graphic race track on the stage. I didn't think it was a good idea; in fact I thought it was tacky and stupid. At this point I had a strong suspicion the producers were trying to make a joke couple of us. I wished I had the balls James did and could have just said no and stuck up for myself and Iwan, but we did as we were told. I wasn't surprised when we only got seventeen points, including a three from Craig.

The following week we did the Cha Cha Cha to Sexy And I Know It. I was given a dress I recognised from an earlier series, which had had a bit of fringing added to it, and I wasn't happy about this because everyone else had a new dress. It didn't seem fair and I felt bad it in.

'Why don't you just wear a catsuit and go out in it on the live show?' James said naughtily. 'What are they going to do? They can't take it off you live in front of millions of viewers!'

I didn't, of course. Iwan and I were given a two by Craig, a four each from Darcey and Len and a three from Bruno. With just thirteen points we were in last place and became the first couple to be eliminated, which was my worst-ever result. Looking back, I'm convinced our fate had been sealed with the negative media coverage. Iwan and I seemed to have everything stacked against us. The lack of training time, coupled with the set, costume and music choices we were given, compounded matters. I don't think we stood a chance.

I was gutted when it was announced we were to be the first couple to leave the competition and, in that moment, I think I knew my Strictly career was over. As I've said before, it felt like half of me had already left when James left the show, and now it was like the other half of me left the building. I was so disappointed, and I felt sorry for Iwan that his Strictly experience had been cut short like this.

I discussed everything with James and told him the time had come. After ten years, I was finally ready to quit.

'Are you absolutely sure, Ola?'

'Yes, it feels right. I just don't want to do it anymore. I feel like you did two years ago. I've had an amazing time and now it's time to go.'

It was liberating to have made the decision, and one of the first things I did when I had some time to myself was to tackle my skin problem. James had done a lot of research as he'd promised and he took me to one of the top dermatologists in the country. She advised me to keep cutting out wheat and dairy and swap caffeine for water, and she put me on a new type of medication I'd never had before. I had been convinced that stress had caused the outbreak of boils, and it seemed the pressure I'd been under all year following my knee injury probably did have a part to play. However, that was only part of the problem, because the new medication actually worked, and it worked quickly. The spots began to clear, and it's now nearly a year on and my skin is still spot-free. I can hardly believe it, and I wish I'd seen this particular dermatologist many years before.

I wanted to give the people at home who had supported me for years on Strictly an honest explanation about the background to why I was leaving. I gave a newspaper interview and said very truthfully what I thought. I didn't hold back, because I felt I owed it to the public to give the real reasons for my departure. I talked very openly about how I believed the judges' marks were used to manipulate positions on the leaderboard, to prevent certain couples from being eliminated after the public vote.

'Some of the marking is way off,' I said. 'People are over-marked and under-marked… In my opinion they know how many votes people scored in the previous weeks and then they try to influence their position on the leaderboard. If the show is not fair, it takes the fun out of it.'

The BBC responded by saying any suggestion the scores were fixed was nonsense. 'Each judge scores each dance independently, based on its merits and on their expert opinion,' a spokesperson said.

I also talked about how I believed certain couples got preferential treatment when it came to routines and song choices and I explained how, in the early days, the producers would never know how good the celebrities were at dancing until everyone had been paired up.

'Now they watch training for the opening group dance so they can see who's good and who's not and how people learn. It's unfair because it means they can decide which professionals will stay in the competition longer.'

I said that Jay McGuiness, who was doing really well in that series, was clearly the best dancer, and that I believed he was strategically partnered with Aliona Vilani, who went out in the first week for the last two years. 'If they didn't care which pros went far, why don't they do it the old way and base it on height and personality? Now they base it on ability. Why do they need to know how good they are? It allows them to control it.'

I'd posed for a glamorous calendar that had recently been launched. I'd done this for many years and had set a bit of a trend, as several other dancers had started doing calendars too. To prepare for the shoot I worked really hard, watching every mouthful I ate and pushing myself to the limit in the gym. I was proud of the results but Craig had been critical in the press, saying he thought my calendar was too raunchy for a star of a family show. I don't know why he did this – my calendars were always sexy and this had never been an issue before. None of the other dancers had ever been criticised for their calendars either. In fact, when one of the young male dancers did one recently it was held up in front of the studio audience and got a lot of positive praise from people on the show, including some producers.

Inevitably, I was asked what I thought of Craig and his comments, and again I told the truth. I said he did nothing but get in the way as creative director of the Strictly live tour and added: 'I think Craig is childish and pathetic making comments about my calendar.'

Incidentally, I've heard on the grapevine that pro dancers are going to be banned from doing calendars from now on, because of mine supposedly being too raunchy. I hope it isn't true; why should the dancers be told what to do in this way? I don't see what is wrong with it at all. I'm very proud of all of my calendars and I've always had great feedback from fans of Strictly. I think this is just another way of the BBC trying to control the pro dancers.

I knew that once I'd given this big interview and gone public with my views, that really was the end of my Strictly career. Inevitably headlines said I accused Strictly of being 'fixed', but I never said that. I would not go that far; I just felt the show was being over-produced. The reason I did the interview was because I believe in fairness. I love Strictly and just wanted everything about the show to be on a level playing field, and to be real and honest, as that is what the viewers and all the contestants deserve.

I announced on Twitter that I was quitting, and a few days later Jamelia spoke on Loose Women about her departure from Strictly the week before. She and her partner Tristan MacManus had left the competition after a dance-off with Peter Andre and Janette Manrara. Jamelia claimed the bosses fixed it for Peter to stay, faking a standing ovation from the audience after his performance, following which Craig, Darcey and Bruno voted to save Peter. Strictly denied any wrongdoing, but I was glad Jamelia had spoken her mind and expressed her view; it was time people did.

I wasn't asked to take part in the Children In Need special, which is normally given to the dancers who go out early, and I was left out of the Christmas special. This meant my last ever performance was in the opening group dance with Iwan for the final show, to Whitney Houston's I Wanna Dance With Somebody. I enjoyed the dance as it was a very fun, upbeat routine but I had a heavy heart. I'd miss this, but I knew deep inside I'd made the right decision.

A lot of people speculated that I'd quit because of James and many blamed him for my departure. I found this annoying. I'm not a big, loud character like James but that doesn't mean I'm not my own person, and it was absolutely my decision to go. James was never jealous of me still being on Strictly, as some reports tried to make out. I was there for two years on my own, with James's full support, so that is a crazy suggestion. It was simply time to go. I'd had an amazing decade, made great friends and worked with some fabulous pro dancers and crew. Yes, I think things had soured between me and the producers since James left, but that was not his fault. I think it had more to do with the fact I was now standing up for myself more than I ever had before.

'Here's to the future!' I said to James when I returned home from my last-ever show.

'I'll drink to that,' he said, smiling and raising a glass.

In that moment felt relieved and full of excitement to have finally left, and I was really looking forward to what the future held. I had no regrets or fear; my decision felt one hundred per cent right.

James and I have the most brilliant memories of our time on Strictly and that night we reminisced about some of the incredible moments we'd enjoyed. When we were immersed in Strictly we took it all in our stride, but in hindsight we could really relish the memories and enjoy reflecting on how amazing so many of our experiences had been.

For example, in our very first year, James and I had the honour of dancing to Meat Loaf, which made us both tingle on stage. 'Oh my God!' we giggled together afterwards. 'Was that real?' When we were dancing it had felt like it was just the two of us in the room with Meat Loaf and we couldn't believe we'd performed in front of millions, sharing the stage with such a huge star. We had a similar feeling dancing to Westlife the following year, which was also a very magical, spine-tingling experience.

'I've got goosebumps,' I said to James during that performance.

'Me too,' he confided. 'Mad, isn't it?'

Kylie Minogue was also a guest on the show that same year, 2007, and the plan was that all the pro boys would dance on stage while she sang. Then Kylie had an idea, and she asked if she could dance with one of the pro dancers just before the end of the number.

'Of course,' the producer said. 'You are Kylie Minogue, you can dance with who you like! You choose.'

Incredibly, Kylie chose James, even though he was one of the new boys on the block.

'Remember Brendan's face!' we laughed when we recalled that moment. 'It was priceless!'

It was a similar story when Girls Aloud came on. 'I want to dance with Cheryl – she's so hot!' James had said beforehand. To his astonishment his wish came true, and he also got to dance with Kimberley Walsh. He was in heaven.

In 2010 I had the surreal experience of having to dress as Goldilocks in a blue frock and white ankle socks, to perform a solo dance number while Brucie sang with Lance Ellington, one of the singers from the Strictly band. Brucie had especially requested me to perform the dance and I'll never forget when the producer explained it to me.

'Here's Bruce's home number. He'd like you to give him a ring so you can have a chat about it.'

I called Bruce and had the conversation, and even though I felt nervous about doing a solo dance like this, as it was something I'd never done before, of course I agreed to everything Bruce wanted.

'Make sure my boobs aren't going to fall out of the dress,' I told the costume girls. 'I can't have anything going wrong with this, especially as I'm supposed to be Goldilocks!'

Meeting Robbie Williams was one of the highlights of my time on Strictly. I'm a massive fan, and when I was training with Robbie Savage he popped into the green room as they are good friends and he'd been passing on some dancing tips from his Take That days. I felt really shy and my legs went to jelly, and it was the one and only time I ever asked a celebrity if I could have a photo with them. I got two pictures actually, as Robbie was really friendly and very happy to pose. I couldn't believe my luck.

The last time James and I danced together on Strictly was in the 2013 series, during which we had the great honour of dancing to Earth, Wind & Fire in the results show. We both had a very good idea that that would be our last ever performance together on Strictly, even though James's departure was not yet signed and sealed. It was amazing, and I can remember that I looked at James that night and thought about how far we'd come from the first time we danced together, in my old school in Poland. I thought about how I'd imagined back then that James was like a knight in shining armour, whisking me to England to make my dreams come true. He certainly hadn't disappointed. I'd had a ball, and what's more I also had a glitterball trophy sitting on display in our lounge.

Strictly had been an incredible experience and given us more fun and enjoyment and rewards than we could ever have imagined or wished for. Now it was the perfect time to move on, and how lucky was I to still have my knight in shining armour at my side, supporting me every step of the way?

James is the love of my life, and I can't wait to see what the future holds for us. Whatever happens, as long as we are together I know we will be happy. We will always keep dancing but, most importantly, we will keep smiling.

Epilogue

I'm looking forward to watching Strictly this year, from the comfort of my sofa, with James beside me. We always loved being viewers whenever we had the chance, and we'll be glued to the TV every week, enjoying the performances, the glamour and all the razzmatazz of the competition, and cheering on our old friends. It would be fantastic if even one of our comments about how the show is produced had been taken on board and improved it, because we want Strictly's success to continue, and to keep growing.

When I first started dancing as a child, Ballroom and Latin were nowhere near as popular as they are today. Strictly deserves so much credit for reviving its popularity and I'm very proud to have played a small part in this victory. If I hadn't watched dance competitions on TV as a small girl, I may not have found my passion and my vocation, so I hope I've returned the favour and encouraged other people to take to the floor and have fun dancing, or maybe even make a career of it.

I can hardly believe I was on Strictly for a whole decade, and when I look back at my twenty-three-year-old self I can see how much I've grown up and changed. I'm more self-assured and assertive, and I've also learned a lot about how other people tick – an inevitability when you're thrown in a training room for ten or twelve hours a day, getting up close and personal with other pro dancers and a very mixed bunch of celebrities!

I want to be a mother now. As I've already said, James and I have been talking about having children for a while. Now I think the time is right for us to start a family so we hope we will be lucky and get our wish. I know James will be a brilliant dad. There have been times in our marriage, and particularly in the last few years, when I've despaired at the way he's doggedly stuck to his belief that 'honesty is the best policy', even when I could see how speaking his mind was going to land him in trouble. I do admire him for sticking to his principles, though, and I'm in the fortunate position of knowing him better than anyone. I know that beneath his bolshy, outspoken image is a very kind and sensitive soul. Without James's belief in my ability, and his generosity, I wouldn't have had the chance to follow my dream all those years ago. I'm very grateful to him for believing in me and I really hope I can help him fulfil his next goal in life, and make him a dad.

Dancing will always be a massive part of my life and I'm going to continue performing and teaching as much as I can. I have a lot of exciting jobs in the pipeline and I'm looking forward to exploring plenty of new opportunities. I know I would not be in such a great place if it wasn't for Strictly, and the show will always have a very special place in my heart, whatever the future brings.